The Sky Is Falling

ARTHUR WEINGARTEN

GROSSET & DUNLAP
A FILMWAYS COMPANY
Publishers • New York

Copyright © 1977 by Arthur Weingarten
All rights reserved
Published simultaneously in Canada
Library of Congress catalog card number: 77-72626
ISBN 0-448-14411-5
First printing 1977
Printed in the United States of America

For Bobbe

Contents

Author's Note

The dialogue used throughout *The Sky Is Falling* has been drawn directly from personal interviews with the survivors, relatives and friends of the victims; it was also taken from the official investigation and report of the disaster which is still suppressed by the United States Air Force and its agencies.

When I began my research in 1975, thirty years after the crash, it was with no small surprise that I discovered the official Air Force report of the event was still classified "Confidential." The normal avenues of information flowing from government agencies to writers were mysteriously dammed. My routine requests for a copy of the 1945 Army Air Forces findings were consistently met with form letters regretting that all records of the crash,. including the investigation and the resulting report, were ' unavailable." With each communique, I received the same two-page typewritten summary of the facts surrounding the event taken from contemporary newspaper accounts. Suggestions were made that I might obtain further information by contacting the newspapers and wire services that covered the story.

My intuition prodded me to conclude that for some inexplicable reason the report was still being considered "hot" by the Air Force. At my request, an officer in the Air Force office of information in Los Angeles attempted to obtain the report through official channels. He was informed that all records pertaining to the crash had been destroyed in a fire that swept the General Services Administration center in St. Louis several years ago. The officer assured me that such a fire had indeed taken place. On numerous occasions he had requested more records from the center, only to learn that they were now but ashen memories. It appeared that I had come to an abrupt and final dead end.

Then quite unexpectedly, and through a source far afield of my search, I was put in contact with an individual who had a copy of the full official report of the crash. This person provided me not only with the entire documentation I was seeking — each of the voluminous mass of pages was stamped "Confidential" — but also with a thick folder of letters and memos relating to the accident.

The letters were from writers who over the years had attempted to gain cooperation from the Air Force and other branches of the government. The memos, many from high-ranking Air Force officers, were interdepartmental instructions designed to block any and all attempts to make the report of the crash public. One highly respected writer, after being given the bureaucratic runaround for two years, appealed to senator Barry Goldwater, himself an Air Force reserve officer. The Senator used his good offices to secure the report —and came away empty-handed. He, like the rest of us, was told that the records no longer existed.

Why, after more than thirty years, is the Air Force still adamantly against releasing this information? The answer, unfolded in this book, shows that no matter how long ago a mistake — or, in this case, a series of mistakes — has been made, the military bureaucracy is not about to assume public responsibility. The report concluded that culpability for this incredible accident rested squarely with the pilot, his superiors overseas, and with civilian and military ground personnel in this country.

As a result of the report's findings, longer and more intensive transitional training was made obligatory for pilots flying back to this country from overseas. Civilian and military ground personnel were given clearly defined areas of jurisdiction. For those who died, and the dozens who suffered these changes came about too late.

Preface

For several days in the summer of 1945, the crash of an Army bomber into the 79th floor of the Empire State Building dominated the headlines. In this country and abroad, the catastrophe shunted aside news of the war still raging in the Pacific, all but relegating Japan's death throes to the inside pages.

The passage of thirty-two years has not diminished my memory of the tragedy which claimed 14 lives and left 26 gravely injured. On that foggy Saturday morning of July 28, I had been brought to City Hall by my father, a New York City fire marshal, to meet Mayor Fiorello La Guardia. Within minutes of entering his office the mayor received word of the crash. Typically, the Little Flower raced off to the scene. And so did I. Overriding my father's instructions to remain where I was, I found myself by childish pleas squeezed into the official motorcade racing uptown. Through a car window a safe block's distance from the crash site I watched the aftermath of an event that even to a young boy seemed improbable. How, I asked, seeing the dead and injured being carried with equal urgency into waiting ambulances, could a plane have crashed into the world's tallest building?

This book is the result of that question. Starting with contemporary newspaper accounts, I began a search for the survivors and relatives of the victims that in eighteen months would carry me from Los Angeles to Iuka, Mississippi; Waltham, Massachusetts; Johnson City, Tennessee; Fort Smith, Arkansas; Sarasota, Florida; Enid, Oklahoma; Mobile and Muscle Shoals, Alabama; Granite City, Illinois; Atherton,

California; Washington, D.C., and back five times to New York City. In all, I interviewed more than two hundred persons involved with the event. In the process, I discovered that we are indeed a nation of the uprooted. Individuals important to the story, who had lived the better part of the lifetimes in one locality, had seemingly vanished. By scouring hundreds of telephone directories, by plaguing federal, state, and city officials, and more often than I care to admit, by sheer luck I tracked down most of those I was seeking.

To a person, they were unstinting in their generosity to travel back in time to recapture the events of that summer morning. Memories, most painful, some surprisingly joyful, and a few forgotten until our meetings, were often partially distorted by the years or an individual's need to maintain graven images. Double, and often triple, cross-checking of personal experiences has led, I believe, to an accurate accounting.

From a journalistic narrative at the outset, the book soon became for me an investigation into what Joseph Wood Krutch called "the great chain of life." The surface drama of the event, the horrible suddenness of an airplane crashing into the world's tallest building, became subordinate to the linkage of the personalities involved.

A.W.
New York City

Acknowledgments

I wish to thank the following people for their invaluable collaboration in the creation of this work: Leonard Kaufman and Hy Steirman, who made it possible; Martha Smith, Robert Smith, His Eminence Patrick Cardinal O'Boyle, Bishop Edward Swanstrom, Ruth Stahlback, Nicholas and Catherine Domitrovich, Major Ron Gruchy, Carl Hinkle, Jr., Major General William C. Garland (ret.), Betty Lou Oliver, Mary Scannell, Ellen Lowe, Therese Willig, Catherine O'Connor, Edward Cummings, Roy Bolton, Sig R. Young, Dr. Melvin Elting, Judge Eugene Canudo, Mrs. Marie La Guardia, John Peluso, Ben and Edith Wollitzer, Peter Pascale, Charles Gelber, Richard Herbert, Uriel Flax, Shirley Robbie, Ralph Byrnes, Robert Allessio, Dr. Jean Mayer, H. Hamilton Weber, Aileen Walker, Anita Terrian, David Hatfield, Charles Bryares, Wilber Snow, Arnold Cane, Kay Parmenter, Annette Fein, Alise Anderson, Phineas Spinrad, Jack T. Cairns, Harry B. Helmsley, Robert Tinker, Jasper F. Frand, and a person who of necessity must remain anonymous but whose contribution was vital; and my appreciation to Robert Markel, Grosset & Dunlap's editor-in-chief, and Larry Gadd, managing editor.

To my parents, Belle and Harry Weingarten, and Tara, Cort, Chris, and Jamie—thank you for your patience and understanding.

CHAPTER I

8:55—The Takeoff

AT FIVE A.M. THE CAULIFLOWER-
shaped cloud had reached an altitude of four thousand feet.

Its birth, less than an hour before, had been rapid. With
swirling, adhesive movements, bits of transparent vapor had
suddenly appeared over this portion of the Atlantic Ocean,
some 300 miles due south of the Rhode Island coastline.

There had been nothing. And then the vapor. It was
siphoned from the ocean's surface by currents of warm air. The
heat had been provided by the sun, which was still hidden
behind the eastern horizon.

This Saturday morning, July 28, 1945, sunrise was an
hour away.

But the air and the water had already sensed the sun's
approach. Deep in the ocean, layers of warming salt water
tumbled upward to the surface. Inches above the wave crests,
a southeasterly wind scooped up the mositure-laden air.

In a pecking order preordained at the creation, the water
droplets, warmest first, were lofted above the ocean on a rising
column of air. At a critical moment, as unique for this cloud as
it had been for its uncounted ancestors, the heated air suddenly
chilled. At that precise instant the vapor appeared.

Separated and unguided, the puffs of moisture expanded,
sought each other out, and clung together. The cloud took on a

1

bubbling motion as it grew gray and swollen. Its top, twisted into an anvil shape, soared thousands of feet above the broad, flat base. It rose higher, fed by a continual stream of fresh vapor pulled from the ocean's surface.

And it was moving quickly now, pushed by the southeast wind. At nine thousand feet, almost two miles above the ocean, it joined an identical column of clouds being herded along the same course. As if on an invisible track, the thunderheads were drawing toward a violent section of sky 50 miles to the west.

Towering 40,000 feet over the ocean, the massive squall line sent barrages of lightning through the black clouds. Whipped by hurricane winds, the torrential rain made a denting, thwacking sound as it struck the ocean at a sharp angle.

The summer storm had traveled more than a thousand miles from the Caribbean to reach this destination far off the tip of Montauk Point, Long Island. Within an hour it would absorb the column of thunderheads coming from the east, leaching their moisture, sending it back into the turbulent ocean with frightful power.

Mariners and airline pilots had been warned well in advance to steer clear of the storm's boundaries. With calipers and rulers they had fixed its position on their charts, giving concrete dimension to a fluid and troubled atmosphere. Those who had business on or above the sea would give the storm a wide berth.

But for those on land, the sailor's adage that "weather makes weather" held true this Saturday morning.

Hundreds of miles ahead of the storm front, masses of unsettled air reacted in various and seemingly arbitrary ways. Over random areas, from Maine to Florida, the moon and a few scattered stars could still be clearly seen in the early-morning sky. Other sections were thickly blanketed by low-hanging clouds and fog.

Over towns and cities all along the Eastern Seaboard, thunderstorms were moving into position.

*   *   *

At five a.m. New York City was bathed in a fine mist.

It hovered above the damp pavements of Rockefeller Center. Yellowish halos around the street lights created a gas-lit effect in the narrow canyons of Wall Street.

Down at the Battery, at the southern tip of Manhattan, the ferryboat *Mary Murray* eased from its berth and headed into a dense fog that rolled in from the Narrows. Sounding the foghorn, her skipper began to navigate the five-mile run to Staten Island more by instinct than compass.

At Fifth Avenue and 34th Street, a lowering field of stratocumulus clouds moving south released a light rain. The first drops to touch the city splattered against the rounded tower of the Empire State Building, 1,250 feet above the street. Within seconds, the two red aircraft warning lights on top of the RCA television antenna were blacked out by the eddying vapor. The layer of cold air above the clouds pressed them still lower. The building's 102nd-floor observation tower disappeared.

*   *   *

At five a.m., Brookline, Massachusetts, a Boston suburb 200 miles north of New York City, lay under a thick cloud cover. In a corner room on the top floor of the Hotel Beaconsfield a telephone rang.

Bill Smith was instantly awake and snapped on the light.

"Colonel Smith." His graveled Southern accent, dipping and rising, made the name sound like the title of a folksong.

Lying next to him, his wife, Martha, had also awakened with the shrill ring. Groggy, shielding her eyes from the harsh glare of the light, she thought it was their wake-up call. But instead of hanging up, Bill swung his legs over the side of the bed and stood up, the phone still pressed to his ear. He wore a puzzled look.

"I didn't get that," he said. "What about the B-25?"

Martha was fully alert now. The mention of the B-25 had brought back the feeling of dread. Fear had accompanied her into a fitful sleep. Now it was there again. Stronger. She felt a dull, throbbing headache.

Bill was shaking his head. "I'd like to help you, sergeant, but I'm not taking any passengers."

He was unbuttoning his striped pajama top, revealing a mass of curly black hair against walnut-hued skin. Tucking the phone between his shoulder and ear, he slipped out of the top and began to fold it neatly.

The pressure in her temples was increasing. As she had done last night, Martha forced herself to think. To blot out the feeling of impending disaster, she sought refuge in facts.

He looked thinner, she noticed, than the last time she'd seen him, a month ago. Mostly around the middle. He was short-waisted, with most of his six feet settled in his long legs. The weight loss made him seem taller.

Nothing would go wrong. He would be perfectly safe.

Or was he trimming his mustache differently? That was it, she realized. He had let it grow to the corners of his mouth, thinning it more in the center. She remembered when he had decided to grow it back in flight school—the ribbing he took about trying to look like Gable. He had laughed off the accusation, but she secretly thought his classmates had come close to the truth. Bill had always been a bit of a peacock.

Premonitions are stupid. I'm being stupid!

God, the hours she'd spent trimming it for him, both of them cracking up as she tried to follow his instructions while he tracked her progress in the mirror. When most brides were discovering how to boil an egg, she was learning to be a barber! Actually, once the mustache had grown in he did bear a striking resemblance to the movie star. Bill's lips were thicker, but the color and texture of their hair and skin were the same. Bill's ears even jutted out at a similar angle.

B-25. Weather.

It wasn't working. The impatience in Bill's voice had cut through her thoughts. She felt her temples pulsing harder. He sounded almost angry.

"Look, Sergeant McCarthy, you'll just have to find yourself another flight. I told you, I'm not taking any passengers this morning. Sorry."

Martha watched him drop the receiver onto the cradle harder than he had intended. He scowled, annoyed at his abrupt reaction. She sat up, turning the sheet back, drawing the braided straps of her blue nightgown over her shoulders. She wished she had brought along some aspirin.

"What was that all about?" she asked, hoping she'd hit just the right level of casual interest.

Bill grunted a laugh and shook his head. "A lady Marine. Bedford Operations told her I was going to Newark Field. She wanted to hitch a ride home."

"Why didn't you take her? There's plenty of room on that monster."

She had to strain to keep her voice even. The anxiety was making her breath come in shallow, rapid spurts.

Dammit! I don't believe I'm doing this!

She had never put stock in premonitions before. Hers or anyone else's. She was an intelligent woman, she kept telling herself, a nurse, trained in modern science—not one of her bogey-ridden Irish ancestors her mother was always joking about. She didn't cross herself when she broke a mirror, or spit at mention of the Devil.

And yet it had come to her yesterday afternoon. They had been out for a drive, listening to the war news on the car radio. The weekend weather report had come on as Bill was saying how strong and healthy the baby looked.

Suddenly, a sensation of terrible dread had swept over her. No—not over her. *In* her. Like a cry in her heart. That was the only way she could describe it. With it had come the knowledge—again, that was the best description she could give herself of the event—that if Bill took off Saturday morning, she would never see him again.

It had not been a vision. No picture had flashed in her mind to identify the catastrophe. She had just been given blind knowledge. And she believed it.

"Not today," Bill said.

He had moved to the window and raised the venetian blind. He was peering out at the barely lightening sky.

"What?"

"That Marine, the hitchhiker. I don't want to bother with all those passenger forms they make you fill out over here."

Over here. He made it sound as if home were a foreign country. He had come back from overseas a month ago, but in a dozen small ways she was realizing that he had not yet made the transition. She would have to be patient. It couldn't be all that easy for him after having been gone for a year and a half.

She rose slowly from bed, crossed to the dresser, and began to brush her long chestnut hair, digging the bristles against her scalp in hard, massaging strokes. It was a full-blown headache now, the pressure centered directly behind her eyes. She glanced out the window past him to the heavy clouds moving over the hotel. There was no doubt in her mind that what she was seeing now would not get any better as the morning progressed.

"What's it look like?" she tested.

He turned from the window and grinned. "A typical English morning," he said, jerking this thumb toward the leaden sky. "In fact, they'd call that sunshine."

She laughed with him.

It had been a ridiculous attempt, made with the full knowledge that Bill was a consummate actor. He would never admit that his concern about the weather ran as deep as hers. After three years of marriage she had learned that his fears were very private, kept at all times under tight security.

Most of his bravado, his attitude toward danger, was pure male. That much she knew. But she attributed a portion of it to his being a Southerner, brought up with the myth that bold men shield fragile women. Sometimes, like now, it took great willpower to hold her Boston Irish temper in check; to keep from demanding that he share *all* of himself with her. Not just the emotions and attitudes that came easily— his gentleness, the deep love he showed for her and their baby—but his fears and doubts as well. In time, she thought, after the war was over, when they were spending years, not hours, together, she would work on that with him. With time he would see that it took nothing from his manhood to share those hidden parts with her.

Christ, let me be the fool. Make me wrong.

He gave her behind a grabbing pinch.

"Hey, come on, shake a leg. I've got a son to see and a plane waiting."

He was climbing into his summer tan uniform, one of three he had had custom-tailored at Brooks Brothers before he went overseas. For no particular reason, she suddenly remembered the day they had gone into the store on Madison Avenue for his final fitting. Bill had stood at attention in front of the mirror while the tailor made pinning adjustments. A passing salesman had stopped. He had given Bill a long measured look, then turned to Martha and said: "That man was born to wear a uniform." He was right, she thought, as she watched Bill button his jacket, the silver wings glistening above the rows of rainbow-colored combat ribbons. She couldn't imagine him in a business suit, going off to work in a starched white shirt and a sober tie. An image popped into her head—those picture cards they showed in psychology class, the professor asking which of the men was the bank robber, the college president, the wife beater. She wondered how Bill would fare in such a lineup, just his face, no uniform. She had always mismatched the face and the profession. Her bank robber was guaranteed to be a renowned scientist, or a policeman. What if William Franklin Smith, Jr.'s picture had been on one of those cards? Funny thought.

"Bedford Field, please."

The first whiff of cigar smoke hit her as she was pulling the nightgown over her head. Bill fanned the match slowly in front of the cigar, making certain the flame caught the tobacco evenly. He switched the phone to his other ear as he dropped the match into an ashtray, then drew the cigar from his mouth and critically examined the ash.

"Since when did you start smoking before breakfast?" she asked. The smell nauseated her; her head felt as if a jackhammer were at work.

"It's not botherin' you, is it, darlin'? I'll put it out if it is."

She watched him poise the cigar over the ashtray, ready to do her bidding.

"No," she lied. "I just think it's a bad habit to get into."
He was making another phone call to the airfield. It was his
fifth since dinner, and by now she could predict his dialogue.

"Operations, please." He drew on the cigar, savoring the
heavy taste as he waited for his connection. She busied herself
with folding the sheer nightgown, bought especially for this
weekend, worn two nights, Thursday and Friday; and now,
Saturday morning, it would be put away until he came home
on leave again. She opened the dark leather briefcase she had
given him for his graduation from West Point and tucked the
gown next to his maps and shaving kit.

"This is Colonel Smith. I've got an 8:30 takeoff filed to
Newark. . . . That's right, the B-25, serial 0577."

It had been the same last night, each call to the airfield
starting off with his concern for the servicing of the plane—
minutes of technical talk she didn't begin to understand. . .
checking magnetos, bleeding the hydraulic lines, something
about the right brake, etc., etc.

He said it all, she thought, with great authority, as if he
had spent the larger part of a lifetime issuing orders. She knew
people were surprised when they learned that Bill was only
twenty-seven, one of the youngest lieutenant colonels in the
Air Corps. It gave her no end of pleasure to read the respect on
her friends' faces when they saw his battle ribbons and
discovered that he had flown more than fifty combat missions
over France and Germany.

She knew it was coming.

"Looks to me like I'll be goin' Instrument." He had
carried the phone as close to the window as the cord would
allow, forcing him to view the sky in a half-crouch. "What's
the latest update?"

As with all of the other calls, his voice gave nothing away
as he asked about the weather. The question had been put in
the same calm, professional manner each time. And yet she
knew he was worried. No one single thing made her certain;
but that was it—the small, seemingly inconsequential remarks
he made about the weather and the plane had to be taken out of
context. Bill's trademark was total self-assurance. Some called

it cockiness, but she had learned that his manner was nothing more than a deep, honest confidence in his abilities as a pilot and an officer. Like a talented ballplayer he took pride in making the hard ones look easy. Where others questioned, Bill made statements. She was just beginning to understand where to place some of his question marks.

"Say again? I didn't get the visibility past Hartford." Bill had carried the phone back to the night table. He sat on the edge of the bed, his back to her. Martha listened to his noncommittal grunts, translating them to mean that nature was in no mood to cooperate with her husband this Saturday morning.

Why? Why is he worried?

If the answer was rooted in fact, it eluded her. Just last night Bill had called the short flight to the New Jersey airfield a "milk run"—one he could phone in with his eyes closed. It was nothing, he assured her, compared to the flight across the Atlantic he had made a month ago, when he brought his B-17 back from England.

The beginning, she thought for the hundredth time; if she went back to the beginning, took it step by step, pulled the moments apart, then maybe she would find the linkage between Bill's concern and her pervading sense of doom. She began again. .

Thursday morning. Two days ago, almost to the hour. Bill had called from the base in South Dakota to tell her that he was coming in for a quick visit. Colonel Rogner, his commanding officer, had put together a party of men whose families all lived in the New York area. Bill would drop them off at Newark, then continue on to Boston to see her.

Thursday afternoon. She had had trouble starting the car. Bill had already landed by the time she arrived at Bedford Field. The flight had been fine, Bill said, just perfect, except for some rain over Cleveland. He was in high spirits, insisting that she look over the B-25. He loved the way it handled, he said, and was looking forward to flying it back to South Dakota.

Thursday night. After dinner with her parents they had gone directly to the hotel. They had made love and then both of them had fallen into an exhausted sleep. But even that aside, if there had been something, she would have picked up on it. She was certain; Bill had been anything but worried Thursday night.

Friday morning. Bill had played with the baby. A month ago, the first time he had laid eyes on the son born while he was overseas, the baby had cried every time Bill picked him up. Yesterday morning little Billy had laughed and reached out for his father. "He knows me! He knows I'm his daddy!" Bill had shouted with pride. Nothing there. Happiness.

Friday afternoon. Just the two of them. Lunch and a leisurely drive through Boston. Bill picking out memories as they passed Faneuil Hall and the Latin Quarter nightclub, where they had blown a month's pay to celebrate his promotion to first lieutenant. The weather report on the radio. She kept getting stuck there, locked into her own instant of fear. Could she be wrong? Was she putting off on him her own insecurities? No. His signals were too strong. She was convinced that he sensed *something*. The calls to the airfield. His constant glancing out the window to check the weather. And that hitchhiker. Why wouldn't he give her a ride? Why did he sound so upset with her? He was the most even-tempered man she knew. It was almost a point of honor with him not to show anger. And yet a simple request had put him on edge.

The sergeant! Why hadn't she thought of him before? He had made the trip with Bill all the way from South Dakota, and this morning he would be going back with him. Bill had called him before they had gone to bed. She had only half heard Bill's part of the conversation, but that could be the key. Maybe the sergeant had told Bill something. What was his name? It sounded Polish. Dom-something. She would find a way to talk to him alone. Then she would have the answer. The ammunition. The logical, unemotional reason she needed to ask Bill to delay the flight. Saturday was the problem. Not any other day. Bill had to stay with her until today passed. Then he would be safe.

Bill was laughing into the phone. "From what you're sayin', lieutenant, it's wet all the way. That B-25's gonna be cleaner'n ivory by the time she gets home. Thanks, I'll check in with you at seven."

He was still smiling as he hung up and turned to Martha. She was using the mirror, bending over the dresser as she blended in the last traces of rouge with a powder puff. The headache had started to subside with her plan about the sergeant. She felt buoyant, as if a crushing fist had suddenly let go of her heart. She watched him move in behind her, the cigar clenched in the corner of his mouth, making the grin on his face all the more devilish as he raised his hand in mock threat.

"Lady—I swear this is gonna land smack on your pretty little butt if you don't get movin'."

Her eyes flicked to him in the mirror. "Why, colonel," she said, attempting a Southern accent, "I'm shocked. I'll bet you wouldn't even treat your wife that way." She turned to him and batted her eyes coquettishly. "And after I let you have your way with me!"

He stood there laughing and shaking his head.

"You are one crazy woman. And you're wrong—that's exactly how I treat my wife," he said, taking the cigar out of his mouth. He laid it on the marble dresser top, then suddenly reached out, pulled her to him, and delivered a slap on her backside. She let out a squeal, more in surprise than hurt, and struggled to break his hold.

"You miserable . . ." she laughed.

He held his finger in front of her nose. "Ahh, ahh . . . remember, rank has its privilege," he warned, moving his finger to tap the insignia on his shoulder.

She stiffened to attention, swinging her hand up, palm out, and gave him a snapped British salute. "Yes, suh, Colonel Smith, suh!" She gave him two quick birdlike pecks on his cheek.

"Sexy," he said, unimpressed.

"Rank has its privilege," she shrugged, then, in a husky whisper: "Now if you were a general, sugar . . . " She arched her body against him and began to nibble his ear with a low, moaning sound. He laughed and pushed her away.

"Wicked Irish. Suppose the Pope saw you standin' there like that?"

"Being a gentleman, *he'd* find someplace else to put his eyes." She grabbed up her dress from the back of the chair and held it protectively in front of her, feigning a modest look.

"Martha," he said, shaking his head and dropping his voice to sound more serious, "you get playful at the darnedest times." He shot his arm out, exposing his wristwatch, and tapped the crystal.

"See what time it is?"

She nodded solemnly. "11:56."

"It's exactly 5:30," he said patiently. "I'm goin' downstairs and check us out. If you are not in the lobby in five minutes, I will go home and tell our son that his mother has abandoned us—that she can be found languishin' in the Hotel Beaconsfield with God knows who."

He picked up the briefcase, crossed to the door, and slipped off the chain.

"Blackmailer," she said poutingly, then giggled.

He opened the door and turned to her. "I'm bein' serious, Martha. Five minutes." He held a hand up, fingers spread graphically for added impact, then closed the door behind him.

She smiled, satisfied with herself. It hadn't really been an act. She actually was feeling euphoric, almost as if a dose of morphine were rushing through her veins. The headache was still there, she could feel her temples drumming, but it was like a phantom pain, amputated from the rest of her. She slipped into a black-and-white cotton print dress, watching herself in the mirror as her fingers fastened the white buttons. She noticed that most of the tension had drained from her face. She was going to make it, going to hold herself together while Bill said goodbye to the baby. She glanced at her watch. In an hour she would see the sergeant.

*   *   *

The baby's shrieking laughter brought Martha out of the house in time for her to see Bill toss him high in the air. She waited until Billy was safely in his father's arms before shouting: "Bill Smith—stop that! You'll make him throw up."

"Throw up?" He held the squealing one-year-old above his head and wiggled him around. "This boy's a born flier. He's gonna be like his daddy, aren't you, Willie Three?" He pulled the youngster down and hugged him tightly, then turned to Martha's mother, standing beside him on the lawn.

"Mother, I'm gonna give you a job while I'm gone. You've gotta promise to give my boy some time in the air every day. Like this." He tossed the baby up, even higher than before, and caught him in a scooping sweep low to the ground.

The older woman laughed with fright and shook her head decisively. "Not on your life, Bill. And I want you to stop that right now! While that child's still in one piece. You play too rough with him."

Martha smiled with relief as her mother took the baby from Bill's arms and cuddled him protectively. She felt good standing there on the porch, watching the generations blend into a protective shield against time past and future.

She had been born in the house, and now her son was growing up there. Bill had been overseas when he was born, and two weeks ago he had been unable to come to his son's first birthday party. Recently she had made the mistake of totaling up the number of days she and Bill had been together in the three years of their marriage. From the ceremony at the West Point chapel, to a month ago, when he returned from overseas, the time barely amounted to a respectable honeymoon.

The depressing calculation had led her into self-pity, a mood she allowed to deepen each time she glanced at the four service flags her mother proudly displayed in the parlor window.

But last night at dinner it had been different. Bill was home. Her two brothers and her brother-in-law were also home on leave. At Sunday-morning Mass, for the first time in three years, Martha and her parents would not have to light candles for their safe return from the war.

As she helped her mother carry platters of food into the dining room, Martha noticed that the four young men were wearing their uniforms. Little Billy was seated in his highchair next to Bill. Across from them were her sister Mary, Mary's husband, Ralph, and their new baby. Her father was enthroned at the head of the table, his rimless glasses, as always, in a precarious balance between his nose and the soup bowl. The house vibrated with the easy comfort of a family together. It was a Norman Rockwell cover, she thought, patently poignant, but indelibly memorable. The only thing missing was the startled look on her mother's face when the butcher had tallied up the number of ration stamps she owed for the huge roast.

After dinner the men went into the parlor. Bill handed out the expensive Havana cigars he had brought back from England. The men sipped brandy as they discussed what would happen at the Potsdam Conference now that Roosevelt was dead and Churchill had lost the election to Attlee. As she cleared the dishes, she heard Bill say he was convinced that Stalin would now dominate the meeting. Truman was still an unknown quantity, he said, too new at the job, and certainly, as far as he could tell, without Roosevelt's experience or persuasive charm. From all accounts in the newspapers, Attlee seemed to him a dull, plodding sort, not at all up to dealing head to head with Stalin as Churchill would have. Why the British had voted Winnie out of office was a mystery to him. Every Englishman he had ever spoken to over there revered the man, Bill said, thought of him as an institution, practically a god.

The men sat silently smoking and drinking their brandy, yielding the floor to Bill's forceful authority.

He *sounded* so intelligent, Martha had thought, as she carried in a tray of coffee. It wasn't so much his grasp of the facts as how he presented them: theatrically, his rich, resonant voice instinctively selecting which words to emphasize, so that his thought became the property of his audience. It was partly cleverness, she knew, an inborn facility he recognized and used to his. profit. But it was also unconscious, this need to command attention, a natural extension of his having been born in a region where oratory was often weighed equally with the deed; how something appeared was important.

She set the tray down, aware that Bill had suddenly stopped in midsentence and was staring at her, as if he were seeing her for the first time. Then, leaning over to his father-in-law, he rested his hand on the older man's arm. He said it artlessly, exactly as the thought came to him.

"You know something, Dad—I've got everything I want in life . . . the perfect wife, the perfect son, and the perfect career. What more could a man ask?"

It must have shown on her face, because her father laughed and pointed at her with gentle accusation. "Hey, Martha's blushing," he said. "You've embarrassed her, Bill." The men laughed, dismissing the color in her face for admirable modesty, and someone picked up the conversation again.

But the flush was anger, and as she poured their coffee she had fought down an almost uncontrollable urge to scream its source to them.

She would have said that Bill's remark was vicious and unthinking; the voiced need of men—not just him, but all men—who equate their desires with possession, and the hell with those possessed. In that one softly spoken declaration of love and contentment, Bill had denied *her* existence, her pain, for the past three years. He had carried her overseas tucked securely in his wallet, her smiling face frozen by the blink of a camera's shutter; and in that unmoving image he had all that he needed from her—gathered by him privately in *their* time together. She was instantly available to him, unchanging, the sum of her parts to be selectively conjured up when he felt the need to be comforted and reassured in his identity as a husband and father.

She and the photographer, in a kind of unpremeditated conspiracy, had given immortality to Bill's fantasy. The photo was his memory of her, fixed by chemicals, made all the more endurable by time and circumstance. The picture was undeniable proof of a happy woman—carefree, painfree, pliant—finding her reason and strength in the man for whom she was smiling. Gone in a hiss of the photographer's airbrush were the faint lines radiating from the edges of her eyes—lines removed without the subject's approval, an assumed obligation to deliver a universal standard of unquestioning serenity. In that sense it was a work of art, reality heightened for easy digestion; like the baby's zwieback, neither bread nor toast, but *something* nutritious, satisfying needs and therefore valuable. Real.

But Bill's incautious statement to her father had instantly collected her pain. Its one-sidedness. The perfection of his goals his only concern. There had been no recognition of what she had gone through in those three years; of what she had left unsaid in her letters so that he could have his peace of mind, his emotions uncomplicated by her needs or fears. She had left him free to do his job. He had not recognized the gift she had given, or the cost to her.

Had they been alone, just she and Bill, would she have said all that to him? Probably not, she thought. Most likely she would have found some excuse to leave the room and quietly cry it out by herself. But they had not been alone, and so she had continued to serve the coffee and chastised herself for dwelling on the cruelty of the situation. She and Bill would spend the rest of his leave together, the words unsaid, and in the morning they would once again find themselves saying goodbye.

"Don't, Billy! You'll tear your daddy's uniform," she heard her mother saying reproachfully.

Martha saw Bill holding his son, the boy tugging at the silver wings with a look of frustration that she knew would soon dissolve into tears.

Bill laughed, loosened the baby's grip, and kissed his hand with a loud, smacking sound. "Hey, Martha, didn't I tell you he's a born pilot?" he said, beaming up at her. "You want to fly before you can walk, don't you, Willie?" He held the boy at arm's length and spun him around, growling in imitation of an airplane taking off. The baby squealed with delight and kicked his legs, not wanting the ride to stop.

"We'd better get going, Bill," Martha said, checking her watch as she moved off the porch. "It's almost 6:20." She said it offhandedly, the prodding natural, a fact of time. They were to meet the sergeant at 6:30.

Bill hugged the baby and kissed him on both cheeks. "You be a good boy now, Willie. Mind your mama and grandmother, you hear?" He kissed his son again and handed him to his mother-in-law. "I'll be talkin' with you next week, Mother. Take care," he said, then kissed her gently on her forehead.

Bill backed their Buick convertible out of the driveway and beeped the horn twice, waving to the pair standing on the lawn. He shifted gears and drove off down the tree-lined street, his eyes darting back and forth to the rear-view mirror. Martha swiveled around in the seat and looked out the back window. She saw her mother holding Billy, helping him to wave goodbye.

*   *   *

Sergeant Christopher Domitrovich was, as usual, precisely on time. The chimes drifting across the deserted Cambridge streets from St. Mary's steeple confirmed the 6:30 hour.

Domitrovich was waiting in Harvard Square, directly opposite Harvard Yard. His GI-issue uniform shirt hung loosely on his shoulders, making the thirty-one-year-old airman seem shorter and thinner than he actually was.

A light rain began to fall. He reached into his canvas carryall, pulled out his Class A cap, and carefully fitted it over his blond crewcut. The cap, its stiff brown visor seated at the regulation angle over his forehead, seemed to heighten Domitrovich's Slavic heritage. It wasn't a happy face; still, the sharply etched lines around his eyes and mouth revealed a depth of character often missing from smoother, less troubled features.

Until Thursday morning, Domitrovich and Colonel Smith had never met. And as far as the sergeant could tell from their brief conversations, he and Smith had only two things in common: both had fought in the air war over Europe, and now each of them was temporarily attached to the base at Sioux Falls, South Dakota, awaiting reassignment to the Pacific.

Any further attempt to draw similarities between them, the sergeant knew, would be laughable. To Domitrovich, the colonel was an honest-to-god hero. A glance at the decorations on Smith's uniform had broadcast to the sergeant an embarrassment of bravery and recognition: the Air Medal with three Oak Leaf Clusters, the Distinguished Flying Cross with four Oak Leaves, a Presidential Citation, and the Croix de Guerre with Palm.

Domitrovich had also won a couple of medals, but he considered his to be flukes compared to Smith's. What he had done hadn't been bravery, but pure survival. The colonel had been the deputy commander of a famed bomb group; Domitrovich had served as crew chief on C-47s, hauling cargo and paratroops with plodding, anonymous efficiency.

And then there was the matter of their backgrounds. Smith not only had the regal aristocratic bearing of a Southern gentleman, but he was a West Pointer. To Chris Domitrovich, who had quit Granite City High School after a year and a half, their educations alone set them universes apart.

He had just lighted a Lucky Strike as the Buick pulled up. Out of deference to Martha, Domitrovich flicked it away, his hand continuing up in a snapped salute to the colonel as he opened the door and slid into the back seat. He offered the Smiths a shy smile.

"Mornin', Chris . . . that remind you of somethin'?" Smith was pointing through the rain-flecked windshield at the murky sky.

"Looks just like England, colonel," Domitrovich said in his flat Midwestern accent.

It suddenly struck Martha that whenever the sergeant talked to Bill he lowered his head and spoke slowly, as if choosing his words as much for careful diction as for content. She had met him only once before, when he and Bill had flown into Bedford Thursday afternoon. Bill had offered to put him up at the Beaconsfield, but Domitrovich had said he had made plans to stay with friends living near Harvard Square. For some reason, Martha was sure that "friends" meant a girl. Why the sergeant needed to conceal this she didn't know, but somehow it fitted in with his bashful, self-effacing manner. Now, as on their first meeting, Martha felt that there was something awfully sad and lonely about the man.

Smith put the car into gear and swung across the street in a tight U-turn.

"Are we going Contact or Instrument, colonel?" Domitrovich asked.

"Instrument. It's too socked in down the line to eyeball it." Smith said. It was raining harder now. He reached over and turned on the windshield wipers. The rubber blades scraped protestingly for a few strokes, then settled into a smooth, sweeping motion.

Martha sat stiffly, her eyes fixed at the point where the blades met in the middle of the windshield on their downward swing.

He doesn't know anything!

The sergeant's question and Bill's answer, each voiced quietly, almost indifferently, had literally numbed her. In that moment's exchange all her hopes of proving a collusion—a blood oath sworn between the men against her—had been dashed. Once again she was having trouble breathing. The air she drew in through her clenched teeth became blocked in her throat, thick, unacceptable. *Breathe deeply*, she warned herself, *or you'll choke ... force the air down!* She could feel her chest tighten in anticipated rejection. *Breathe!*

She jammed her heels against the floorboard and forced her body upright, slanted back against the seat. At the same time as she pretended to straighten her skirt she sucked the air in hard, forcing it past the constriction in her throat and deep into her lungs. Almost instantly she felt her lightheadedness vanish. To avoid suspicion, she made a few extra smoothing motions before sitting down again. She stole a glance at Bill. He was discussing technical details of the flight with the sergeant. He hadn't noticed. She stared out the side window, willing her breathing to become more regular.

They were moving through the old cobblestoned section of the city, the heavy car cushioning the rough surface into a lulling rhythm. She was filtering out their words, listening only to the sound of the men's voices, analyzing the timbre, the emotional flow, the length of their thoughts. She had been right—the sergeant and Bill were not transmitting on a secret wavelength. There was no plot. She was convinced now that

the premonition was hers alone, of her making. Its solution—
if any—was her responsibility.

"Off again, on again. Sure can't seem to make up its
mind," Bill said. He switched off the wipers.

Martha looked out the windshield and saw that it had
stopped raining.

"I wonder what it's like in New York?" she asked.

"Latest report said showers," Bill answered. "I hope Rog
leaves himself enough time to find a taxi. You know, some of
those New York cabbies don't like taking fares to New Jersey.
They sure can be uppity," he added with a laugh.

Rogner. The Barclay.

The dashboard clock read 6:50. Harris Rogner, Bill's
commanding officer, was staying with his wife at the Barclay
Hotel. They would be having coffee together now, she
thought, in the small dining room where she and Bill had
grabbed a hurried breakfast the morning after their wedding. It
was too much, she knew, to wonder if Rogner's wife was even
thinking about the flight her husband was about to take. *But if
it was raining in New York!* If it was raining, if the weather in
New York was as dark and unsettled as here . . . *Rogner might
decide to delay the flight.* For all she knew, he was calling
Bedford Field now, leaving a message for Bill saying, "Take
your time—no hurry—the weather's lousy here. We'll wait
until it clears up. No sense taking chances."

"Good morning, sir."

Martha was suddenly aware that they had stopped.

"Mornin', corporal," Bill said, returning the MP's salute.
He opened his billfold and showed the spit-and-polish guard
his ID card. She realized that they were at Bedford Field. Off to
the left, beyond the parking area, she saw the B-25. A red fuel
truck was backing up to it.

"Thank you, colonel," the guard said. He saluted again,
then stepped back as Bill gunned the car onto the gravel road.

What if there was no message from Rogner? Then she
would have to find the right way of approaching Bill, suggest
that it might be wise for him to check with Rogner before he
took off. It would be a shame, she would say, if he landed at

Newark only to find out that Rogner had decided to delay the flight. A simple phone call might give them a few extra hours together, she would say casually.

The Buick glided to a halt next to the gate leading onto the field.

"Grab my briefcase back there, willya, Chris?" Bill said, opening the door. He walked around to Martha's side and helped her out. He took the briefcase from Domitrovich, then looped his arm through Martha's and guided her through the gate.

As they walked toward the plane, Bill said, "Make sure they worked on that brake, Chris. I don't trust these boys here worth a darn."

Domitrovich nodded. He shared Smith's distrust of the Stateside maintenance crews. Most of the mechanics had never been overseas, had never seen a plane limp back from a mission with engines shot out, daylight pouring through gaping holes in the wings and fuselage. They could not know, not really, how many lives depended on an extra turn of a wrench, a second look at an oil line. For the most part they did their work by rote, bored, waiting for their discharges. Domitrovich had learned not to put his life in their hands.

"I'll double-check it, colonel," the sergeant said.

They reached the plane. The fuel-truck driver had climbed onto the left wing and was hauling up the thick rubber hose. Martha watched as he unscrewed a filler cap and fitted the hose nozzle into the gas tank. He squeezed the trigger. The high-octane fumes instantly engulfed her. She grimaced, fanning the acrid smell away with her hand.

"That's pretty rich first thing in the mornin'," Bill laughed. "Would you rather wait in the car?" He opened the briefcase, took out his swagger stick, and tucked it under his arm.

"No, I'm interested. I'll stay here with the sergeant—if he doesn't mind." She turned to Domitrovich questioningly.

"My pleasure, Mrs. Smith." He said it with the barest trace of a smile, yet he seemed genuinely flattered at her attention.

"Be back soon, darlin'," Bill said. He turned and walked off toward the Operations building.

She watched as he shifted the briefcase to his other hand, amazed at how he kept his back coat-rack straight while the rest of him seemed to move with a gliding, dancing motion. Long ago she had decided that it was all right for her to think of him as being beautiful. Of course she would never tell him that—not the man who had once proudly spent an hour detailing for her every sprain, cut, and bruise he had suffered en route to becoming an All-American lacrosse player. But that's how she thought of him. Handsome, rugged, manly—none of those words captured his powerful, animal-like grace, or the way he went about his life with a quiet gentleness.

If Rogner had not left a message delaying the flight, then she would devise a way to keep Bill with her. For some reason, which she refused to examine, she was feeling confident. It was this sense of security that allowed her to watch with genuine interest as the sergeant began to inspect the plane.

*   *   *

Smith scowled as he studied the weather map mounted on the wall just below Truman's portrait. As the Weather Officer chalked in the latest data, he saw that conditions would get even worse within the next hour or so. A squall line, moving in from the Atlantic, was pushing dense clouds and rain against the coastline.

Smith turned from the map and crossed to Lieutenant Curtis' desk. The Airdrome Officer was just hanging up the phone.

"No go, colonel. Boston Control won't okay your 8:30 Instrument direct to Newark."

"Did you tell them that Colonel Rogner was expecting me to pick him up no later than ten?" Smith asked, visibly annoyed.

"Yes, sir. With all due respect, Boston said they didn't care if Eisenhower was waiting for you. They've got too much Instrument going into Newark. They suggested if you can hold off, they'd slot you direct for an eleven o'clock takeoff."

Smith pulled the swagger stick from under his arm and tapped it impatiently against his thigh. It was an expensive one, covered in rattlesnake skin. He had bought it in Dunhill's, on a weekend in London, to play a practical joke on Rogner. The prank over, the stick had remained as a permanent part of his uniform.

He glanced over to the weather map and peered at it thoughtfully. La Guardia Field was close to Newark, about 15 miles northeast, less than five minutes' flying time across Manhattan to the New Jersey airfield.

"What's it like at La Guardia?" Smith asked.

Curtis picked up a teletype sheet from his desk and ran a pencil point down the mass of weather information.

"As of ten minutes ago, La Guardia reported Contact, 1,500 foot ceiling, lifting to 6,000, local fog and light rain."

"Contact" meant that Smith would have to fly below the cloud cover, keeping in visual contact with the ground at all times. If the ceiling dropped to below 1,000 feet, he was aware that regulations called for the flight to be terminated. He would be forced to return to Bedford Field.

Smith studied the weather report, weighing his decision with a brooding expression, the swagger stick beating a restless tattoo on the desk top.

"Have Boston Control clear me Contact to La Guardia," he told Curtis. He lifted his briefcase onto the desk and opened it, absently pulling out Martha's nightgown as he rummaged through his maps. After a moment Smith realized that the lieutenant was staring at him with a bemused grin. His eyes fell on the gown lying on the desk.

"My wife's," Smith explained, his face instantly reddening. "I forgot to drop it off at the house." He snatched it up and hastily stuffed the embarrassment deep into the briefcase, then busied himself with selecting a sectional map from the stack in his case. He noticed with relief that Curtis had the good sense not to comment. The young officer had picked up the phone and started to dial, then stopped and looked at Smith hesitantly.

"I hope you're aware, colonel, that you've got to have official business with the base unit to land at La Guardia. It's a new order, came in last week." His tone clearly doubted that Smith's flight complied with the edict.

Smith looked up from his map and gave Curtis a reassuring smile. "I've got official business, lieutenant," he said evenly.

Curtis still looked troubled. "I'm afraid I'll have to ask you to sign a statement to that effect, Colonel Smith."

"No problem there, lieutenant." Smith nodded understandingly, then flashed a smile, and tapped the phone with the tip of his swagger stick. "After you get my clearance, of course." He turned his attention to the map and began to plot his course. A moment later he heard Curtis dialing the phone.

*   *   *

The air was still heavy with the aroma of gasoline as Martha watched the fuel truck pull away. Her gaze drifted to where Domitrovich, squatting like a snake charmer, was examining the right landing gear, probing it with a long screwdriver, pressing his face close and squinting into it.

For the past half-hour she had followed his every move, impressed with his meticulous inspection of the entire plane. He seemed to take nothing for granted. When the refueling was completed he had climbed up onto the wings, and using a dip stick, checked each of the gas tanks, gauging their fullness against the gallons registered on the truck's meter. Then he had stooped under each wing and opened a valve, letting a small amount of the pale-red fuel drain onto the ground. He was checking for water that might have seeped into the tanks, he explained, anticipating her unasked question. He offered her that shy smile, then added that the presence of water in the fuel tanks could be very dangerous, starving the engines of critically needed power at the moment of takeoff. The thought crossed her mind that he sounded as if he was reciting from textbook memory—the precise terminology accepted but really alien to his instinctive knowledge.

The sergeant struck her as one of those men women called "handy with their hands"—the kind who could fix or build anything in a garage workshop. A man children would be attracted to because he spoke little and offered no judgments. Though they had hardly talked at all, she felt comfortable around him. She had no doubt that he could be entrusted to keep a confidence—and yet a dozen times she had stopped herself from revealing her fear, from asking him if her sense of doom had any basis in fact. Perhaps it was because he seemed so totally unconcerned with anything but his work. He appeared to take no notice that the sky had darkened considerably in the last ten minutes.

Bill's voice startled her.

"You about ready, Chris?"

There had been no message from Rogner. She turned and saw that Bill had taken off his jacket and was wearing his dark flying glasses.

Domitrovich emerged from under the wing, wiping his hands on a cloth. "All set, colonel. They tightened up that brake okay."

Bill nodded and handed his jacket and briefcase to the sergeant. "Stow that for me, willya, Chris?"

"Have a good flight, darling," Martha said, putting her arms around his waist and hugging him tightly. "Call me tonight if you get a chance, huh?"

It had taken her last ounce of courage not to bolt and run to the car—to make her words sound breezy, as casual as saying goodbye to a friend after a bridge party.

"Hey, where you runnin'?" he said, surprised. "I thought you wanted to see me take off."

She was trapped by a promise made Thursday, when she had missed watching him land. One thing or another had always prevented her from seeing him fly. Once, during his training in Florida, she had caught sight of him in the air, as he swooped low over their rented house, buzzing her. But that was not the same, he pointed out with bruised pride, as actually seeing him behind the controls, lifting his ship off the ground. Saturday morning, she had promised.

"I didn't want to get in the way," she said, aware that her voice came out sounding helpless; a child powerless to intervene in the adult world. He would take off. Given the fact, all she wanted now was to absent herself. To take her fear and her impotence from the scene.

"There's nothin' to get in the way of," he said, grinning at her foolishness. "Just stand back over there"—he pointed to the wire fence—"an' I'll show you how that ole eagle takes to the air."

She felt detached, out of body, as if she were in a darkened theater watching a March of Time newsreel. He was embracing her, promising to call when he landed at the base. Then he was gone, swinging up into the plane through the open belly hatch. A moment later he appeared in the cockpit and slipped on a set of headphones the sergeant handed him. He gingerly placed the padded cups over his ears, making several adjustments to the band arched over his head. His ears were bothering him again, she thought, all that high-altitude flying in freezing weather. They would probably never stop giving him trouble.

She saw the man at work framed in the cockpit window, his hands busy, his head turning back and forth as he checked the instruments. She heard a whining sound and saw the left propeller begin to turn, grudgingly, then it spun into a blur. The man started the second engine, sending a blast of wind back to her, molding the thin dress to her body. She brushed the hair away from her eyes. The engine noise became painful.

Now she saw something moving toward the plane. A gray-colored jeep. It halted a short distance away from the spinning blades. A baby-faced sailor jumped out, raising his hand in a "hold it" gesture to the man in the cockpit. He broke into a trot around the wing to the pilot's window. She saw that he was carrying a small canvas bag like the sergeant's. His blue uniform was a shade too light for his compact body, the jumper hiking up, exposing his white skin as he ran. She watched the pilot slip off his headphones and lean out the small window, straining to catch the sailor's words over the roaring engines. The sailor opened his bag and showed a slip of paper to the pilot. The pilot nodded and made a waving motion.

She saw the hatch under the plane open and the sailor toss in his bag, then hoist himself up through the narrow opening. It suddenly struck her what was happening.

Bill is giving him a ride. Why? Why the sailor and not Sergeant McCarthy?

The hatch closed. She saw the pilot talking into his microphone.

"Army 0577 . . . you're cleared for taxi to runway one eight . . . wind south-southwest steady at ten knots . . . altimeter setting reads two nine nine five."

Corporal Frederick Harrison released the button on his microphone and watched the B-25 as it began to roll under his glass enclosure in the control tower.

"Roger, tower . . . thank you," the pilot's voice drawled over the loudspeaker.

Harrison followed the Mitchell as it turned onto the taxiway. He could make out the name *Old John Feather Merchant* emblazoned under the cockpit. The .50-caliber machine guns had been stripped from its Plexiglas nose and top turret, giving the aluminum-sheathed bomber a rather peculiar, almost neutered look. And yet, even with the armament missing, the blunted, ramrod sweep of its fuselage transmitted unmistakable power. It was, Harrison thought, exactly what it looked like—a craft designed for a lethal purpose.

He raised his binoculars as the plane neared the northern edge of the runway and turned into the wind. Even at that distance he could clearly see the men seated in the cockpit.

Smith eased back on the throttles and allowed the painted runway numerals to disappear under his wings before applying the brakes. The twin Cyclone engines took shearing bites of the damp morning air as Domitrovich, buckled into the right-hand seat, continued to read off the check list.

"Autopilot . . . "

Smith reached over the control pedestal and rocked the switch back and forth. "Off and locked."

"Fuel booster pumps . . ."

"On—six pounds' pressure."

"Oil pressure . . . "

"Eighty-two pounds—steady."

"Mixture . . . "

The colonel's right hand grasped the two levers and pushed them forward. "Full rich."

Hunched behind them in the small jump seat, the sailor, Machinist's Mate Albert Perna, listened to the seemingly endless detail required to lift a plane off the ground and keep it in the air.

"Flaps . . . "

Smith looked down at the lever markings, then shot glances out both windows at the wing surfaces. "Down— twenty degrees." He rolled the throttles slowly forward, his eyes locked on the tachometer. The needle climbed to 2,600 rpm as he pressed the levers snugly in place. The bomber's wings were trembling under the strain of the howling engines. Smith looked over his right shoulder and checked to see that the sailor's seat harness was fastened, then turned his attention toward the far edge of the field, where Martha was standing next to the gate. He extended his arm out the window and waved, the gesture sweepingly exaggerated to carry the distance. He saw her wave back.

"0577 . . . you're cleared for takeoff."

Smith picked up the microphone and brought it close to his mouth. "Roger, tower . . . thank you."

His eyes traveled the instrument panel, halting momentarily at each dial and gauge as he noted the pressure and temperature readings, then continued on to the switches and levers, forcing himself to remember that he was behind the controls of a B-25. It was a conscious precaution. For more than two years he had flown the giant four-engine B-17 Flying Fortress. Its array of instruments and controls had become engraved in his mind, as familiar to him as his own face.

This Saturday morning, for only his second time, he was flying the smaller, lighter, and much faster B-25. Although the instrumentation of both planes was basically the same, there were specific differences—lever settings, temperature readings, placement of gears and switches. It was because of these differences that he forced himself to override a thousand hours of instinct—to keep his hand from automatically converting this stranger into a friend.

He released the brakes. *Old John Feather Merchant* rolled forward and rapidly gained speed. As it shot past the 3,000-foot marker Bill Smith lifted the twelve-ton machine smoothly into the gray overcast. Keeping his eyes on the tachometer, he reached down with his right hand and pulled the gear lever to the up position. Under the drone of the engines he felt a hollow thump as the hydraulics drew the tricycle landing gear into the fuselage. He glanced at the airspeed indicator, then retracted the flaps, his eyes darting from the wings to the panel indicator as the metal slats rolled back into position.

Normally, these technical details—the preflight check, radio contact with the tower, trimming the craft in flight—all should have been the shared responsibility of the copilot, the man usually occupying the right-hand seat. The pilot gave his orders, the copilot carried them out.

But Sergeant Domitrovich was not a pilot. He had been assigned to the flight as an engineer in charge of the mechanical maintenance of the aircraft. His job was over long before they left the ground. Bill Smith was flying the bomber solo—as both pilot and navigator.

Clearing the airfield's outer marker, Smith banked the plane into a climbing left turn. Even at their low altitude, scattered patches of fog and clouds partially obscured the ground. He reached over the control column and redialed the radios to the tower and broadcast frequencies used by La Guardia.

Martha turned with the sound, peering up into the bank of clouds hovering directly overhead. The B-25 was still so close she could actually feel the pulsing throb of its engines, but except for a glimpse of the bomber's twin tail, it had already been swallowed by the overcast.

Reluctantly, she turned and started toward the parking area. It was done, over with. Out of her hands. But the strange, momentary sensation of relief was settling into an uneasy guilt—it smacked of rationalization; the kind she imagined people must use when they let their fingertips slip from a rock ledge, or felt the unequal pull of the street below the rooftop. Letting go, the act of unalterable commitment, surprisingly brought with it no solace. The engines were a faint buzz now, like a bad phone connection, almost dissolved in the sounds of the airfield. She was rummaging through her purse for the car keys and not finding them.

Bill has the keys!

The flash of memory was correct. She remembered seeing him drop the keys into his jacket pocket as he opened the car door for her. It had been so casual, so automatic a gesture that she never questioned it.

                    *   *   *

"Army 0577 . . . this is Bedford Tower. Please contact."

Martha watched Corporal Harrison as he flipped the console switch to "receive" for the third time. She stared up at the loudspeaker, listening to the crackling silence. Harrison turned to her and shrugged.

"I'll try a different frequency." He dialed the radio to another band and depressed the "transmit" key.

"Bedford Tower calling Army 0577 . . . Army 0577. Do you read?"

She glanced at the clock. It was one minute past nine. Bill had been gone six minutes. She had started to calculate how far he could travel in those six red sweeps of the second hand when Harrison answered her question.

"He should be west of Providence by now." He swung his eyes from the clock to Martha. "Still well within range."

"Why doesn't he *answer*?!"

Harrison pushed his chair back and swiveled to face her. He was grinning, shaking his head in mild rebuke. "Because he's probably switched to the New York frequencies. About the only thing you can do now is phone ahead to La Guardia." He picked up a clipboard and scanned a typewritten list. "We've got three flights from La Guardia scheduled to land here later this morning. Your husband could get the car keys on one of those."

Martha relaxed a bit. Harrison's explanation for the silent loudspeaker seemed plausible. She was already thinking of how she would word the call. The part about the keys was easy. The nightgown, which she remembered that Bill had also forgotten to give her, was another story.

*   *   *

At 1,000 feet the bomber was scraping the swollen bottom of the cloud cover. Smith glanced at the airspeed indicator. It read 230 miles per hour, the tach needle steady at 2,100 rpm. He reached down to his left and depressed the button on the radio compass control box, then fine-tuned the frequency dial to the Providence Beacon. A green light flashed on, and at the same time a steady tone entered his earphones. He was on course.

In the distance, under his left wing, was the city of Providence. Farther off, lying dark and sullen under a bank of storm clouds, was Narragansett Bay. He checked the panel clock. In fifty minutes, if the weather held, he would reach the New York area. At two minutes past nine it was a coin toss where he would land—La Guardia or Newark.

CHAPTER II

The Pilot

To THE NAVY HITCHHIKER, ALBERT Perna, who had been in a plane only once before, it must have seemed as if the wing tip had been suddenly and quite mysteriously sheared off. The bomber was flying heeled over on its right side, the leading edge of the left wing sucked high into the solid gray vapor.

Smith watched the compass rotate to 225 degrees before releasing his foot from the right rudder pedal. He leveled out, the altimeter showing that *Old John Feather Merchant* was now flying 1,000 feet above the lush green of northern Connecticut.

It was familiar country. A month before, Smith had flown a B-17 across the Atlantic from England, landing at Bradley Field in Windsor Locks. That day, as on this Saturday morning, the Connecticut River had raced past the small town, running a snakelike course to the distant Long Island Sound. Although its color was slate gray and not red, its meanders longer and more gentle, the river reminded Smith of another, more remote in geography and removed in time.

For a boy growing up in Latham, Alabama, the Tensaw River provided all the mystery and adventure of the Spanish Main. The rural town sat close to the river, on earth rich in iron oxides which colored the waters rust red.

In 1918, the year Bill Smith was born, Latham's citizens would stroll along the river bank on a hot summer's night and discuss the war—not the one for which Irving Berlin had just composed a bugle call, or which Sergeant Alvin York was turning into a turkey shoot, but the Civil War, the conflict that had ended fifty-three years before and had changed their lives for all time. The city of Mobile, with its wide, deep-water port, flourished only 25 miles away, but inland, Latham and surrounding hamlets like Little River, Rabun, and Perdido were the legacy of the lost South. Abandoned farms and shuttered mansions lined the path which Bill and his younger brother, Bob, took down to the river, where they skinny-dipped and dug for bloodworms to catch the bottom-feeding catfish.

The Smiths lived on a small farm near the edge of the town. Black tenant families tended the few seasonal crops, and Bill, like all white kids in the area, had "Nigra" friends. There was no prejudice in Latham, he would argue in later years to Northern acquaintances, simply because both blacks and whites knew their place. The Ku Klux Klan rarely had need to don their hooded bedsheets; when they did, the midnight visit was more often paid to a white farmer thought to have mistreated his wife or daughter. Principles, like tradition, ran deep in Latham, and an honest application of tar and feathers made a workable preservative.

Except for when he was six, when a rabid collie bit his face and he had to undergo the long and painful series of Pasteur shots, Bill Smith's life in the small town was a "Penrod and Sam" idyll. But Dolly Mae Smith's plans for her son went far beyond the dusty boundaries of Latham.

Bill's mother was determined for the boy to have all the advantages due him. Her people had come to the South with the first English settlers. With her marriage to William Franklin Smith, Dolly Mae could then proudly claim not one, but two links to the infamous Fort Mims massacre.

Located two miles from Latham, Fort Mims was, in 1813, the southernmost barricade in a string of forts built to protect settlers from the warring Creek Indians. On August 20th of that year, 553 men, women, and children were jammed into the small blockhouse and surrounding log stockade. Their long rifles were primed and cocked. Outside, hidden in the tall grass and rushes bordering the Alabama River, were one thousand Creeks. Among them was a warrior named Red Eagle.

Probably the illegitimate offspring of a Creek mother, Red Eagle had been abandoned when only days old. He was found by a militiaman named Weatherford and taken into Fort Mims to be raised as William Weatherford. Educated by the whites, he had managed to live peacefully in both worlds—until the chiefs of the Creek Nation decided that all-out war was the only way to halt the settlers' encroachment on their territory. Forced by circumstances to choose a side, Weatherford painted his face with the red clay of the river bank and took the name Red Eagle. By noon that August day, his final attempt to avert bloodshed had been ignored by both the Creeks and the settlers.

The massacre took five hours. At sundown, of the original 553 inhabitants of Fort Mims, 36 remained alive; only Negro slaves and halfbreeds had been spared butchery by ax and scalping knives. Weatherford, sickened by the carnage, had left the battle after a few hours, but not before begging the warriors to spare the women and children. Again, his pleas went unheeded.

Among the women killed that day was Dolly Mae Smith's great-great-grandmother. Red Eagle went on to become chief of the Creeks, leading them to a final and lasting peace with the settlers. He took up farming and married a white woman. One of his sons was William Franklin Smith's great-great-uncle.

Bill Smith grew up hearing that story from his mother time and again, and like a hand from the grave, it was to have a determining grip on his future. "Duty, Honor, Country" had a greater depth of meaning to Dolly Mae than mere embroidery on dimestore samplers. The Smiths' roots went far into the country's foundations, and so by the time he was eight, Bill could tell anyone who asked that he had already decided on a career in the Army. "After you graduate from West Point," Dolly Mae invariably added.

Mr. Smith was a railroad man. Precise, yet easygoing and genial, he was comfortable in his job as general agent for the

Alabama, Tennessee and Northern Railroad. He was given a promotion when Bill was ten, and the family moved up to Birmingham.

On weekends, Mr. Smith entertained his railroad clients with long hunts on horseback, his prize pack of bird and rabbit dogs never failing to impress the deskbound executives. But try as he would, the elder Smith could never interest Bill in hunting. He had no stomach for killing animals, the boy told his father over and over—especially for sport. The more he resisted, the more exasperated and insistent his father became.

"How can you have an Army career," Mr. Smith would ask, bewildered, "without knowing how to hunt and shoot?"

Bill finally gave in. The morning of the hunt a heavy mist covered the ground. With a .22 cradled over his arm, Bill was following the lead of his father's favorite hound. The boy stumbled over a rock. The gun went off. The dog howled like a banshee as the bullet plowed through his foot. And that was the last time Mr. Smith ever mentioned hunting to his son.

If guns were no part of his life, girls and sports quickly filled the void. At Woodlawn High School, Bill firmly entrenched himself as the Big Man On Campus. Virginia Seaforth was his steady girl, and Bill became the envy of his buddies when the tall, strikingly pretty blonde would pick him up after school in her convertible. Virginia was the prototype for a string of girls that in the years to come were attracted to Bill's dark handsomeness. "It's probably the Indian in me," he'd say poker-faced whenever friends grumbled that Smith always got the prettiest girl.

Everything, in fact, seemed to come easy to Bill Smith. He was a natural dancer, and no matter how new or complicated the step or rhythm—from the Big Apple to the Stomp—he learned it effortlessly. The bookshelves in his room sagged under the weight of trophies won in city and statewide dance contests. When he wasn't dancing to the latest pop tune, Bill was playing it in the Woodlawn Band—on either the clarinet, saxophone, trumpet, or trombone, instruments which he mastered after taking only a few lessons.

He was a member of the debating team, and employing the same agility and grace he displayed on the dance floor, he won several state championships. Theater was another passion, especially Shakespeare, and he starred in Drama Club productions of *Hamlet, Macbeth,* and *King Lear.*

With a single exception, Bill had Dolly Mae's blessing in everything he attempted. The lone disagreement was football. Miraculously he had reached the far side of his teens without breaking any bones; she did not want to tempt fate just so Bill could hang another varsity sweater in his closet. He would have to content himself, she told him with finality, with the letters he had already won for tennis, baseball, and golf.

To his brothers in the Mikado Club, a quasi-fraternal order dedicated to malt drinking and girl chasing, Smith was a constant source of frustration; whatever he wanted, he seemed to get. Backed to the wall, they would admit that Bill worked harder and longer than most for his rewards. Still, even his closest friends felt there was something uncanny about his success. No matter how far back he started, whether in academics or in sports, Smith always managed to come out on top. It was no surprise when the graduating class of 1936 asked Bill to give the valedictory speech.

With a certain predictability, he chose his theme from Carlyle's poem "To Thine Own Self Be True." Weighed in literary terms it was not exactly a spine-tingler. And yet, as if prophetically parting a curtain into his future, Smith invoked the poet's caution that "the ordinary man looks to external circumstances for things that can only be found in himself. We must choose for ourselves, think for ourselves, and above all— trust ourselves."

As his uncle had done before him, Bill prepared for West Point by attending Marion Military Institute. He breezed through the two-year course with honors, emerging as Captain Adjutant of the Corps. On the competitive exam for the Point, Bill received the highest score of any Alabaman.

On July 1, 1938—while Hitler was preparing to annex Austria—Cadet William Franklin Smith, Jr., Serial Number

12879, entered the Long Gray Line of the United States Military Academy at West Point. Dolly Mae Smith's dream had come true.

*   *   *

Rain splattered against *Old John Feather Merchant*'s windshield as the bomber approached Hartford on a south-southwesterly heading.

The fuel-gauge needles were barely off their "full" marks. Domitrovich had taken the precaution of filling the four wing tanks to their 974-gallon capacity because of the uncertain weather conditions. If necessary, Colonel Smith could land, pick up his passengers, and fly on to Sioux Falls without refueling.

Smith had carefully checked out his fuel load on the Aircraft Clearance form provided by Lieutenant Curtis back at Bedford Field. He had affixed his signature to the form directly below the typed-in statement: "I have official business with the 1338th Base Unit at La Guardia Field. I am familiar with the danger areas in my line of flight."

CHAPTER III

9:05—The People

CROSSING UNDER THE MASSIVE GLASS and blackened steel dome, Paul Dearing noticed that Penn Station was virtually empty. Even the commuter train, usually crowded on a Saturday morning with suburban matrons coming into the city to shop, had been half filled. The rain, he concluded, had kept most people at home.

Following his daily ritual, Dearing stopped at the Union Newsstand's out-of-town rack. He tossed the *Times* he had read on the train into the trash bin and bought a copy of the Buffalo *Courier-Express*. The thirty-five-year-old Dearing was the New York City correspondent for the upstate paper, and, except for his conservative double-breasted gray suit and dark tie, he looked and acted like a reporter. His lanky openness and quick wit had often positioned him to land a scoop for his hometown paper. But "stringers"—part-time journalists— were notoriously underpaid. Dearing held down a full-time job as the public-relations director for the Catholic War Relief Services.

Emerging on Seventh Avenue and 33rd Street, Dearing's eyes instinctively swept up to the Empire State Building. A glance told him it was going to be one of those "soupy" days. The graceful limestone building was only a block away, but a swirling canopy of clouds and fog had already sliced the towering structure almost exactly in half. Dearing knew that somewhere behind that mass of gray his secretary had just turned on all the lights in his corner office on the 79th floor.

*   *   *

As long as she was shooting up and down in the car, Betty Lou Oliver felt reasonably cool. But now, as the petite, blue-eyed elevator operator opened the doors to let the two maintenance men out, the mugginess in the Empire State Building's lobby hit her. As she stepped out of car Number 6, her hand brushed against the wall and came away wet. Even the tomblike Rocheron marble, normally chill to the touch, was beaded with a thin film of sweat.

But the last thing on Betty Lou's mind this morning was the weather. By this time tomorrow she would be on the train to Norfolk, Virginia, for a reunion with her Navy husband. She had not seen him for two years, and when Oscar's surprise call had come a week ago, on her twentieth birthday, it had been weeks since she had received a letter. Newspaper reports had told her that his destroyer was part of the vast armada shelling the Japanese Home Islands. Although the accounts vividly described the total destruction of the Nipponese war machine, Betty Lou had also read about the waves of kamikaze pilots willing to make the final sacrifice for their emperor.

She was staying with her aunt and uncle in their spacious apartment on upper Broadway. Their daughter had been visiting with her in Fort Smith, Arkansas, during the past six months. When her cousin decided that she had had enough of small-town life, she had invited Betty Lou to come to New York with her and await Oscar's return. Her uncle, a Navy captain, had assured her that the war in the Pacific would be over in a matter of weeks. To occupy her time he found her temporary work through a friend with connections at the Empire State Building.

Today, her last day on the job, Betty Lou was bursting with excitement. And it was infectious. Even the normally staid head starter, Chauncey Humphrey, had grinned at her and winked as he made his rounds of the G bank of elevators. She had worked there for only six weeks, but her vivaciousness quickly made Betty Lou a favorite with the tenants and her fellow workers. Throughout the week her "regulars," as she called them—tenants and employees who poured into her express car every morning—had been saying goodbye; some even gave her small gifts of perfume and candy in appreciation for the cheerful, breezy way she started their workday.

Still, although she knew it was silly, even childish of her, most exciting of all this morning was the new outfit she had bought for the trip to Norfolk: a navy-blue suit and a pair of blue-and-white spectator pumps—an extravagant purchase on her $32-a-week salary. They were in her locker in the fifth-floor employees' lounge. At noon, after saying her last goodbyes, Betty Lou would change out of her brown uniform dress and meet her cousin at the Russian Tea Room for a farewell lunch.

*   *   *

Monsignor Patrick O'Boyle awakened at 6:15 with a sense of urgency. The police ambulance clanging past his windows in the rectory of St. Malachy's Church on 49th Street, west of Broadway, prompted him out of bed a little faster than he would have liked; but this morning he found even that impelling sound appropriate. Today he was having lunch with the Archbishop of New York, Francis Cardinal Spellman, and the Italian Ambassador. It was an important meeting for the monsignor. As executive director of the War Relief Services of the National Catholic Welfare Conference, O'Boyle was setting up a vast emergency relief program for war-ravaged Italy.

Since 1943, his organization had shipped thousands of tons of food, clothing, medicines, and books throughout Europe. The aid had been distributed by the International Red Cross to Allied prisoners of war, as well as to the destitute civilian populations. Within the past month the monsignor and his assistant, Father Edward Swanstrom, had inaugurated full-scale civilian relief programs in France, Germany, and many other European countries. Italy was next on his agenda; but O'Boyle, and the Vatican, had first to overcome an unforeseen problem. The Italian Communists, virulently anti-

Church, were rapidly growing as a political power. They would have to be either won over or neutralized before the relief program could operate without fear of sabotage. That was to be the topic of the monsignor's noon luncheon.

But first there was seven o'clock Mass, and after that confessions to be heard. Thus it was a few minutes past nine when Monsignor O'Boyle hailed a cab on Broadway. On his lap was a thick folder of notes he had made the night before concerning Father Swanstrom's upcoming trip to France and England. His plan was to dictate the handwritten pages to his secretary and have them typed in time for his 11:00 meeting with Swanstrom.

As he reviewed the notes, something shiny caught the monsignor's eye. It was his right pant leg. His housekeeper had pressed the black clerical suit that morning, but obviously had overlooked the glaring defect. A fastidious, exacting man, O'Boyle wouldn't dream of appearing before the archbishop in such condition. He shot a vexed look at his watch. With any luck, the new suit he had bought earlier in the week at Rogers Peet wouldn't need further alteration. He could change there, and then proceed to his 79th-floor office in the Empire State Building.

*   *   *

Waiting for the 34th Street light to change, Therese Fortier discovered that once again she was staring at the gold ring on her left hand. It was a recent and, she thought, disturbing habit. Although she had received the ring some months ago, time had only increased, not diminished its presence. It was a simple enough piece of jewelry, quiet and in good taste. The small red stone strongly resembled a ruby, but Therese had no illusions; her boyfriend George was an Army private.

What troubled the nineteen-year-old secretary for the Catholic War Relief Services was wearing the ring as she did; it gave the appearance of engagement, and yet she and George had no formal agreement. They had discussed marrying before he went overseas, and the topic constantly came up in their letters; but she still found herself wavering. For as devout a Catholic as Therese, marriage could never be induced by anything so mundane as war.

She was a strikingly pretty girl, and so it was perfectly natural that the two young Canadian soldiers would fall in beside her as she crossed the wide avenue. With her shoulder-length natural-blond hair and not a trace of makeup, Therese, they were sure, was either an actress or, at the very least, a Powers model. She left them at the entrance to the Empire State Building, still disbelieving that the large brown envelope she carried contained religious song sheets, and not cheesecake photos.

*   *   *

It was impossible to mistake Father Edward Swanstrom for anything but a dyed-in-the-wool New Yorker. At forty-two, the tall, powerfully built cleric paced along the sidewalk with the same direct, no-nonsense determination that he had exhibited on the Fordham track team back in the '20s. There was no hesitation, no sense of indecision; he had a mission. At the moment it was to get a haircut and shave at his favorite tonsorial parlor.

As he had done every Saturday morning for years, Father Swanstrom threw open the door to the Two Park Avenue Barber Shop and was waved into the waiting chair by Danny Fumarola. This was a happy and relaxing ritual for the priest. Under the soothing hot towel he and Danny would trade jokes and gossip. This morning the talk centered about Swanstrom's visa problem.

Red tape had held up the necessary papers for the War Relief Services mission on which he and his two assistants were to embark Tuesday. Although the war in Europe had been over since mid-May, the bureaucratic log jam continued. Political corners needed to be cut, and a friend in the British Consulate had agreed to help. When Danny's ministrations were finished, Father Swanstrom would walk the two blocks to the Empire State Building, pick up his assistants, and then hop a cab to the English outpost in Rockefeller Center.

*   *   *

The 34th Street crosstown bus was blocking the intersection of Fifth Avenue, directly behind the shiny black horsedrawn Victoria carriage. Pounding his horn in impatient, staccato bleats, the bus driver succeeded only in making the horses even more skittish. In a publicity stunt designed to attract suburban shoppers, Saks 34th Street had just initiated the unique pickup service from Grand Central Station to the Sixth Avenue department store. It was not only convenient, the ads promised, but it was also patriotic: "Our horses don't consume precious gasoline."

Standing in the exit well at the front of the bus, Monsignor O'Boyle's secretary, Kay O'Connor, found the situation laughable. The harder the liveried coachman hauled on the reins in an attempt to maneuver the carriage around a double-parked delivery truck, the more stubbornly the horses refused to move. Traffic was backed up in all four directions— hundreds of idling engines gulping great, unpatriotic quantities of rationed fuel. With a frustrated shove the bus driver hit the door handle and waved Kay out into the middle of the street.

Protecting her blue straw picture hat with both hands, the tall, patrician secretary dashed through the rain into the Empire State Building's Fifth Avenue entrance. A hurried glance at the lobby clock warned her not to stop at the cigar stand and pick up a pack of Old Golds. The monsignor was a stickler for punctuality, and Kay was in no frame of mind to endure another of his lectures. Just last week she and O'Boyle had had a minor blowout over his practice of placing a red check next to the names of late-arriving employees. She pointed out to the monsignor that as his executive secretary she felt it was denigrating to be included, as she put it, on his "eccentric scorecard." She had stopped short of adding that at thirty-seven, she could hardly be mistaken for a schoolgirl, especially with her prematurely snow-white hair.

As Kay rounded the corner to the G bank of elevators she spotted Paul Dearing entering the Number 2 car. The operator, Mary Scannell, saw her and, grim-faced, urgently motioned her into the car. Involuntarily, she broke into a trot.

"He's in already?" she asked the plump, red-haired operator.

Mary gave Dearing an impish wink, then turned to Kay and pealed a trilling giggle. "Not yet," she said in her County Cork brogue, "but you should've seen your face . . . even your rouge went white."

Dearing shook his head and laughed. "She got you again," he said, patting Kay's shoulder in commiseration.

He, like just about every other long-term resident of the building, had more than once borne the brunt of Mary's practical jokes. But the War Relief Services people were her favorites; not even the formidable O'Boyle escaped her attention. Just the day before, as Dearing and the monsignor were being rocketed up on an express run to the 79th floor, O'Boyle asked Mary if she had ever timed how long the almost 1,000-foot ride took.

"One Hail Mary and two Our Fathers," she had instantly shot back.

Although she had been in America for ten years, the twenty-seven-year-old Irish girl still spoke with an accent thick as peat. Operating an elevator in the Empire State Building was a step up for Mary after working as a waitress in Schrafft's Restaurant; not only was it more prestigious, but the higher salary went far in helping to support her eight brothers and five sisters still living in the Old Country. Besides, piloting a monsignor, she once told Kay, put her a heck of a lot closer to "you know who" than serving watercress and cucumber sandwiches every day.

Instinctively, Mary eased the brass control handle toward neutral and brought the speeding car to a gliding stop at the 79th floor. Just as Dearing and Kay O'Connor stepped out, the car's buzzer sounded and a red light flashed on the panel, indicating a call from the 86th-floor observation deck. Mary sighed and shook her head in mock weariness.

"Until you two came along, things were quiet. I'm going to get even with both of you for making me work," she said, wagging a finger at them as she closed the doors.

A sharp left turn brought Kay and Dearing to 7907, the frosted glass double doors of the War Relief Services office located on the west side of the corridor.

Inside the simply furnished reception foyer, Lucille Bath was seated at the switchboard answering a call. Dearing pushed past the wooden gate next to the reception desk and headed for his office in the northwest corner of the building. As Kay stopped to pick up a large stack of mail sitting on top of the switchboard, she noticed that the shapely nineteen-year-old blond receptionist was wearing a sheer white blouse, her brassiere straps clearly visible. Kay couldn't help smiling; the monsignor would go straight up the wall when he saw Lucille in that outfit. O'Boyle had talked to the young newlywed several times about wearing "risqué" attire; on the last occasion Lucille had come to the office in an off-the-shoulder peasant blouse, showing a bit more cleavage than perhaps even the designer intended. Kay had attempted to mollify O'Boyle's indignation, but the monsignor had an unswervable sense of decorum; men and women, he insisted, should dress like ladies and gentlemen—especially if they worked for the Relief Services.

For a brief moment Kay thought about saying something to Lucille, then decided it would be fruitless; even if she wanted to, what could the youngster change into before the monsignor arrived?

*   *   *

Occupying the entire west side of the 79th floor, the War Relief Services office overlooked 33rd Street to the south and 34th Street to the north. Glass-partitioned executive offices rimmed the walls, with the wide center areas to the left and right of the reception foyer given over to the side-by-side desks of secretaries and bookkeepers. The furnishings were monastic, reflecting Monsignor O'Boyle's personal taste as well as his strict adherence to the charity's tight budget. Anything that had not been donated was rented on a monthly basis: the dark oak desks and chairs, adding machines, filing cabinets, typewriters—even the ancient water cooler located outside Father Swanstrom's office.

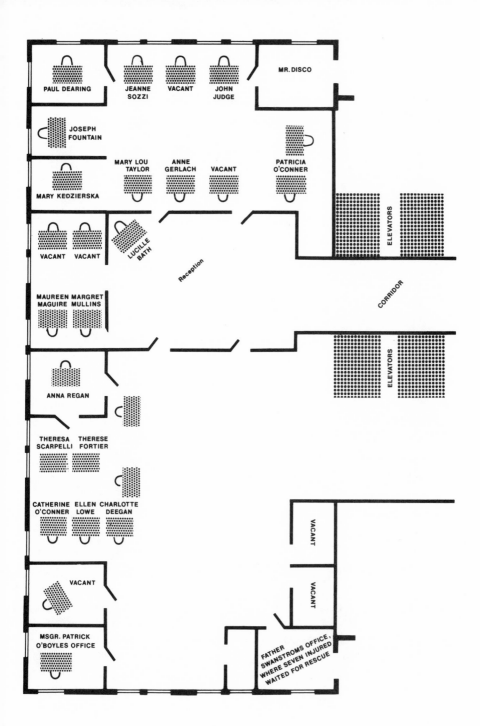

This morning, following their usual alternating Saturday schedule, more than half the weekend staff of twenty were already at their desks. Saturday was a short work day, and like most Manhattan offices, the Relief Services would close at noon.

As far as John Aloysius Judge was concerned, his work day might as well be over. The forty-year-old former Christian Brother had made the long train trip in from Bell Harbor, Long Island, specifically to dictate an important report to his secretary, Ethel Reidy. But Ethel, Father Swanstrom's sister, had just called in sick. Seated at his desk overlooking 34th Street, Judge gloomily stared out at the fog pressing against his windows and reviewed his options: he could catch the 9:35 at Penn Station and spend the rest of the day at home with his wife and children; or he could attempt to pry Jeanne Sozzi loose from Dearing and ask her to take down the report. He swiveled his chair in time to see the short, olive-complexioned secretary carrying a file folder into Dearing's office. He checked his watch; if Jeanne was not out in ten minutes, he'd call it a day.

Reaching across his desk, Judge snapped on his Philco portable and tuned in WQXR. The newscaster announced that Mississippi Senator Theodore Bilbo planned to introduce a bill in Congress which would force all U.S. Negroes, including those who served in the armed forces, to emigrate to Africa.

* * *

Pacing his office, Joseph Fountain pulled off his glasses and angrily slapped them against the cablegram in his hand.

"Nine million packages," he said bitterly. *"Nine million!"*

Her pencil poised above the steno pad, Fountain's secretary, Mary Louise Taylor, shook her head in disbelief. The cable from the International Red Cross headquarters in Paris had just arrived. Its brevity only heightened the horror of its message: nine million packages of food, medicines and clothing destined for Allied prisoners of war in German camps had been discovered rotting in a Nuremberg warehouse.

Many of the packages had been sent by the Relief Services to the Heppenheim POW camp on the outskirts of the ancient Bavarian town; Heppenheim was infamous, Fountain knew only too well, for its high death rate from starvation and medical neglect.

The balding director of the Prisoner of War Project stood speechless for a moment. Then, as his eyes filled, he quickly turned and crossed to a window facing Sixth Avenue. In that instant, Mary thought the forty-seven-year-old executive had aged at least ten years.

Although she was only working as a summer temporary, the delicately pretty nineteen-year-old Bronx girl had quickly become attached to Fountain. Despite their age difference, they had much in common: both were deeply religious, and unlike her parents, Joe Fountain eagerly blessed Mary's intention of entering a convent in September.

In fact, they had been discussing just that subject before the cable arrived. After going to early Mass, Mary and her father had taken the subway to work. Mr. Taylor was an electrical engineer for Westinghouse, and for the past week he had been overseeing a rewiring job in the building. During the half-hour ride Mary had listened in silence as her father again attempted to argue against her lifelong goal of becoming a nun. She was an only child, and could well understand her parents' feelings; but as she had just reaffirmed to Joe Fountain, come September, she planned to take her first vows in the Carmelite Order.

Blankly peering into the field of gray fog hanging outside his window, Fountain was devastated by the news in the cable. He was a man of indelible conviction in the basic sanctity of life; but two years with the Relief Services had opened his eyes to the possibility that every so often the human condition became toxic. Each day now, the aftermath of the European war brought equally shattering reports of German atrocities. In order to remain functioning he could no longer allow himself the luxury of finding each unique. Hereafter, he would refer to the cablegram from Paris as "the Nuremberg incident";

another statistic to be catalogued among the holocaustic behavior of the Germans.

Turning from the window, Fountain glanced at the cable and then carefully laid it on his desk, next to the framed, hand-colored photograph of his wife and four young children. As he put on his glasses, he suddenly became aware that Mary had been studying him with concern. He gave her a reassuring smile, and began dictating a reply to Paris.

*　　*　　*

Cradling the phone between her shoulder and ear, Mary Kedzierska stirred the second lump of sugar into her coffee. The connection to Mexico was bad, yet through all the buzzing and crackling she had little difficulty translating the woman's ungrammatical Polish. Between sips of the steaming black coffee, Mary jotted down the sobbing woman's name, when and where she had last seen her husband and two children, and the number she was given at the Displaced Persons Camp in Mexico City.

To the thirty-four-year-old social worker, the woman's problem was heartbreakingly common. As director of the Polish Displaced Persons project, Mary was not only responsible for food, clothing, and medical attention for the thousands of DPs pouring into the United States and Mexico, but also for acting as an unofficial tracer of missing family members. It was a physically and emotionally back-breaking job; but nothing could have given the slender, dark-haired woman a greater sense of pride or achievement.

Born in lower Manhattan to Polish immigrants, Mary knew early what it was to feel alien. Insults about her name and background had followed her even to Barnard College, which she had attended on a full scholarship. On graduation day, her aunt had given her a diamond ring and a piece of advice: always wear a hat, she told Mary—that way no one would ever mistake her for a salesgirl or a file clerk.

As she hung up the phone, the diamond on Mary Kedzierska's finger caught fire from the desk lamp as she adjusted the long pearl pin stuck into the rear of her beige turban.

*   *   *

Standing behind the ticket booth in the 86th - floor observatory lounge, Sam Watkinson smiled at the appropriateness of the recording being played over the loudspeakers; "Night and Day" perfectly described the weather conditions outside the double glass door leading to the observation deck. About twenty people had bought tickets from Sam, paying $1.10 for adults, and twenty-five cents for children, to see New York City from 1,050 feet above the sidewalk. At the moment, all that was visible was a depressing panorama of bloated rain clouds and wind-whipped fog.

So far, there had only been two takers for Sam's offer of a refund; the others were optimistically staying on the slim chance that the weather would soon clear. Nevertheless, Sam had asked Mary Scannell to take the "Cloudy Today— Visibility Poor" sign down to the lobby and place it in front of the observatory elevators. From long experience, the sixty-nine year-old veteran weather-watcher knew that this morning there was little chance that conditions would change. There was no sense making people take the ride up to the observation deck, he reasoned, only to have them turn back disappointed.

Watkinson surveyed the group as they wandered about the lounge. Some were carrying cups of coffee and snacks out of the cafeteria, taking up vigils next to the windows in hopes of catching a glimpse of the city through a passing break in the clouds. Typical of the tourists were two Sam had just chatted with, Lieutenant Allen Aimen and his wife, Betty. The young Army flier was visiting the city on leave from the Pacific. Today was their last chance to catch a bird's-eye view from the observation deck; in the morning Lieutenant Aimen was shipping back to his unit on Guam. As the couple peered through a fogbound window facing north (the direction the guide book promised would "bring the Art Deco spire of the Chrysler Building within seeming reach"), Sam Watkinson debated a difficult question: should he give the Aimens his tickets to the radio show as a gift for their last night in the city? The program, "Flight to the Pacific," starring Franchot Tone, Captain Ronald Reagan and Lieutenant William Holden, was being broadcast "live" from Town Hall as a tribute to the Air Forces.

The day before, Franchot Tone had brought some out-of-town guests up to the observation deck, .and in appreciation for Sam's attentiveness, the actor had given him a pair of tickets to the 9:30 performance. Now, Watkinson was in a quandary; he had promised his wife a night on the town, dinner and the show. Yet he felt it was almost his patriotic duty to offer the tickets to the Aimens, especially since the weather and the young pilot's schedule made another visit to the observation deck impossible. Besides, the elderly ticket-taker rationalized, his diabetes was acting up; the last thing he needed was a rich dinner in an expensive restaurant. Just as he pulled the tickets out of his wallet, Sam saw the Aimens step into the small elevator which went up to the glassed-in, turretlike 102nd-floor viewing station. They might as well give it a try, he thought; but Watkinson knew the higher altitude would only put the young couple deeper into the surging weather.

*   *   *

Old John Feather Merchant's three-bladed props chewed into the cloud bank, hurling chunks of milky vapor back against the windshield. Smith was finding it difficult to maintain his 1,000-foot altitude; quartering winds and an unexpectedly heavy cloudburst over Hartford buffeted the B-25 in rollercoaster dips and updrafts. Easing the throttles back, the colonel watched the tach needle fall off to 2,000. Decreasing the bomber's airspeed would at least cut down on some of the banging around they were taking.

Leaning his head against the left window, Chris Domitrovich looked down through the rills of fog as they passed over the red-brick factories of South Hartford. As if reaching for the plane, thick columns of pigeon-gray smoke cascaded out of the Colt Manufacturing Company's twin stacks. Had the large sign on the roof not spelled out the gunmaker's name, Domitrovich could easily have mistaken the sprawling plant for one he had seen from the air over Holland less than a year before.

CHAPTER IV

The Sergeant

THE SIGHT HAD STAGGERED THE sergeant. There in front of him, stretching as far as his eye could span, were more planes and gliders than he thought the earth capable of bearing.

Sunday morning, September 17, 1944, had dawned sunny and hot. Because of that meteorological fact, Chris Domitrovich sensed something had to be very wrong with the operation code named "Market-Garden." For more than two and a half months the sun had not made an appearance over his base in the south of England; that morning, the day of the Allied invasion of German-held Holland, for the sun to suddenly shine a benediction seemed a perverse omen to the crew chief. Close-mouthed by nature, Domitrovich was not one to have noiced his thoughts, but as the air crews filed out of the briefing hut, he found an unexpected ally in Captain William Wade, the pilot of his C-47 troop carrier. Wade had glanced at the orange sphere then just edging over the horizon, and had shaken his head.

"Bad news," he muttered to no one in particular. "Those bastards really jinxed us this time."

By "those bastards" Domitrovich wasn't certain if the pilot meant the Germans or the British. During the week of planning and preparation for the massive assault, thousands

of American flying crews and paratroopers had been thrown
into marriage-close contact with their English counterparts.
Had it not been wartime, the divorce rate would have been
staggering. For the first time in the war, entire divisions of
American air and land forces had been placed under a foreign
commander—Field Marshal Bernard Law Montgomery, the
creator and battering ram behind Market-Garden.

Prior to this joint effort, the U.S. Air Corps' relations with
their British hosts had been cordial, if at times somewhat
strained: the two cultures had language in common, but from
there on, in matters ranging from technical to philosophical,
continual top-level puttering with each fighting machine was
needed to keep the parts frictionless. Until the audacious plan
to strike at Germany's heart through the rear door of Holland
was put into action, British and American airmen had spent
endless hours arguing over whose intelligence was the best and
the latest, whose bombs fell with more devastating accuracy,
whose pilots were the hottest and bravest.

With Eisenhower's decision, as the Supreme Allied
Commander, to place Montgomery in charge of
Market-Garden, the sergeant felt the pace of competition
between the English and Americans instantly quicken—and
with a vengeance. The assault on Holland, the British airmen
bragged, would forever bury all questions as to who was top
dog; the plan, English in origin, would naturally be led by
them.

Precisely that fact is what scared the hell out of
Domitrovich and a large number of his comrades in the 72nd
Troop Carrier Squadron. The intensive briefing given the
members of the Ninth Air Force in the early-morning hours of
the 17th fully laid out both the plan and the risks involved in
pulling off Market-Garden.

Incredibly complex, the invasion was divided into two
distinct elements: "Market" was the airborne assault, and
"Garden" the land-based attack; the success of each totally
depended on split-second timing and unquestioned
cooperation. Although the Intelligence officer failed to
mention it. Domitrovich was painfully aware that for a win,
a third ingredient was of urgent necessity: blind luck. The

operation, if brilliantly conceived, was clearly riddled with pitfalls.

Breaking all precedent, the airborne attack into enemy-held Holland was to take place in broad daylight. Intelligence reports from the Dutch underground, backed up with reconaissance photos taken by low-flying Spitfires, proved that the Germans were in retreat all across the southern and central sectors of the Netherlands, pushed to a frenzy by General Patton's Third Army and Montgomery's 21st Army Group's lightning advances toward the Ruhr and Rhine rivers. Underground reports filtering in up to the night of the 16th told of entire German infantry and armored units abandoning their positions and equipment; discipine was falling apart, as the demoralized Wehrmacht forces clogged the roads in a mad scramble for the German border.

What the briefing skipped over was the unsettling rumor racing through Domitrovich's airfield near Newbury, some eighty miles west of London: the exact location of the assault had been leaked, the enemy was expecting them; anti-aircraft guns and Panzer tank units were being rushed in at that very moment to greet the airborne invaders.

The sergeant was used to rumors. In the days and hours before he took part in the Normandy invasion he had heard and discounted dozens. But this time, with this particular rumor, Domitrovich was forced to agree with his navigator, Second Lieutenant Harold Baker. "It's probably a pile of bullshit," Baker had said with a fatalistic shrug, "but I buy it. This thing's too big to come off without a hitch."

Standing well back of the warming engines of his C-47, Domitrovich helped the radio operator, Staff Sergeant George Ellis, into his chute. For hours they had watched in awe as the seemingly endless columns of jeeps, trucks, tanks, rocket launchers—even motorcycles—rolled into the gigantic Hamilcar gliders. Then, as on twenty-three other airbases scattered throughout England, the paratroops had boarded the C-47s and troop-carrying wooden Horsa and Waco gliders. Domitrovich was only half kidding when he said, "They'll never get off the ground."

But they did. At 9:45, exactly on schedule, almost five thousand planes and gliders rose into the morning sun and headed for Holland. It was the largest airborne armada man had ever assembled. In sheer numbers of aircraft and personnel involved, it nearly doubled the D-Day invasion of Normandy.

In the cockpit of Domitrovich's troop carrier, Captain Wade, and his copilot, First Lieutenant Donald Pahlow, saw the orange flare burst over the control tower. They were eighth to roll in their forty-five-plane string of C-47s. In the rear, seated facing one another on wooden shelves, were twenty-two men. Twenty-one were combat-hardened veterans of the 101st "Screaming Eagle" Paratroop Division; the odd-man-out was Corporal Thomas Hoge, a correspondent for *Stars and Stripes*, the armed forces newspaper. This was his first combat assignment. Hoge knew it was useless to hide his nervousness; even though he wasn't jumping with the troopers, no matter how he tried, he couldn't seem to keep his fingers from exploring for the pull-ring on the side of his emergency chute.

Domitrovich's formation of 424 C-47s, plus seventy tow planes and gliders, crossed Allied-held Belgium guarded by a mixed bag of British Spitfires and rocket-firing Typhoons, and U.S. Thunderbolts, Lightnings, and Mustangs. Unlike the 82nd Airborne, destined for the northern route to Arnhem, the men of the 101st in Domitrovich's plane were heading toward the south of Holland, in the area of Eindhoven. The latest rumor had it that this was the most lightly defended portion of the assault zone, a rumor that Corporal Hoge instantly decided had the ring of truth. After all, his reasoning went, how could anyone have survived the pre-invasion attack of 1,500 Allied bombers sent out early that morning to pound the enemy defenses? Domitrovich merely smiled and said nothing; he saw no purpose in reminding Hoge that the same "softening-up" treatment had been handed the Germans at Normandy.

The C-47s had dropped in formation to less than 1,000 feet as they crossed the Dutch coast. Approaching the drop area, Captain Wade signaled for Domitrovich to open the side door. Miraculously, at this point only minutes from the jump zone, they had not encountered any flak, or sighted so much as a single enemy aircraft. As the red ready-light flashed on over the jump door, word buzzed up and down the row of paratroopers now standing and hooking up their static-lines to the overhead wire: maybe the latest rumor was true; for once, it was possible the Germans had packed up and headed for home.

They hadn't. On one of the rare occasions in which a combat rumor contained more than a smattering of fact, the Germans were indeed preparing for the Allied invaders. Through a series of bizarre events, ranging from the determined disobedience of a Wehrmacht general to an eleventh-hour disclosure of the Market-Garden plan to the German high command by a Dutch double agent, the enemy had halted their retreat and were now digging in for a pitched battle.

Domitrovich was standing to the right of the open door, looking down at the flat green farmland rolling only 500 feet below the C-47. Now, for the first time, he and the small, wiry major leading the 101st's jump saw the advance "Garden" forces of the British 30th Corps. Massed columns of tanks, personnel carriers, and half-tracks ribboned out along the dirt roads, their brigade pennants attached to the lead vehicles' antennas snapping in the wind. As the plane shot over them, the Britishers waved exuberantly, holding up their fingers in the V-for-Victory sign. Still no flak. No enemy aircraft. They were two minutes from the jump zone.

Breaking formation, the fighter escorts raced ahead of the troop carriers, screaming down to strafe and bomb the drop area at treetop level; an operation intended to mop up whatever Germans were still on their feet after the pre-dawn bombing raid.

This was exactly the moment for which Lieutenant General Kurt Chill had gambled his career. Thirteen days before, the Wehrmacht officer had blatantly disobeyed his commander's order to collect the remnants of his shattered division and retreat to the German border. Instead, convinced that the Allies would soon swarm into southern Holland through Belgium, the general had dug in this troops along the Albert Canal, just south of Eindhoven—and directly under the path of the northbound C-47s.

As the fighter planes bored in on their first sweep, Domitrovich saw a row of large haystacks explode open, revealing nests of 88mm anti-aircraft batteries and radar-controlled 20mm rapid-firing cannons; the woods below suddenly came alive with tracer-firing machine guns. Not two hundred yards from his plane, Domitrovich watched a black Horsa glider splinter apart as it took a direct hit. Bursting into flame, it nosed down, tearing loose the cable still attached to its tow plane. Exposing himself to the ground fire, the sergeant stood in the open doorway and followed the flaming path of the glider. No chutes appeared before it hit the ground.

Flying low and flat, almost wing tip to wing tip, the C-47s took no evasive action to avoid the devastatingly accurate flak.

Throughout the formation, one plane after another was hit. Those that didn't disintegrate instantly flew on toward the drop zone, some with one or both engines burning, others with wing and tail surfaces shot to shreds. The pilots were determined to deliver the paratroopers smack on target.

The green light flashed on in Domitrovich's plane. He turned to wish the major luck, but he was gone. One after another, like rock climbers spliced to their leader, the troopers were plummeting out of the plane. Domitrovich watched their brown-and-green camouflaged chutes stream out, billow as they caught air, then collapse tentlike as the men hit the ground in what seemed a suicidally short span. The crew chief's job was over. He hit the switch, signaling the pilot that he could begin his turnaround and head for home. As he bolted the door, Domitrovich saw Baker, hunched over the small navigator's table, grinning at him. This drop at Eindhoven was their twenty-second mission together; three more and both men would be eligible for a month's holiday in Scotland.

It was eerie how the shell tore through the floor of the cockpit before exploding against the instrument panel. Domitrovich actually saw the projectile enter, just behind the pilot's seat. The plane was in a climbing left bank as the burst lifted Wade out of the chair and threw him across the copilot. The C-47 shuddered, then seemed to hang suspended on its side for the longest moment.

"We're hit!" Domitrovich shouted.

The cockpit was a blazing, twisted mass of metal and severed cables. He knew Wade and Pahlow had been killed instantly. "Let's get out of here!" the crew chief yelled.

Throwing the door open, Domitrovich instinctively reached for one of the two Thompson submachine guns racked upright across from the hatch. He clipped the heavy weapon to the front buckle of his emergency pack, then turned to check on the others. With Hoge in the lead, Baker and Ellis stumbled through the smoke toward the door. The plane gave a sudden heaving roll to the right. Domitrovich was pitched out, tumbling head first, on his back. There had been no time to attach his static-line. He yanked the ring and saw white silk pour out of his seat pack. The canopy cracked open with a whipping jolt, spinning the wooden butt of the machine gun up against his mouth. The sergeant felt his lip split open, and a moment later saw blood trickling down the front of his flak jacket.

Domitrovich was coming down fast, directly over an apple orchard in the center of Oirschot, a small town on the outskirts of industrial Eindhoven. Facing south, he could see the huge Philips factory complex, and although he had never viewed it from the air, the electrical-appliance plant looked strikingly similar to the steel mill he had worked in back in Illinois.

Just as his boots touched the top branches of a tree, Domitrovich saw two uniformed men running toward him. He covered his face with both arms and crashed through the fruit-laden branches, then abruptly jerked to a halt as the chute snagged. Spinning dizzily for a few turns, his feet only inches off the ground, Domitrovich wondered what it would feel like when the Germans shot him. If their first burst didn't kill him, he was determined to get off a few rounds from the Thompson; yet, instead of reaching for the weapon, he was startled to find his right hand fumbling to unbutton his shirt. All Domitrovich could think of at that moment was touching the St. Christopher's medal hanging about his neck.

The younger of the two unarmed Dutch policemen misinterpreted the sergeant's movements; he thought that the

American airman with the blood running from his mouth was attempting to unlimber his machine gun. Talking fast, in what he desperately hoped was better English than he had spoken in school, the policeman hurriedly told Domitrovich that the Germans had seen him bail out. They had only a few minutes, he explained, to cut the sergeant free and hide him on a neighboring farm.

Since the first day of the German occupation, Louis Termeer's hayloft had served a double duty. The short, heavyset farmer, although himself not a formal member of the underground, was part of a courageous network of Dutch citizens willing to risk anything to be rid of their oppressors.

The week before, a British pilot had peered through the same crack in the timbered siding where Domitrovich now huddled for his second day behind bales of sweet-smelling hay.

Even with his narrowed field of vision, the sergeant had quickly gotten the grim picture. Roughly a quarter of a mile distant he could see a savage battle taking place on both sides of the Queen Wilhelmina Canal. German gun emplacements and tank units had all but halted the Allied advance dead in its tracks. Not a hundred yards from his hiding place, squads of Waffen SS and Wehrmacht troops were uprooting fruit trees and flower beds, replanting the holes with heavy mortars and machine guns. The Termeer farm was surrounded.

He was, Domitrovich told the graying farmer—who had a somewhat less than working knowledge of English—clearly between a rock and a hard place. Termeer knitted his brow; he understood "rock," but the rest escaped him. He had no trouble, however, recognizing with delight the green pack of Lucky Strikes the sergeant pulled out of his shirt pocket. Whispering as they lit up, Termeer explained that he had a sister living in America. Before the war, like clockwork, she had sent him a carton of Lucky Strikes every month.

"You see," Termeer said comfortingly, "we have much in common."

Domitrovich watched the farmer take a last deep drag, then, with micrometer precision, pinch off the burning tip and place the half-smoked cigarette in his pocket.

How could he tell this good, brave man that they actually had nothing at all in common—except, perhaps, the war.

Unlike Louis Termeer, whose family had farmed the same land for uncounted centuries, the sergeant's roots were struggling for a first-generation foothold in the mill grime of Granite City, Illinois. No sooner had he been born in the gray industrial town across the Mississippi from East St. Louis, than Domitrovich's laborer father died, leaving his mother destitute, with no alternative but to place her five young children in a Catholic orphanage. A year later, with the priests insisting that she put the three boys and two girls up for adoption, Annie Domitrovich squeezed a third job into her around-the-clock labors, and managed to bring the family together again.

After a year and a half of high school, Domitrovich quit and, applying his natural mechanical talents, apprenticed in a garage, then took a job in the same steel mill in which his father had worked. Nights, every night, he helped his mother clean offices until the early-morning hours. An occasional beer and a movie with the boys was all he had time for. Annie's gift to her son when he enlisted after Pearl Harbor was his father's St. Christopher's medal.

During his fifth night in hiding, Domitrovich was awakened by the sound of the barn door scraping open. Slipping the Thompson off safety, he inched to the edge of the loft. He could make out the silhouetted figures of two men. The door closed, shutting off the dim spray of moonlight. He aimed in the general direction.

"Chris?"

The hoarse whisper was strangely familiar.

"It's Ellis. . . . Where are you?"

Like the sergeant, Ellis had been picked up by a policeman after landing on the roof of the Duc George cigar factory, only a few hundred yards from a German bivouac area. Now, accompanied by a resistance fighter known only as Vlemminx, Ellis had come for Domitrovich. As he changed into civilian workclothes, the sergeant was brought up to date: Lieutenant Baker was safe, hiding in a nearby monastery; Corporal Hoge had been picked up by the SS—he had literally dropped on the doorstep of their headquarters. After interrogation, the Germans had shipped the war correspondent to Berlin to undergo, as the underground man chillingly put it, "deeper questioning."

Vlemminx's plan was eloquently simple—and dangerous. Employing Termeer as additional window dressing, they would pass through the German lines in the guise of migrant farm workers and collect Baker, then head for the Boxtel Woods, ten miles north, where the 101st Airborne had secured a stronghold.

If they were caught, Domitrovich knew what the Americans' fate would be. After questioning, because they were out of uniform, the Germans would shoot them on the spot. For the Vlemminxes and Termeers of Holland, the local head of the SS, General Hanns Rauter, had reserved special treatment. The Dutchmen would be tortured for information, then they and their entire families, from infants to the bedridden elderly, would be either hanged or shot in the town square.

Domitrovich was aware that Rauter did not make idle threats. On the 18th, the day after the invasion, the SS chief had rounded up twenty-eight civilians suspected of aiding the resistance; among the group were two nuns. Alloting thirty seconds for each, Rauter had them shot one at a time against a fragment of a bombed-out factory wall. Termeer reported to the sergeant that hundreds of citizens of Eindhoven had been forced from their homes to witness the executions.

The four men slipped out of the barn at noon the next day, during the height of an Allied bombing raid near the Queen Wilhelmina Canal. They scurried past German troops who were racing for their guns. No one took the time to question why the four "farmers" were heading across an open field, rather than seeking protective cover. Vlemminx had supplied the Americans with false identification papers, but, he ruefully apologized, they were amateurishly crude; the woman who had been turning out letter-perfect copies of ID cards for more than a year had been captured and shot only the week before. The resistance fighter cautioned Domitrovich and Ellis to make as little use of the documents as possible.

Traveling in pairs along back roads, the Dutchmen, talking and laughing with seeming unconcern whenever they passed German troops, the men reached the walled monastery in Haaren without incident. Baker was jubilant to see his crewmates, but no more so than the youngish abbot, who had hidden the navigator in a secret room in the cavernous wine cellar. A nervous type to begin with, the abbot was on the verge of a total breakdown as a result of repeated searches by the SS hunting for the American airman. The Germans had seen Baker's chute come down near the monastery. For over a week they had all but torn apart the ancient handhewn floorboards looking for him. In the process, the abbot moaned, the soldiers had carted off vast quantities of his hoarded vintage wines.

Locking the group in the cramped room behind a bin of his ravaged wine stock, the abbot was consoled by a single thought: come nightfall, the Americans would be gone; he could get his first full night's sleep in more than a week.

Traveling by night from farm to farm, it had taken Vlemminx and Termeer two weeks to lead the Americans to within a mile of the Boxtel Woods. Twice they had been challenged by special units of the Waffen SS who ranged the countryside searching for downed airmen. Both times the Dutchmen had managed to divert the Germans' attention before the Americans had had to show their papers. So far, they knew, they had been incredibly lucky. Now, within sight and sound of the Allied guns firing from captured pillboxes deep in the forest, it seemed depressingly certain that their good fortune had finally run out.

Ahead lay the bridge of Moergestel, the only route to the woods the group could safely take. In the billowing grain fields on either side, and along the sloping banks of the canals, the Germans had laid hundreds of anti-personnel mines. Relying on information received that morning from another underground member, Vlemminx had expected to see the narrow steel-and-wood bridge free of enemy troops. Instead, an elite unit of the Ninth SS Panzer Division had suddenly moved in and set up a roadblock on the southern approach to the span. The black-booted troopers, at least half displaying Iron Crosses on their spotless gray tunics, were checking the papers of everyone, soldier and civilian, who attempted to cross the bridge.

Vlemminx had taken the precaution of moving his charges along the road singly, spaced a few hundred feet apart. The average German conscript, the underground man knew, would not have given more than a cursory glance to the three Americans wearing farmer's clothes and carrying battered cardboard suitcases tied with rope. But the troops guarding the bridge were not average—and to make matters worse, their officer, seated in an armored carrier, had seen the men approaching. To turn the airmen back now would certainly arouse his suspicion. On the other hand, for them to go forward, the resistance fighter realized, was inviting disaster.

Vlemminx stopped to fill his pipe with a pinch of the dark Belgium shag he carried loose in his jacket pocket, hoping the familiar action would somehow provide an inspired solution.

His eyes had been fixed on the charred bowl of the pipe when the catcalls and whistles suddenly erupted. Looking toward the bridge, the underground man couldn't believe what he saw. Sprawled on the wooden decking in the center of the roadway was a slim young woman who had tumbled off her bicycle. Her bright-blue skirt had hiked up clear to her waist, and at that moment every German eye was touring her anatomy. Even the Prussian-looking officer had leaped from his vehicle and was rushing to aid the unharmed but flustered cyclist. Who she was, and why she had chosen that precise instant to cross the bridge, Vlemminx would never know, but as he quickly motioned the men forward, the resistance fighter was convinced that God sometimes took the form of a Dutch girl with glorious legs.

Flashing his ID card in the best offhand manner he could muster, Domitrovich sauntered past the distracted guards. He was thinking of how many times he had seen similar scenes in movies, and had laughed them away as being ridiculously contrived. And yet, there he was, his life being saved by just such an incident.

As he would later remark to Baker, this was one story he could never tell back home. Who would believe it?

At dusk, the American airmen were safely behind the Allied lines, wolfing down plates of lukewarm C-rations to the deafening accompaniment of the captured guns. Domitrovich had amazed himself by eagerly accepting an Airborne corporal's offer of a second helping. One of the things he had dreamed of while in hiding—if he got out of Holland alive—was never having to eat another bite of food out of an olive-drab can. Now, as he slid the last slice of spam onto the stale biscuit, the sergeant would have been more than happy to round off the meal by eating his words for dessert.

He reached into his pocket and took out a single, slightly crumpled Lucky Strike. It had been Louis Termeer's parting gift, carefully preserved since the night, two weeks before, when Domitrovich insisted that the Dutchman have the last smoke in his pack.

*   *   *

Domitrovich watched as Colonel Smith tapped the cylinder-head temperature gauge several times with his index finger. The needle had suddenly climbed past 425 degrees, but then, exactly as the sergeant had predicted, it dropped back to just a shade under 400 and levitated there quiveringly. The *Feather Merchant* had her peculiarities, Smith was discovering, and Domitrovich apparently was on intimate terms with each eccentricity.

But contrary to the usual affection most crew chiefs exhibited for their charges, the colonel had been surprised to learn that Domitrovich had little love for Army 0577. During the flight from Sioux Falls, the sergeant had gone over the B-25's technical manual with Smith, preparing him to take over the copilot's seat. Learning that Smith had never flown a Mitchell before, Domitrovich had given him a few words of advice not included in the manual.

"Treat her like a pregnant lady, colonel—nice and gentle, no surprise moves. Otherwise," he had said grimly, "she'll bite the ass off you!"

Smith had laughed. "Sounds like you're tryin' to tell me somethin', sergeant."

Domitrovich had pondered for a moment, running through his recent experiences with the plane in order to select a definitive example. Finally, "See those oxygen tanks, colonel?" The sergeant's finger had swept the six large cylinders bolted to the walls throughout the aircraft.

"About two weeks ago, on a flight over the Rockies, this young pilot got kinda lazy and drifted off course. The next thing I knew he was pulling straight up to miss a mountain peak. We kept on going straight up, until this machine flopped on its back. Every last one of those tanks tore loose and came straight for me."

Domitrovich had shaken his head gravely. "I'm here to tell you, sir—this plane wants to be a P-38, but in a stall she floats like a bank safe."

CHAPTER V

9:15—The Plane

Approaching New Britain, Connecticut, the bomber crabbed to the left as an unexpected blast of wind sliced under the right wing. Then, as if a giant plug had been yanked from beneath, the plane was suddenly sucked toward the ground.

They had hit an air pocket, a nearly vertical downward stream of air that forced the B-25 to drop a hundred feet in a startling and, Domitrovich felt, sickening instant. The phenomenon was common to all things which fly through the air, birds as well as planes. But the sergeant's experience with turbulence was limited to C-47s. In his opinion, there was no finer, more reliable machine in the air than the stolid, no-frills, twin-engine troop carrier. On the other hand, as he told Smith, he was convinced that the B-25 had been designed in a berserk and totally successful attempt at defying the laws of aerodynamics. It was thunderously noisy, uncomfortably cramped for space—but worst of all, it seemed to handle with the stability of a Mexican jumping bean.

Aware of Domitrovich's silent plight, Bill Smith casually reached down to his right and made a slight adjustment to the trim wheel, balancing the bomber more solidly in the unsettled air. Like the sergeant, he too was partial to a single airplane; there never was, or could be for the colonel, a sweeter ship than

67

the B-17. But, surprisingly enough, Smith was enjoying the *Feather Merchant*; she was fast, responsive, and for a craft considerably lighter, he found her almost as unskittish as his first love.

In the two years, two months, and four days of its existence, Army 0577 had submitted to the hands of many masters. For the three men now riding in her cabin, the 25th of May, 1943, held no special significance.

On that Tuesday afternoon, while the drab-green B-25 was being towed out of the North American assembly plant in Kansas City, First Lieutenant William Franklin Smith, Jr., was completing his training as a combat operations officer at Wendover Field, Utah; Albert Perna was about to graduate from high school in Brooklyn, New York; Corporal Christopher Domitrovich, on a troop ship in the mid-Atlantic, was bound for Liverpool, England. For all three men, the birth of *Old John Feather Merchant* would remain an anonymous event.

Right from the start, when the first B-25 was test-flown in 1940, it was a foregone conclusion that the medium bomber was destined to become the backbone of the Air Corps. During the Spanish Civil War, American military observers had clearly seen the devastation rained on cities such as Guernica by Germany's fast medium-range bombing planes. Within a year of the first squadron's delivery, the B-25 was the only bomber the United States had in the air capable of avenging Japan's attack on Pearl Harbor.

But it took the daring and imagination of two men for the plane to acquire a humanizing identity.

In the years following the First World War, the General Staff's thinking was still mired in constructing larger and more complex armies and navies. Brigadier General William "Billy" Mitchell, an intelligent—and outspoken—air pioneer, set out to disprove their theories as dim and archaic. In a series of graphic tests, covered by the press and newsreel cameras, Mitchell showed the world that a single aircraft could send a battle cruiser to the bottom, or play equal havoc with troops of infantry. He overwhelmingly won his point—at the cost of his career. In 1926, publicly embarrassed by Mitchell's scathing criticism, the General Staff contrived to have him court-martialed.

Sixteen years later, from the pitching deck of the aircraft carrier *U.S.S. Hornet*, lying some 700 miles off the coast of Japan, another pioneer, General James Doolittle, launched a raid on Tokyo. His squadron of B-25s, the only bombers at that time capable of taking off from the carrier's 467-foot deck, were flying gas tanks; every conceivable inch of space not taken up by the five-man crew, or by bombs, was converted into carrying fuel. Even armament was sacrificed; pairs of broomsticks painted black replaced the rear turret guns, which had been removed to make room for a collapsible gas tank.

In the thirty seconds Doolittle's B-25s were over their target, America's morale, sinking because of the unbroken string of early Japanese victories, was given an enormous boost. The success of the surprise raid proved that the Japanese were not only vulnerable but could be beaten at their own game. Mitchell had been vindicated. In gratitude and recognition, the men of the Air Corps dubbed the bomber the Mitchell, a name synonymous with victory and courage.

To her pilots, the B-25 seemed capable of carrying out any mission. In the South Pacific, flying scant feet over coral reefs, the versatile Mitchells strafed beaches and jungle roads with the agility of a single-engine fighter—then soared miles high to bomb, with pinpoint accuracy, oil depots or heavy cruisers. In North Africa and China, over Italy, France, and Germany, B-25s flew, bearing not only the American star, but also the colors and emblems of Great Britain, the Netherlands, and the Soviet Union.

Army 0577 had cost the government $181,074. Like her more than two thousand predecessors, she was considered a bargain at a shade under $7.50 a pound.

Within three days of her delivery to the Army, twin-barreled .50-caliber rapid-firing machine guns had been inserted in the top turret and bombardier's Plexiglas nose compartment. Stowed midway in the plane's 53-foot fuselage were the navigator's and radio operator's equipment. Installed under the 67-foot wings were special racks for rockets and additional bombs. With its five-man crew, the plane could deliver a 5,000-pound bomb load to a target more than 1,000 miles distant; it could fly above most weather at 21,000 feet, at speeds in excess of 280 miles per hour. Army 0577 was now ready to go to war.

It was never to happen.

From the moment the ferry pilot put her down at Randolph Field, in San Antonio, Texas, 0577 became embroiled in a paper war. Originally intended as a replacement aircraft for the 12th Air Force, fighting in North Africa, the plane was impressed into emergency service to train combat crews. A year later, still listed as on "temporary" duty, 0577 had logged over 1,350 hours in crew training. Her machine guns, barrels drilled mirror-smooth by scores of neophyte gunners, had been replaced twice. Three sets of tubeless 47-inch smooth-tread tires had worn bare during hundreds of takeoffs and landings. Her Wright Cyclone 1,700-horsepower engines were completely overhauled after completing a thousand flying hours. A total of thirty-two combat crews had learned the business of war in 0577. From Randolph Field they were dispersed to the compass points, picking up fresh Mitchells at their foreign bases. But Army 0577 stayed in Texas, and with Germany's surrender, her days as a war plane came to an end.

In June 1945 she was flown to Cincinnati and placed under the Military Air Transport Command, Her guns were removed, and, a final ignominy, the bomb-bay doors were bolted shut. She was to be a "fat cat," a ferry craft used by military and civilian VIPs on briefcase-carrying hops around the country.

In the closing days of the war, hastily constructed bases had been set up to receive the masses of fighting men returning home, some to be reassigned to the Pacific, others waiting for release from the service. One such reception center was Sioux Falls Army Air Field, South Dakota.

Under the command of the second Air Force, the 211th Base Unit had been thrown together around the nucleus of the old Sioux Falls municipal airport. On June 8, virtually unnoticed, Army 0577 winged over the sprawling base and settled down on the 5,700-foot runway. Only two men were officially on hand to welcome the new arrival: Captain John Kemp, the officer in charge of aircraft maintenance, and Technical Sergeant Christopher Domitrovich.

Domitrovich had arrived at Sioux Falls the month before and was waiting for reassignment to the Pacific. Kemp, astutely sizing up the crew chief's experience with twin-engine aircraft, handed him the job of keeping the airfield's small fleet of ferry planes in flying condition.

While mechanics performed an inspection teardown of her engines, Domitrovich set about having 0577's olive-drab paint sanded down to the original bare metal. Inside, carpenters and sheet-metal workers ripped out bulkhead walls and refitted bench seats along both sides of the bomb-bay area. If 0577 was going to carry VIPs, Colonel Sig Young, the base CO, decreed they would ride in style.

A week later, with 0577's facelift completed, a young pilot assigned to take the aircraft up on a check flight approached Domitrovich outside the transient hangar. The lieutenant, looking barely out of his teens, cocked a jaded thumb at the gleaming Mitchell.

"This Kemp's new feather merchant?" he asked.

Domitrovich had no idea what the lieutenant was talking about. Not only had he never heard of the mythical little people, notorious for their laziness—a band of slackers who shirked honest labor—but the sergeant was ignorant of the fact the pilots applied the derogatory term to all noncombat aircraft.

The name intrigued Domitrovich—so much so, that by the next morning, in honor of Captain Kemp, 0577 had been christened *Old John Feather Merchant* in the paint shop's best vermilion red.

Since returning from Holland, a curious change had taken place in the sergeant. Before being shot down he had counted each and every day spent in combat, tabulating them with a bank teller's precision into the points necessary for his separation from the Army. The government had rewarded him with an Air medal for his escapade with Market-Garden, and an Oak Leaf Cluster to add to the Bronze Star already won for the Normandy invasion. Domitrovich's assignment to Sioux Falls was an additional pat on the back, designed to keep the sergeant safely in the States, yet on tap if his expertise was needed to hammer Japan into submission. As to how or why the metamorphosis came about, Domitrovich was in the dark; all he was aware of was a strong desire to stay in the Air Corps, and to be transferred as quickly as possible to the Pacific. No one was more surprised by his decision than the sergeant himself.

Throughout June and into July, while his request for immediate reassignment sludged through channels, Domitrovich logged time in *Old John Feather Merchant*. Flying as crew chief, he sat alongside dark-suited Senators making publicity-seeking inspection hops of the reception centers; ferried USO entertainers and bands to and from the base; talked shop with pilots during the long cross-country flights they needed to maintain their flying status. As a side benefit, Domitrovich was seeing the vastness of his country for the first time. He was also experiencing a burning desire with each flight of Army 0577 to make it his last.

*   *   *

A good five hundred feet above and about a mile to his right, Smith watched a Trans-World Airlines DC-3 lower its wheels as it descended en route to Hartford. There were jigsaw-shaped gaps in the towering banks of stratocumulus clouds off to the northwest, but dead ahead of *Old John Feather Merchant* lay a murky palisade of dark haze and industrial smoke.

Gripping the control column with his left hand, the colonel fitted the headphone cups against his ears, then switched the filter control dial to "range." The beacon signal out of New Haven, still almost fifty miles away, was weak, but steady. He cranked the dial to "voice," picking up the middle portion of the Army Flight Service's weather report. The woman's voice droned on mechanically.

"...seven-tenths stratocumulus with tops at 2,500 feet... visibility four miles...winds northwesterly at ten to fifteen miles per hour..."

Smith switched off the report. The forecast was at least a half-hour old. At that moment, Smith judged Army 0577's forward visibility, at 1,000 feet, to be less than three miles. The rain, peppering the windshield like beads of mercury, was being driven by gusts easily double the reported velocity. His appraisal of the situation back at Bedford Field had been correct: flying Contact into the New York area would be a race against time.

CHAPTER VI

The Sailor

ALBERT PERNA HAD NEVER BEEN IN A B-25 before, and therefore he had no way of knowing just how uncomfortable the small jump seat behind the cockpit could be in rough weather. He was hemmed in on either side by two of the yellow emergency oxygen tanks mounted on the wall exactly level with his forehead. By now, twenty-odd minutes into the flight, he had learned to hunch forward whenever the aircraft rolled or dipped; to do otherwise meant having his skull brought into sharp contact with either or both of the heavy metal cylinders.

But comfort was the last thing on Machinist's Mate Perna's mind this morning. Three days shy of his twentieth birthday, he was going home to Brooklyn on the saddest mission of his young life.

In his carry-all bag, along with an emergency two-day pass, was the telgram he had received from his father late the night before: "ANTHONY CONFIRMED DEAD-STOP-CAN YOU COME HOME?"

Perna was shattered by those three words. Of his entire family, he alone had possessed the unshakable conviction that his brother would be found alive. Two weeks before, the Navy Department had cabled Vincent and Rosa Perna that their twenty-two-year-old son, Anthony, serving aboard the destroyer *Luce*, was reported missing in action. The ship, taking part in the Third Fleet's invasion of Japan's Inland Sea, had come under kamikaze attack. One of the suicide planes, hit by ack-ack fire, plummeted directly into the *Luce's* bridge. Anthony Perna, Carpenter Second Class, was one of the sixteen men listed as "missing—presumed dead."

Even now with the confirming news, Perna still found it difficult to accept that Tony was gone. He had been so certain, with a faith inexplicably deeper and beyond even his devout Catholicism, that his brother would somehow survive the facts.

To support his rejection of Anthony's presumed fate, Albert had created a series of elaborate scenarios as to the possibilities. Perhaps his brother had been blown over the side by the concussive blast of the exploding plane, and, after floating unconscious for hours, had been picked up by another ship his ID tags—and memory—gone. A second possibility, following the same overboard theme, resulted in Anthony's capture and internment by the Japanese. Still another; the Navy had the wrong Anthony Perna, there was a snafu, and another man with the same name was dead. Any minute now, Albert kept reassuring his family, the mistake would be resolved by the Navy Department's telegram of abject apology; this to be quickly followed by the *real* Anthony Perna's cabled declaration of safety and health.

But in the early-morning hours, alone in his off-base boardinghouse room, reading and rereading the slabs of blue cablese pasted on the gray-white Western Union form, Perna concluded that perhaps his father had been right all along. Vincent, who had seen action in the Italian navy during the First World War, had bitterly announced to his family that "God marked him . . . He spared me so He could take my Anthony."

Typical of the Jewish and Italian families in the Bensonhurst section of Brooklyn, the Pernas were close-knit. "Rich in family, poor in the bank" was the way Albert succinctly described his background. His father, a master carpenter and woodcarver, owned a small furniture company in Queens, a business he fervently hoped both his sons would enter after the war.

It was a neighborhood of small two-family houses and railroad flats over kosher butcher shops and radio-repair stores; a place where a kid like Albert, playing stickball in the crowded street, never paid much attention to the surrounding historical lore. By the time he was born, successive waves of immigrants had all but obliterated the last traces of the Dutch village of New Utrecht, first settled in 1652. A few scattered odds and ends of those more pastoral days remained, such as the Van Pelt Manor House, built in 1664, and used by George Washington as a field headquarters during the Revolution; and the New Utrecht Reformed Church, which dated back to 1667.

But these New World artifacts were of little interest to the Perna family. Their lives centered on their church, St. Frances de Chantal, where Anthony, Albert, and their sisters, Joanna and Teresa, had been baptized, and where bingo and a cunning game of bocce could be had on Wednesday and Saturday nights with old-country *compares*.

By the time he was a senior at New Utrecht High School, Albert was going steady with Dolores Reggio, spending weekends riding the Tornado rollercoaster at Coney Island's Steeplechase Park, and downing hot dogs and chow mein sandwiches at Nathan's Famous just off the boardwalk. Like Anthony, who had joined the Navy only hours after hearing of the attack on Pearl Harbor, Albert counted the days until his graduation. One month short of his eighteenth birthday, with his father beaming at his side, Albert enlisted—underlining on the Navy recruitment form in double strokes of black ink the words: "For the Duration."

After completing his boot training in Newport, Rhode Island, Perna was transferred to the Navy Pier in Chicago, where he studied diesel-engine repair and maintenance. He enjoyed the course, getting top scores in his written and manual examinations. But somewhere along the way his instructors determined that the Navy could make better use of Perna's talents in aviation mechanics. Although he had no preference between working on diesel or gasoline engines, the thought of being around aircraft—and perhaps even going up now and then—intrigued him. Perna had never been in a plane; in fact, until his arrival at Squantum Naval Air Station, near Boston, Albert's closest contact with flying had been a craning view of the Heinz "57 Varieties" advertising blimp as it made its twice-weekly, low-altitude passage over Brooklyn.

By February 1945, Perna had advanced to Aviation Machinist's Mate Second Class—and the closest he had yet come to flying was sitting in the cockpit of a hangared aircraft. But unbeknownst to him, at that moment plans were afoot which would soon grant the young sailor's wish to fly at least once, or perhaps twice, before leaving the service.

Perna had never heard of Special Project Unit Cast. In that regard, he had a vast amount of company; in the three years of its existence, knowledge of the top-secret radar project was limited to a select handful of scientists and pilots.

From the outset of the war, scientists from M.I.T. and Harvard were working on flight applications of microwave radar. Within a short time they had developed in-flight techniques for blind flying, night bombing, and aircraft interception. Radar-equipped planes used in the tests were based in a highly guarded section of the Bedford Army Air Field. When he received word that he was being transferred to Bedford, Perna had no idea that he had just undergone and passed a month-long FBI scrutiny into every facet of his life. Each member of the ninety-six-man "Cast" section, from the chief project scientist to mechanics like Perna, had top security clearances.

The Navy had chosen the right man for the job. He was basically a loner; with his quiet, even temperament, Perna could be counted on to repair and maintain the test planes' engines—and to keep what the aircraft were being used for to himself. Like his newly found friend Robert Alessio, a machinist's mate also transferred from Squantum, Perna lived off the base in nearby Arlington. Whenever the men grew homesick for a solid Italian meal, Alessio would invite Perna to his home in Everett, where his mother would cook enough for the "still-growing boys" to eat their fill, and even have leftovers to take back to their rooms.

On off-duty weekends, Perna would join a car pool of New York-bound seamen and visit his folks—but only after first attempting to hitch a ride on a flight heading for the city. Each time, for one reason or another, he never flew. Then came word that Anthony was missing. The Unit Commander arranged for Albert's emergency leave—and a seat on a ferry flight going to New York. The ride had thrilled him, but terrified his parents. "We have one son missing," his mother told Albert. "We don't want to have to worry about you."

"Ma, don't even think about it," Albert said placatingly. "When it comes, it comes—and nothing can change it. But I swear, nothing's going to happen to me."

Now, on this rainswept Saturday morning, for the second time in his life, Albert Perna was in an airplane.

Uncomfortable as the conditions were, he felt lucky to be on the *Feather Merchant*. When he had checked with Bedford Operations shortly after dawn, he had learned that there was only one plane, a B-25, going into New York. But, the Operations Officer warned him, the pilot was a "hardass"—for some reason he was refusing to take passengers.

"What the hell," Perna told Alessio as they drove out to the bomber. "I'll tell the guy my story. If he says no, I'll still have plenty of time to catch the train." ˙

*   *   *

As the Mitchell cut a diagonal across Meriden, Smith peered down on a sea of billowing white cheesecloth sheltering acres of Connecticut broadleaf tobacco from the drying rays of the sun. Smith knew from newspaper stories that New England farmers had seen only two days of sunshine in July. The month was finishing up to be one of the wettest and cloudiest in recent years.

Ahead, just a trace southwest, lay New Haven and the broad reach of Long Island Sound. Farther beyond, still hidden behind an impenetrable veil of fog and rain clouds, stretched the New York shoreline.

Smith reached for his sectional map tucked into the slot just under his window. A glance at the inked lines traversing the chart reaffirmed his flight plan: once past New Haven, he would gentle the right rudder and follow the sound down the Connecticut coast to Stamford; then a hard left would sweep him across a stretch of open water, placing *Old John Feather Merchant* on its designated path to La Guardia Field.

The panel clock indicated that the maneuver would take place in twenty minutes.

CHAPTER VII

9:25—The Mayor

JOHN PELUSO SAT BEHIND THE WHEEL of the green-and-white prowl car parked in the circular drive and studied his watch, then looked off toward the mansion's front door.

That's funny, he thought, almost nine-thirty, and still no La Guardia. In his twelve years of chauffeuring the mayor, Peluso could have counted on one hand the number of times his boss had been late for an appointment. Quixotic, totally unpredictable, La Guardia would normally juggle a crushing day's schedule with the boggling elasticity of an India-rubber man. But late? Hardly ever. Peluso toyed with the idea of asking Juanita, the housekeeper, to remind the mayor of his 10:15 appointment at City Hall. Then, as he had done a half-hour before when he drove past the policeman guarding the front gate of Gracie Mansion, Peluso glanced at the black Lincoln parked at the end of the driveway. Whoever the owner was, the chauffeur made a mental bet, at that moment he was no doubt getting an earful from the Little Flower.

Peluso was right, as a small number of tourists and neighborhood regulars peering through the wrought-iron fence surrounding the colonial mansion on 88th Street could attest. Ignoring the light rain, they had collected to watch one of the best free shows in town—Fiorello H. La Guardia at his breakfast table. As usual, through the south dining-room windows, they could see the stubby dynamo in a blur of motion, while his guest sat rigidly unmoving throughout La Guardia's performance.

Even seated, Newbold Morris, at six-five, towered over the squat mayor. An aristocrat from an old-line Republican family, Morris was relieved to be nearing the end of a session that had begun almost two hours before.

He had come to ask for La Guardia's answer to a simple question: should he run for mayor of New York City now that La Guardia had decided not to seek a fourth term?

Athletically trim, Morris sat across from La Guardia and watched him pack away his usual morning meal of eggs, bacon, several onion rolls heavily layered with cream cheese, and a few forkfuls of pickled herring. Morris sipped coffee— and listened.

Obviously up at the crack of dawn, La Guardia had already consumed the morning newspaper. Before addressing himself fully to Morris' problem, the mayor sprinkled political advice between bits and pieces of his personal view of the state of the world.

"About time!" La Guardia had pounded the table for emphasis as he launched into the Senate's impending ratification of the United Nations Charter. "We diddled with it back in the twenties—and all it got us was another war. Maybe now they'll learn that talking's better than bullets!"

Spearing the last roll with his fork and waving it in front of Morris like a New Year's Eve noisemaker, La Guardia then hurtled directly into his favorite news item of the morning: Hermann Goering's heart attack.

"I told you every last one of those Kraut punks were cowards!" he said, adding gleeful emphasis on the word "told."

Morris had no recollection of any such conversation, but long experience cautioned him not to derail La Guardia's garrulous enthusiasm with trivia. Besides, he had read the entire acount of Goering's heart seizure; as with much of the mayor's retelling of the news, he enjoyed hearing La Guardia's colorful version of the "facts."

"A little lightning storm and that Nazi pansy goes crazy. You know he's a dope fiend? Sure, they found over seven hundred codeine pills in his luggage when they captured the louse! And what about that pal of his? That SS queer in Poland—Frank! That's his name, *Doctor* Frank."

La Guardia shot his index finger into Morris' chest and rolled his eyes with derisive amazement.

"Some doctor. When they nabbed *that* little bastard, all he had on was a pair of black lace panties! Some superman! Some heroes!"

La Guardia stopped attacking the air between Morris and himself long enough to disengage the onion roll from the fork, tear it open, and slab the top half with a hunk of herring and a slice of onion. Morris had quickly put his finger on the mayor's jubilant preoccupation with the Germans this morning. He had just received word that his sister, Gemma, would arrive in the United States in the next few days. Trapped in Europe at the outset of the war, and married to a Jew, she had been interned in the Ravensbruck prison camp for women. Throughout the war, La Guardia had had no idea if she was dead or alive.

The muffled drone of an approaching airplane invaded the antique-furnished room. Instinctively, La Guardia's eyes darted toward the windows facing the East River. Fog and a syrup-thick ground haze obscured even the nearby tugs churning past the northern tip of Welfare Island directly opposite the mansion; but the mayor's attention was focused on the plane's invisible point of departure, La Guardia Field, some four miles across the river in Astoria, Queens. Opened to coincide with the 1939 World's Fair, the airport had been named for the mayor in recognition of his constant efforts to make New York the center of commercial aviation on the East Coast.

Often on clear days, when his two adopted children, Jean and Eric, were younger, La Guardia would lie on the east lawn with the youngsters and watch the planes taking off from the distant field. As each one barely cleared the horizon, he would shout its identity: "Douglas DC-3!"; "That's a United Air Lines 247!"; "Oh look—there's a honey of a Lockheed Vega!"

After a few flawless identifications the children's interest would wane, but not La Guardia's. Since his days as a bomber pilot in the First World War, he had maintained his enthusiasm for aviation.

Now, with the sound of the plane almost directly over Gracie Mansion, Newbold Morris seized on the momentary distraction to wrench a decision from the mayor.

"Well, Fiorello," he asked, "give me the bottom line. Yes, or no?"

Asking La Guardia for a one-word answer was like asking a barfly to quit after a solitary peanut. The situation was complicated by the fact that the mayor was, as usual, at odds with both the Democrats and the Republicans, even though he had ostensibly been a lifelong Republican. However, his rabid hatred for Tammany Hall, the inner circle of corruption that for decades called the shots of New York's Democratic Party, surmounted all other negatives. But then, with less than six months left in office, La Guardia had startled politicians and citizens alike with his offer to back the Democratic candidate, William O'Dwyer—if he would run independent of Tammany bosses and drop his all too obvious flirtations with underworld characters. O'Dwyer refused, and La Guardia instantly pulled his support.

This overcast, drizzly Saturday morning, La Guardia leaned across the table and offered up not only his political advice, but much more; he granted Morris a priceless audience with his soul.

"The Republican ticket's closed to you," he said, wagging his finger in cadence with each word. "They've already got their bum. You could probably cut yourself into the Democrats' deck, and with some smart finagling, maybe even convince them out of O'Dwyer. That would be the clever thing to do."

His round, jowly face took on a deadly-serious cast, then just as quickly softened into an almost childlike appeal.

"But, Newbold, you *can't* do that. *You couldn't live with those people!*"

"Then what do you suggest?" Morris asked.

"There's only one thing you can do. Run independent!" the mayor said, slamming the table with his fist, his high-pitched voice spiraling as if he were addressing not an old friend across his dining-room table, but a vast throng at a political rally.

"You're a decent man with a clean record. The people deserve a better choice than between two chiselers. Don't trade off your integrity," he warned Morris sternly, "for a free print job on the ballot!"

To knowledgeable New Yorkers traveling the East River Drive, the police car with the five white stars on the door panels signaled that their mayor was on the move. Over the years they had grown accustomed to seeing him darting to or from any of the five boroughs; absolutely nothing he did—or said—could surprise them. At least one day a week, the newspapers featured photos of La Guardia, crowned with his personal fire helmet, directing the quenching of a four-alarm blaze, or wielding an ax in the vanguard of a police raid on an illegal numbers parlor. Eight million New Yorkers expected La Guardia to do the unexpected.

Southbound traffic was light, but Peluso drove with extra caution over the rain-slicked roadway, staying just within the speed limit as La Guardia insisted he do.

The mayor was sitting in the front seat. Since moving into Gracie Mansion in 1942, as the first occupant of the newly renovated official residence of the city's chief executive, La Guardia enjoyed riding along "his" river, watching "his" city whip past in a kaleidoscopic sweep of history. And it was his city. Not merely by accident of birth, or elected title, but because he had poured his entire adult life into making it a safer, healthier, and happier place for "an average Wop-Jew like me to live in," as he once said in a moment of personal reflection.

Born in the heart of Greenwich Village in 1882, Fiorello ("Little Flower") was the product of an Italian-Catholic father and an Italian-Jewish mother. At age three, the first of an endless variety of incongruities entered his life. From a

cold-water tenement on Sullivan Street, La Guardia was
suddenly transported to the barren wilds of Sully, South
Dakota. His musician father had joined the Army as a
bandmaster. For the next dozen years, Fiorello—undersized,
overweight, and as Italian-looking as a ripe gorgonzola—
spent his time on Army posts riding horses, shooting carbines,
and dreaming of the day he could turn Frederick Remington's
romantic paintings of the American cowboy into a reality. And
if he couldn't be a cowpuncher, then he definitely would
pursue a career as a jockey. Clearly, young La Guardia felt his
prowess as a horseman would overcome any burden his weight
might place on the thoroughbreds.

But the Spanish-American War cut short Fiorello's
ambition—and his father's life. The mainstay of Achille La
Guardia's diet, as for all the American soldiers in Cuba, was
tinned beef. The meat, much of it already spoiled or cut from
diseased cattle, had been sold to the government by
profiteering contractors who delivered it packed in large sealed
tins, knowing full well that each can was as potentially deadly
as a time bomb. After weeks of storage in flithy warehouses, the
"embalmed beef," as the soldiers called it, was shipped to the
battlefront in the steaming holds of transports. Those tins that
did not swell and pop open in the ovenlike temperatures were
considered fit for consumption. Of the 6,500 who died in the
"glorious little war," as Teddy Roosevelt called it, most were
victims of disease and unsanitary conditions.

La Guardia's father, sickened by the rotten beef, was
mustered out of the Army with an $8-a-month pension. Broken
in health and finances, Achille took his family to Italy, where
he spent the last six years of his life in a futile attempt to
overcome his illness and poverty. Meanwhile, eighteen-
year-old Fiorello had already begun his political career as a
clerk in the American Consulate in Budapest.

Getting the job, through a friend of his father's, had been
relatively easy; but La Guardia quickly discovered that rising
in the consular service to any position above peon would take
far more than a friend in court. For one thing, he had no
college degree, much less one from a prestigious institution

such as Harvard or Yale which regularly spawned career diplomats. Another strike against him was his lack of foreign languages; the consul, a Harvard honors graduate, sympathetically pointed out to La Guardia that half the time he even spoke English ungrammatically. Still another stumbling block to his career in the diplomatic corps was his almost total ignorance of world history and foreign affairs.

Another eighteen-year-old might have soberly agreed with this dismal accounting of his deficiencies and humbly folded his tent. Not La Guardia. Within two years, by studying night and day, he more or less mastered Italian, French, German, and Croatian. Between language studies he devoured texts on world history and diplomatic machinations, and every local and American newspaper and magazine he could lay his hands on. The midnight oil paid off; before his twenty-first birthday, La Guardia was elevated to the post of consular agent in Fiume, Hungary's largest shipping port. It took only a few months for him to become infamous, at least to one State Department official, who tagged him "the worst headache in the history of the department."

La Guardia had found his legs—as a muckraker, iconoclast, and tenacious champion of the common people. He took on any and all comers: giant corporations, exalted personages, entire governments—his own, as well as anyone else's—if he found that either the law or local tradition had denied someone his basic human rights.

One of the people La Guardia leveled his lance at was Her Imperial Highness the Archduchess Maria Josefa of Austria. When she arrived in Fiume for a short visit, Hungarian officials decided that she might like to view a few hundred peasants who were emigrating to the New World. Because of her tight schedule, this display meant they would have to board the ship a full three days before it was due to sail. La Guardia pointed out to the officials that United States health regulations decreed that once the passengers were on board, he would have to inspect both the ship and the emigrants and issue a health certificate; the certificate would be invalid if the peasants left the ship after the archduches's entertainment had concluded.

"Then they'll just have to stay on board, won't they?" shrugged a high-ranking official.

La Guardia was enraged by the casualness with which hundreds of men, women, and children could be sentenced to imprisonment in the reeking hold of a cargo ship for the sole purpose of providing Her Highness with a sideshow. He curtly refused to allow the boarding to take place. Pressure came from all quarters, including his own government, demanding that this small cog get off his high horse and let the pageant proceed as planned. He rejected even a personal plea from Maria Josefa for him to take tea with her and watch the embarkation.

"Tell the archduchess," La Guardia barked at her emissary, "that she may boss her own immigrants—but she can't boss the American consul!"

Three days later, as scheduled, the passengers boarded the ship and a smiling La Guardia cheerfuly signed the bill of health.

But even an ambitious and hard-driving young man like La Guardia realized that without the benefit of a formal education, he was forever doomed to wander the basements of government service. He decided to become a lawyer, a "semicolon boy" as he snidely called members of the legal profession, in order to get a rung up the diplomatic ladder. He had distrusted all lawyers and politicians, solidly lumping the two together, since his childhood days in the West. Between witnessing the evils of Indian agents and their legal aides, and the political corruption that led to his father's death, La Guardia had a firm foundation for not wanting to practice law, but rather to use his knowledge to combat its shortcomings.

After a variety of jobs, including a stint as a stenographer for Abercrombie and Fitch Sporting Goods (he mastered a shorthand course in one month), La Guardia entered New York University Law School. He attended classes at night, working days as an interpreter at Ellis Island to pay for his tuition. With more than five thousand immigrants streaming into New York harbor each day, La Guardia worked a seven-day week, then studied all night.

It was a killing schedule, but in his three years with the Immigration Service he gained firsthand knowledge of just how really corrupt was the collusion between vast numbers of police, lawyers, and judges. In his last year on the job he had been assigned to a night court dealing with cases involving aliens charged with vice offenses. The inspector in charge of his division took La Guardia aside his first night and offered him a hardnosed look at reality.

"You can get experience in this job," he told La Guardia, "or you can make a great deal of money. I don't think you'll take the money. But, remember, the test is if you hesitate. Unless you say 'No!' right off, the first time an offer comes your way, you're gone."

Night after night, La Guardia had plenty of opportunity to say "No!" He never once hesitated.

After graduating from law school and passing the bar, La Guardia reversed himself and began practicing his new profession with the passion of a mongoose tracking a cobra. The years spent on Ellis Island had spotlighted the injustices; his law degree now provided him with a way to strike back at the system. He became a "people's lawyer," handling cases for newly arrived immigrants, and usually for little or no fee. The Triangle Shirtwaist Factory fire, in which scores of Italian and Jewish workers were killed because the appalling sweatshop conditions were condoned by law, jogged La Guardia into politics.

In 1912, he joined the garment workers' strike as both lawyer and a line-walking picket. It was a daring and dangerous step. Not only could he get his head split open by employers' goons, but the strike had been judged illegal; La Guardia was risking arrest, and possible disbarment. With his typical "punch 'em first" attitude, La Guardia publicly dared the police to arrest him; he wanted to turn the strike into a test case. The police, advised by both the employers and Tammany Hall, refused to accommodate him. The last thing they wanted was to turn the unknown "little loudmouth Wop" into a publicized martyr.

With or without a boost from the police, La Guardia's reputation as a tough infighter for liberal causes won him a seat in Congress as a Republican Representataive from Manhattan's Upper East Side. For ten years, including time out for flying service in the World War (he retained his seat by unanimous approval of his constituents), La Guardia ranted from the floor of the House against the Ku Klux Klan; made home brew on the sidewalks of New York to point out the futility of Prohibition; tore wafer-thin ham sandwiches out of his pocket to demonstrate how inflation had affected the nation's nutrition. He bolted the Republican Party countless times, taking a maverick stand on issues that he considered vital and basic to the well-being not only of his city, but of the country as a whole.

It was during the Depression that La Guardia gained a national prominence. To the disgust of his fellow Republicans, he embraced Roosevelt's New Deal. Time and again, La Guardia took the floor and hammered away on a single theme: get America moving—put people back to work. But in one major area he differed with the President. Roosevelt's New Deal provided federal funds for the destitute—the dreaded "dole," as the Republicans termed what they considered to be a giant step into socialism. La Guardia was less worried about giving the funds a political name; he was against Roosevelt's program simply because he believed that handing out money to people, without their working for it, stripped them of dignity and ambition.

In the midst of a heated debate on just this issue, La Guardia sprang out of his seat in the House and in total frustration shouted:

"I can go down to the market and buy a parrot for two dollars. And in one day I can teach it to say 'Dole, dole, dole.' But that parrot would never understand an economic problem—much less a human one!"

"Will You Love Me in December (As You Did in May)?" was written in 1905 by Jimmy Walker and Ernest Ball. By 1926, Walker had given up part-time songwriting to become the part-time mayor of New York.

No one symbolized the Roaring Twenties more than the dapper, wisecracking, extraordinarily handsome Walker. Created and owned by Tammany, James J. Walker was probably the most blatantly amoral politician since Boss

Tweed; but the people loved him. Whad did it matter that
he showed up at City Hall only two days a week—and then
hung around for less than an hour? Whose business was it
that he flitted from one speakeasy to another in a $17,000
Duesenberg—the gift of an "anonymous" admirer—with a
ravishing showgirl in tow, while his wife ate herself into
solitary oblivion? He was "Jimmy the Jester," "The Jazz
Mayor," "The Playboy of City Hall," and the press, like the
voters, sparked to his madcap style. He was flawlessly urbane,
as a buxom matron discovered when the Irish mayor showed
up at a Jewish fund-raising dinner wearing a yarmulke.

"Jimmy," she asked, as he made his way to the dais,
"circumcision next?"

"Madam, I prefer to wear it off," he shot back with a
winning grin.

Just about everybody, Republican as well as Democrat,
cheered Jimmy and what he had done for the city. During his
first administration, sandwiched in between his social
engagements, Walker had actually accomplished some real
work; under his guidance the City Fathers had voted into being
popular projects such as the Midtown Tunnel, the Triborough
Bridge, and 100 miles of new subway lines. But what the public
didn't know—or perhaps didn't care to know—La Guardia
knew; and he told it all in his sidewalk speeches.

"He's a Tammany bagman!" Congressman La Guardia
shrilled about Walker. "He's a tinhorn dandy handing out
favors to the boys in the back room, while the citizens pay for
it!"

La Guardia was right, and he knew it. So did a handful of
others, who agreed with him that it was time New York had an
honest man sitting in City Hall—and on a daily basis. That
man, La Guardia convinced them, should be La Guardia. In
1929, the race for the mayoralty of New York was betwen the
"Wet Wop"—as Tammany labeled anti-prohibitionist La
Guardia—and the "American Prince of Wales," Jimmy
Walker. La Guardia was embarrassingly defeated by almost
three to one. The city, like the country, was riding a high; by
preaching honesty and social concern, La Guardia had
threatened to burst the bubble.

He went back to Congress, but his heart no longer pumped the old excitement when he introduced a new bill or fought to pass a needed piece of social legislation. Over his years in the House, La Guardia had set a record of introducing more amendments than any other Congressman; some had even passed after years of erosive struggle.

Increasingly, when one of his more radical bills was shunted aside, La Guardia grumbled: "It's damned discouraging trying to be a reformer in the wealthiest land in the world."

The House had 435 members; but New York had only *one* mayor. La Guardia realized that if he were ever to have a real chance at reforming the Establishment, he would have to carry the banner from City Hall.

1932 swept in the cleansing wave of the New Deal—and carried La Guardia out with the debris. He was out of a job; Roosevelt's overwhelming victory placed a Democrat in La Guardia's seat in the House. Again, the incongruous entered his life. Roosevelt, the man whose ideals La Guardia had worked so arduously for, was the ultimate cause of his defeat. But the ennobling atmosphere created by the New Deal had also managed to seep into the conscience of the average New Yorker. Voters had found Jimmy Walker amusing and lovable in 1929; they now suddenly discovered him to be intolerable—and criminal. Always the song-and-dance man, Walker picked up his cue and beat a hasty retreat before the cell door opened. In his place was an interim Tammany clod, John P. O'Brien. A physical giant, O'Brien looked and sounded like a Neanderthal. When the press asked him who he would pick as his police commissioner, O'Brien ponderously shook his head and said: "I don't know. I haven't got the word yet."

The 1933 municipal election was La Guardia's chance. He grabbed it, electioneering in six languages—he had picked up Yiddish while at Ellis Island—and kept hammering at Tammany until he was sworn in as the ninety-ninth mayor of New York City.

Nothing epitomized the height of the Depression more than the city's treasury; La Guadia had inherited a virtually

bankrupt government. Corruption riddled every department.
The city's credit was nonexistent; miles of completed subway
lines lay idle because funds needed to connect the rails to the
existing system had been either stolen or squandered by Walker
and his cronies.

But no matter what he said about the deplorable situation
in public, privately, La Guardia was ecstatic; the chaos was
tailor-made for his pent-up energies. Pumping his arms like a
long-distance walker, he harangued Roosevelt to release
federal funds for slum clearance and the construction of low-
cost housing. When a wildcat trucking strike was threatened,
he quickly settled it by announcing that the city's garbage
trucks would be used to bring food into the markets. He weeded
out the Civil Service deadwood, and kept the police on their
toes by every so often turning in a false riot alarm to test their
efficiency. Where Walker had two beautiful secretaries—
neither capable of recognizing a typewriter—La Guardia kept
six at their wit's end, as he spewed out reams of letters,
speeches, staff memos, and notes for his weekly radio talks to
the people.

Now, this fogbound Saturday morning, as La Guardia's
car rolled past the white ceramic-tiled buildings of New York
Hospital, his gaze drifted up to the 325-foot chimney towering
over 70th Street. Every morning on his way downtown, the
soaring stack of interlaced bricks drew his attention. Although
the tapering column was aesthetically pleasing, the mayor's
focus of interest was always rooted on a particular section of
the chimney, about a third of the way up. A quiet, satisfied
smile would come on his face; he was remembering a day back
in 1938, when he and a hundred other anonymous donors had
contributed $1,000 to have swastika-like designs removed from
the structure. Greek crosses replaced the innocently ancient
symbol that Chancellor Hitler had embraced for his "New
Order."

In his twelve years in office, that silent gesture had to be
the only unpublicized act La Guardia had committed.
Whether it was the simple signing of a routine document, or
cutting the ribbon at a public ceremony, the mayor basked in

the sudden glow of a photographer's flashbulb. During his administration, La Guardia had bullied, charmed, strong-armed, cajoled, jailed, and wooed to put his city back into solid financial and social shape. He had carried out most of his campaign promises; and where he couldn't deliver, he gave sensible-sounding reasons for the breach of faith. But the machine was beginning to show signs of fatigue. His boundless energy, which once had encompassed everything from the price of chickens to advising Winston Churchill over the city radio station, was noticeably geared down. He was sixty-two, and there had been some recent disappointments.

Throughout their terms in office, Roosevelt and La Guardia had maintained close contact. The President not only appreciated La Guardia's support for his programs, but he genuinely liked and respected him. When war was declared, La Guardia, discontent with being just the mayor of the largest city in the nation, wanted to get into the action. He bought some uniforms and began to barrage Roosevelt with letters and phone calls asking, and sometimes demanding, that he be given a commission and sent overseas. If he could no longer fight, he told FDR, he could at least advise Eisenhower on some vital points he thought the general had overlooked. For a time, it seemed that Roosevelt was actually going to commission La Guardia a brigadier general; but then he backed off when advisers, notably Harry Truman, warned that the mayor's uncontrollable pyrotechnics might create, rather than solve, problems. Instead, Roosevelt handed La Guardia the job of Director of Civilian Defense, and placed his wife, Eleanor, as his assistant. The work was important, but hardly what the former Air Service major had in mind. The crowning blow to his ego came when Roosevelt commissioned Brooklyn district attorney William O'Dwyer and sent him overseas to fill the post La Guardia had hoped for.

For several months, La Guardia pouted over Roosevelt's denying him a chance to get into "the real fight." He lamely struck back, refusing to comply with the nationwide curfew that ordered all places of entertainment to close down at midnight in order to conserve electricity. His argument, carried all the way to the White House, was that the boys home on leave deserved a brightly lighted New York to greet them. Roosevelt good-naturedly avoided an argument with La Guardia; he simply had the Army and Navy place any club or restaurant that failed to keep the curfew off limits to the military. Then, on April 12, the running squabble between the mayor and the President ended. FDR was dead; and with his sudden passing another fire in La Guardia went to embers. In six months he would vacate Gracie Mansion and move back into his old sixth-floor apartment on the unfashionable upper end of Fifth Avenue.

But there were still some important matters he had to take care of before leaving office. One of them concerned flying— specifically, military aircraft.

Since his days as a Congressman, La Guardia had pressed for more stringent federal aviation controls. After the First World War, the barnstorming craze had swept the country. Ex-Army fliers bought surplus planes for a few hundred dollars and set up flying schools in pastures and fairgrounds. For $50 and a few spare hours, anyone could learn to fly; how well, was left completely up to the individual. By the mid-1920s, New York City was a favorite target for joy-riding amateur and military pilots. As the city's buildings soared in height, so did their daredevil antics. Weekend birdmen, flying brightly colored biplanes, cavorted through the canyons of Wall Street; some chased each other around the spire of the Woolworth Building, then the city's tallest skyscraper; others, including several military aircraft, flew under the Brooklyn Bridge. It was all great fun—a terribly modern lark designed to thrill both the pilots and their gaping earthbound audiences. Federal regulations called for all aircraft flying over the city to "maintain a safe altitude." "Safe for who?" La Guardia demanded to know. "The pilot, or the people he might crash into on the ground?"

There had been a few close calls—some forced landings on parkways and golf courses—but nothing for anyone, except La Guardia, to raise a fuss about. Then, on November 20, 1929, Charles L. Reid, a wealthy concert manager and amateur pilot, had the unique misfortune of becoming the first flier to crash into a New York City building. Up on a sightseeing flight with two friends, Reid was skimming his biplane across Manhattan at less than 500 feet when he lost control. He slammed into the West Side YMCA building at 64th Street, killing himself and his passengers. La Guardia suddenly had a great deal of company urging the Civil Aeronautics Administration to set and enforce a safe minimum altitude for planes entering New York's air space. The government agency quickly put into effect a 1,000-foot minimum for all planes, civilian and military, flying over Manhattan.

For a while, that seemed to end the problem. But then, in 1931, a new attraction opened in New York—the Empire State Building. Its 1,250-foot height was an instant, irresistible magnet for pilots. Totally disregarding the regulations, planes buzzed, rolled, sideslipped, and dive-bombed around the building with maniacal regularity. Almost daily, the CAA received urgent calls from panicked tenants telling of some pilot playing "chicken" (seeing how close he could bore in before veering off) or sightseers who were circling the tower for a terrifyingly close look. The CAA would dispatch chase planes; once identified, the offender either had his license suspended for a long period, or lost it permanently. The sport soon lost its attraction.

But then, as the rumble of war grew louder, La Guardia found himself in an air battle with the military. Single-engine fighter planes and large bombers were being flown into the city's airfields with alarming frequency. Crisscrossing Manhattan on their approaches to La Guardia, Mitchell, Floyd Bennett, or Newark airports, the planes often deafened office workers as they came in well below the minimum altitude. By the early part of 1940, Brigadier General C.P. Kane, in charge of the Air Technical Service Command for the New York area, had grown weary of fielding La Guardia's insistent complaints about the low-flying aircraft. Tragically, the mayor's prediction of disaster came true on June 17, 1940. While practicing formation flying over Queens, two twin-engine B-18 bombers collided in midair over a densely populated area. Miraculously, only the eleven crew members and one woman on the ground were killed. La Guardia raced to the scene. Sickened by the charred, dismembered bodies strewn among the wreckage, the mayor could only say, "I told them . . . I told them it would happen."

As the war escalated, so did the incidents, with heavier concentrations of military planes descending daily on the New York area. La Guardia himself was an angry witness to one of the violations. During the last game of the 1943 World Series between the Yankees and the St. Louis Cardinals, the mayor was seated in a box in Yankee Stadium. At the top of the fifth inning, a sudden thundering roar swept over the ball park. With a single reflex, 67,000 fans ducked as an olive-drab B-17 buzzed the playing field at less than 300 feet. Not satisfied with the one high-speed pass, the pilot wheeled the huge Flying Fortress around in a sharp turn and swooped down on the stadium twice again.

*   *   *

The twin peaks of the Queensboro Bridge faded in and out of the mist as Peluso threaded the prowl car through the merging 59th Street traffic. La Guardia checked his watch. He would have ample time before his appointment to read Dr. Wallace's memo. The day before, Friday, the 27th, La Guardia had arranged a meeting between Marcel Wallace, president of the Panoramic Radio Corporation, and the engineering staff of the Empire State Building. Wallace had invented an electronic device called the Stratoscope, a radarlike instrument he claimed would give pilots early warning that they were approaching either tall buildings or other aircraft.

Dr. Wallace had called La Guardia late Friday afternoon. He reported that his meeting had gone well. The building engineers and executive staff had agreed to install a test model of the anti-collision device on the Empire State observation tower the following week.

CHAPTER VIII

The Pilot's War

THE CLOCK EMBEDDED IN THE FACE of the New York Central Building read 7: 22; the hands had frozen in that position since the evening before. Workmen in yellow rain slickers were now on a scaffold high above Park Avenue replacing a rusted pin bolt.

Two blocks uptown, on the corner of 48th Street, "Hub," Hinkle and "Judy" Garland stood smoking, idly watching the suspended yellow figures laboring in the dismal half-light to repair the timepiece. The men, both lieutenant colonels in their late twenties, still addressed each other with the nicknames handed them in their plebe year at West Point. In William Garland's case, creativity yielded to the obvious; Carl Hinkle's more imaginative "Hub" was the upperclassmen's best imitation of the stammering, gulping sound he had made when being hazed. The officers had just returned from a stroll around the block. The rain had momentarily halted, replaced now by a suspended mist which washed the city with the muted grayscale of a Japanese scroll.

"Hell, there's a good chance Smith won't even be able to get in," Hinkle said, his gaze scanning the solid overcast. He scowled and tossed the cigarette into the gutter.

"I still can't figure out why Rogner's so hot to get back today."

"Maybe they need the plane back at Sioux Falls for a flight going out tonight." Garland shrugged.

Like Hinkle, Garland had questioned Rogner's reason for returning to the base early Saturday, rather than on Sunday. With his typical distance, Colonel Rogner answered by repeating what he had told them before: they were to meet him at the Barclay Hotel at 9:30 Saturday morning; they would take a cab from there to Newark Field to meet Smith. End of conversation.

The two men turned and started down the street to the Barclay. From force of habit, Garland field-stripped his cigarette, splitting it open, scattering the tobacco on the ground, then rolling the paper into a tiny ball before flicking it away. As they entered the lobby they saw Rogner talking on one of the house phones. He spotted them and waved them over.

"That was Newark Operations," Rogner said, replacing the receiver. "They don't have Smith up on the board yet."

"Are you sure he left Bedford?" Hinkle asked. "He could be socked in up there."

Rogner shook his head. The movement was crisp, precise. To Hinkle, the commander of the 457th Bomb Group seemed as rigidly starched as his meticulously pressed uniform. He was aware of Rogner's reputation as an excellent combat pilot and top-notch administrator, but the man's aloofness irritated him. True, he and Garland were one grade junior to Rogner, a full colonel, but only a damn fool would even think of pulling rank at their level. Although Hinkle had flown with another bomb group, word had filtered through that Rogner was a strictly by-the-book commander; he avoided personal contact with his men as much as possible, leaving that job to his deputy, Bill Smith. It was Smith's job to translate Rogner's commands into a style and manner guaranteed to produce results without ruffling too many egos, or bruising morale.

"If Smith had a problem, I would've heard about it long before now," Rogner said. He left no room for arguments as he glanced at his watch. "We'll leave in fifteen minutes."

The information, Hinkle thought, had been delivered as a briefing command. He watched Rogner head for the lobby newsstand. He could see now why Harris Rogner would not exactly win the Most Popular Commander of the Year award.

*   *   *

The altimeter needle dipped to 950 feet as Smith released pressure on the right rudder pedal and leveled out. Below the bomber's left wing Domitrovich watched the sandstone cliffs of New Haven merge with Long Island Sound. The ground fog half-hid the deep-water harbor crowded with small freighters and ore carriers.

Approaching New Haven, Smith had run into a dense cloud bank bottoming out at less than 1,000 feet. Now, running just beneath the solid vapor, he saw the fuel-pressure gauge sink below 6 pounds. He reached down to his right and snapped on both fuel booster pump switches. The pressure instantly climbed back to 7 pounds and held. Hedgehopping like this annoyed him. As the weather forced him to lower altitude, Smith found himself constantly toying with the controls, adjusting the mixture, the prop pitch, the cowl flaps, the trim wheel. It was dirty flying—nitpicking the aircraft, troubling it through air too close to the ground, when he and it were meant to soar clean and free.

But a single glance to his left only a few minutes ago had told him that the rest of his flight was to be this way. Moving in from Block Island Sound, off the eastern tip of Long Island, was an unbroken line of ominous black clouds. Even at that distance he could see the rolling, boiling movement of the squall line. The rain had picked up again, and along with it the gusting winds. The conditions were typical of air being violently moved 100 to 200 miles in front of the storm. Ahead, all along the irregular shoreline bordering the sound, the fog banks were growing thicker and higher, as the moist, warm air was being forced up to feed the turbulence. Smith edged the throttles forward a hair, the rpm climbing to 2,200. His decision to increase *Old John Feather Merchant's* speed was based on instinct as much as experience; Smith had once before been caught in a storm like this one. But the, three years before, he had been a passenger on his first flight.

*   *   *

The red Stinson bounced like a football trapped in a wind tunnel. Inside the fabric-covered single-engine plane, Bill Smith gripped the back of the pilot's seat and peered down through the rain clouds at the Hudson River less than 1,000 feet below.

"One more pass," he shouted to the pilot.

The pilot, as much daredevil as his passenger, scanned the storm clouds moving rapidly down the channel and decided to risk it. He kicked the left rudder and banked the feather-light craft inland, leveling out over the southern edge of West Point. He banked again, this time heading north, across the academy's sprawling campus.

"Take a good look, 'cause this is it. We're going home before this storm busts us up!"

Smith nodded absently, his eyes glued to the window as the plane flew over the North Barracks, his home for four years. This was May 1942, and in a few days Cadet Smith would graduate. He had to know if he had made the right choice, and now he was certain; second to marrying Martha Molloy, he wanted to fly more than anything else in life. This one chartered flight had told him all that was necessary—being in the air, even in a stomach-churning storm, gave him a sense of freedom and power he had never before experienced. He congratulated himself; his instinct had been right.

*   *   *

As an Army nurse at West Point, Lieutenant Martha "Molly" Molloy thought she had heard it all; she had been pitched every line in the book by the cream of the Cadet Corps. But then Bill Smith, recovering from a ruptured appendix as a result of a Harvard-West Point football game, invented a new one; he told her they were going to be married the day of his graduation. His bedside was continually swarming with beautiful young socialites from New York, all of whom flooded his room with flowers; she was Catholic and he Presbyterian; they had never so much as exchanged more than wisecracks; and although she thought he was handsome, she also found him insufferably smug and convinced of his lady-killing prowess. And yet in spite of all the negatives, somehow Martha quietly thought Cadet Smith was probably right—they would be married.

On the morning of December 8, 1941, the Boodlers was unusually crowded. The balcony area of Grant Hall served as the Point's coffee shop, the only area where cadets and their dates were allowed to gather on off-duty hours. Without warning, the music coming over the loudspeaker ground to an abrupt halt. A man's voice announced that war had been declared. The speculations and rumors which had been circulating for months throughout the Point were now fact; Bill Smith's class would graduate one month early. The war needed its young officers in an inconvenient hurry. For Bill and Martha, it meant adding their names to the list of more than two hundred couples rushing to be married in the Point chapels. It also meant that Bill would have to tell Martha, ahead of schedule, that he wanted to join the Air Corps instead of the Infantry. He had put off bringing up the subject, afraid, for one of the few times in his life, that someone could keep him from doing what he wanted.

Seated across Cokes and doughnuts at a corner table, Martha searched Bill's face, then asked, "You're sure that's what you want?"

Smith nodded. "But I won't do it if it'll worry you. I couldn't fly if I thought you'd have even a minute's worry."

Martha fixed him with a stern Irish look. "I'm not marrying you so I can worry, Bill Smith. That'll be *your* job!"

On graduation day, May 29, 1942, William Franklin Smith, Jr., received his commission as a second lieutenant. In his four years at West Point, he could look back on moments of glory interwoven with disappointment. He had become a brilliant lacrosse player, the sole member of the Army squad to be elected All-American. Away from his mother's protective eye, he had gone out for football; within a year he had made the varsity. But the honor Smith coveted most, Regimental Cadet Captain, the pinnacle of success for a West Pointer, eluded him. That award went to his lacrosse teammate Carl Hinkle.

As they emerged from the Most Holy Trinity Chapel, moving slowly beneath the crossed sabers arched by somber-looking cadets, the full and sudden reality of the war came home to Martha. She and Bill would have no time for a honeymoon. Second Lieutenant Smith had orders to report immediately to Ocala, Florida, to begin his flight training.

A month later, after receiving her discharge from the Army Nurse Corps, Martha joined Bill at the primary flight school. He had been flying every day in open-cockpit biwing Stearmans. His instinct had been on the button; he was a natural pilot. Once in the air, Smith and his plane became a single entity, a unit welded by the basic elements of design and talent.

The Smiths became gypsies, traveling from one flight school to another in a battered Mercury sedan donated by his father. From Florida, to Mississippi, to Illinois, where Bill Smith had his wings pinned on personally by General Ira Eaker. He met Jimmy Doolittle, and as a result, that very night he tore the wire stiffener out of his officer's cap and spent hours molding the cloth into an exact duplicate of the famous general's nonregulation "go-to-hell" headgear. He was a pilot now, and they were together, and for both of them, the war in Europe still seemed very far away.

Smith's days were spent training in B-17s at Wendover Field, in Utah; a barren salt flat that stretched so unerringly smooth it was possible to see the curvature of the earth. For navigational purposes the pilots pinpointed the area as the exact middle of nowhere; it was 125 miles east of Salt Lake City, and San Francisco lay 500 miles to the west. It was winter, and the freezing winds and ice storms spilled off the Rockies night and day, howling unmercifully across the unbroken flats. For Smith, born in the humid warmth of the South, the constant cold was the most grueling part of his training. For ninety days he flew cross-country navigational missions, practiced bombing runs on targets outlined to scale on the salt flats and high in the Humboldt Mountains, drilled endlessly in evasive combat and emergency techniques. He was learning to master the 38,000-pound killer whose thirteen .50-caliber machine guns had given it the name "Flying Fortress."

In the evenings, Smith, Hinkle, and their Point classmate Bill Snow would pile into the Mercury and drive 60 miles into Nevada, where their wives would have dinner waiting in a small rented house. On the surface it appeared an extension of their life at West Point—the camaraderie, the training, plus the added excitement of new marriages. But, Martha knew, Bill was anxious for this period of his life to end. He was itching to put to use in combat what he had spent a solid year training for. She too, wanted something—a baby. Bill had made some feeble arguments about waiting until the war was over, but he quickly realized that her need went deeper than maternal instinct. She had kept her bargain, never once voicing concern about his flying; he intuited that once he went overseas, Martha would require a replacement for that silence. Weeks had stretched into months with no sign of pregnancy, and the time had come for the Smiths to go their separate ways. Bill had gotten his orders. Within a week he would be in England.

"We tried," Bill said.

"Maybe we tried too hard." Martha laughed, shrugging off her disappointment.

"There are some things," he said with mock seriousness, "that you don't mind giving your all for."

A week later, Martha was home. She had driven across the country, each morning starting off with sickening waves of nausea. The rabbit reported there was no doubt—she was pregnant. She was heartbroken at the thought that Bill would have to hear the news by letter. That same night, breaking tight security regulations, Bill phoned her. All he could say was that he was at a secret base somewhere in the country. They were taking off in a few hours. When he heard that he was going to be a father, Bill's wild rebel warwhoop almost burst Martha's eardrum.

Behind the controls of *Big Time Operator*, Bill Smith flew across the Atlantic from Goose Bay, Labrador. The weeks of classroom and practical navigation by radio and radar were useless; for ten hours, Smith and the others in his formation flew by dead reckoning. The Atlantic was covered by a solid sheet of cloud cover, and German submarines were jamming the radio frequencies. His initial flight to England was a grim introduction to the weather conditions he would be flying in for the next year and a half.

The 457th Bombardment Group was stationed at Glatton Airdrome, a former Royal Air Force base in the tiny parish of Conington, some 80 miles north of London. The base bordered on a road built by the Romans more than two thousand years earlier. For the men of the 457th, and their commander, Lieutenant Colonel James Luper, the gray, drab, mud-drenched base was a depressing letdown after their hardships at Wendover. The weather was continually wet and cold. The small metal Nissen huts used as barracks were heated by coke stoves, which raised the temperature only a few degrees.

But, amenities aside, Glatton provided room at the top for a man with foresight and ambition. Luper, a West Pointer, was commanding an outfit of civilians turned airmen. He naturally looked to other West Point men among his officers for more than just leadership. Within a week of his arrival at Glatton, Bill Smith was named Assistant Operations Officer in addition to his flying duties.

That he was career-oriented, no one, including Luper, had the slightest doubt; but Smith was equally ambitious to prove himself in combat. Before that was possible, however, the pilots and crews of the 457th had to fly several combat missions as observers. The "formality" rankled Smith, but, of course, he went along for the ride. His first flight as an observer was in a B-17 piloted by his classmate William "Judy" Garland. Garland, attached to a different bomb group, had arrived in England a few weeks earlier. With four missions under his belt, he was already considered an old pro. Smith was positioned near the cockpit. In the rear section of the bomber, Bill Snow was crammed in next to the tail gunner. Both newcomers had been warned to keep strict radio silence once they were over the Channel, heading for Germany. As they approached the target, Smith's attention shifted from total concentration on the technical details of the bomb run to the air space above the target. Not a single enemy plane had come up to oppose the formation; what little puffs of flak could be seen were low and wide of their mark. The bombs were dropped. The Fortresses wheeled for home. It had been a "milk run"—the ultimate dream of every combat pilot and crew.

Suddenly, Smith's heavy Southern drawl cut into the crew's interphones. "Where the devil are they?"

"Who?" Garland asked, forgetting his own edict of radio silence.

"The Germans!" Smith said with exasperation. "I thought you guys said it was rough over here."

How rough it actually was, the devastating, terrorizing power the Germans could mount in defense of their homeland, Smith would discover; but not soon enough to suit him.

Smith's impatience to get into the fight was no less than the frustration felt by the man who had pinned on his wings a year before—General Ira Eaker, commander of the Eighth Air Force. While Smith and the 457th waited to fly their first combat mission, Eaker was driving the meteorologists to the far edge of their science, and sanity. For fifty straight days, from the end of December 1943 to the middle of February 1944, storms and thick cloud cover had kept the B-17s from hitting vital factory and airfield targets deep in enemy-held France and Germany. What missions could be flown during the foul weather were against targets of secondary value, lightly defended by the enemy's ground and air forces. The Germans had made good use of the bad weather. In a matter of weeks, they had replaced most of the single-engine Messerschmitt and Focke-Wulf fighters the Allies had shot down—at a fearful cost—over the past six months.

What Eaker was desperately waiting for was one week— seven consecutive days—of good bombing weather over enemy territory. Given the "Big Week," as he called it, Eaker planned to mount a massive assault against the German aircraft production plants and airfields. His reasoning was sound; wipe out the Luftwaffe on the ground, rather than in the air.

Eaker's frustration and Smith's impatience dissolved with the meteorologists' prediction that beginning February 20, the skies over France and Germany would be a bombardier's notion of heaven; the weather over most of the major targets would have less than two-tenths cloud cover. The Big Week was on. The 457th was ordered to hit airfields at Lippstadt and Gutersloh, deep within Germany. For the group's first mission, Colonel Luper chose Bill Smith as his lead pilot.

At 3:30 on the damp, scathingly cold morning of February 21, 1944, Smith awakened and climbed into his heavy leather and wool-fleece flying suit. By choice, he was living in a tent on the perimeter of the field with his driver, Sergeant Roy Bolton. The Nissen huts, even with stoves primed night and day, were miserably cold and damp. The tent, smaller, and with a wooden floor, was easier to heat. Equally important to Smith was his privacy. Because much of the base was still under construction, wooden housing promised the officers was still not ready for occupancy. Smith had been placed in a hut with two other officers, former civilians. They were pleasant enough, but Smith felt that he had little in common with them. What truly appealed to him was the British flying officers' tradition of having private quarters, and a "batman"—an enlisted man whose sole function was to service the officer's needs. Smith had met Bolton at Wendover, and was immediately taken by the lanky, good-natured pig farmer from Iuka, Mississippi. At Glatton, Smith had plucked Bolton from the motor pool and made him his personal driver. With Luper's permission, Smith and Bolton moved into the tent—a transition not unnoticed by certain of Smith's fellow officers who felt the move was motivated more by snobbishness than just escape from uncomfortable living conditions.

Warmed by the coffee Bolton had brewed on their hotplate, Smith filed into the briefing hut for a detailed rundown on the mission. Suspended in the acrid haze of cigarette and cigar smoke was the unmistakable aroma of body odor peculiar to men under tension. The pungent smell, surprising in the hut's frigid temperature, was normally offensive to Smith, even in a locker room; and yet, given the occasion, it seemed appropriate—strangely primal, and therefore comforting. The biting chill of the corrugated hut certainly had once been felt in a glacial cave. The pilots, .45 Colt automatics tucked snugly into shoulder holsters, had undoubted brotherhood with ancestors gathered before a hunt to ask the gods' blessing.

One hundred and thirty men—pilots, navigators, and bombardiers—riveted their attention on the small stage where the briefing officer pinpointed their route and target areas on brightly lighted wall-sized maps. An hour later, with a ricepaper "flimsie" detailing each step of the mission in hand, Smith drove the Bolton to his bomber.

Rene III, named for Luper's wife, was the first up on the flight line. It was a B-17G model, the latest in the long series of continually modified Flying Forts. With his crew chief and copilot, Smith began a probing search that would take him over every square inch of the plane. He walked both sides of the 75-foot-long fuselage, and ran his hands along the leading and trailing edges of the 104-foot wings, feeling for loose fittings or imperfections in the taut metal skin. He checked the fuel load, making absolutely certain that the eight wing tanks contained the critical 2,800 gallons the mission's distance and bomb load called for; that the thirteen .50-caliber machine guns, bristling from turrets, and ports throughout the ship, had been charged with 6,000 rounds of high-explosive ammunition. Standing a respectful distance from the open bomb-bay doors, he had watched the awesome ritual of fusing each of the twelve 500-pound general-purpose bombs. Until the fuses were inserted in the nose and tail, the bombs were totally harmless, even if dropped or whacked with a sledge hammer; fused, so much as a vibration from a nearby plane might set them off.

Up forward in the Plexiglas nose, the bombardier was fitting a Norden bombsight into its special holder. He had carried the top-secret instrument aboard in a locked container—accompanied, according to strict regulations, by an armed escort. The bombsight's design was so jealously guarded by the U.S. command that not even the British were allowed to use it.

Through the bleak, early-morning fog obscuring the airdrome, Smith saw multicolored signal flares burst high over the control tower. He released the brakes, allowing the four 1,200-horsepower engines to hurl *Rene III*'s 68,000-pound weight down the runway. Behind him, as if sucked into his slipstream, the thirty-five other Fortresses lifted off over the flat English countryside.

The first hour of the mission would be nerve-racking for Smith. As lead pilot it was his job to work the thirty-six planes up into formation; two "boxes" of eighteen planes, each divided into six-plane squadrons. Climbing under full power at 150 miles per hour, Smith cut through the fog, flying blind, relying on his instruments to locate a radio transmitter called the Buncher Beacon. While he led his squadron in shallow, sweeping turns about this invisible focal point, the rest of the flight laboriously climbed to altitude and slipped into formation. The slightest mistake on Smith's part—a misread radio signal, or distrust of his instruments—could lead to midair collisions in the thick, mesmerizing fog. Throughout his training in the States and at Glatton, Smith had witnessed the sudden, cataclysmic result of bomb-laden B-17s careening into each other while climbing on instruments to altitude. Finally, after what seemed an eternity to the circling crews, the 457th was in formation. They turned eastward and headed for the English channel.

At 24,000 feet the phrase "bitter cold" loses all human context. The ten men who were riding in *Rene III*, their features obliterated behind oxygen masks and tight-fitting fleece-lined caps, were moving through air registering 40 degrees below zero. At that temperature, warm skin making contact with bare metal forms an instant, inseparable bond. Breath literally crystallizes; perspiration forms beaded icicles. Swathed in bulky electrically heated suits and gloves, power lines plugged umbilical-like into wall receptacles, the men still trembled as over 200-mile-per-hour drafts raced through the plane from the open gun ports and crevices in the bomb bay.

For no medical reason that could be discovered, Smith's ears were extraordinarily sensitive to the sub-freezing altitude. He had become painfully aware of the condition while training at Wendover. But not even the most brutal of Utah's winters seemed to affect him like the damp of northern England. The pain began at 10,000 feet. First, there was a burning sensation as if sandpaper were being brushed across the outer, fleshy portion. At 15,000 feet, the burning subsided, replaced by a throbbing, needlelike jabbing in the cartilage near the canal. At that altitude the pain would come in waves, then subside for minutes at a time. But at bombing altitudes, four to six miles above the earth, the pain was steady, often excruciating. Smith had been to a doctor several times, always minimizing the condition's severity, afraid that he might be grounded for medical reasons. But nothing could be found to explain the problem. The only remedy that seemed to help was to coat his outer ears with vaseline and swab the canals with peroxide before taking off.

On that first mission, however, the pain was all but forgotten as Smith led his formation toward the Dutch coast. The briefing had told him to expect "little friends," as the bomber pilots called their fighter escorts, about mid-Channel. Other elements of the Eighth Air Force had joined formation with the 457th. More than a hundred B-17s, flying in tight boxed squadrons, had almost reached enemy-held territory without sighting the desperately needed fighter protection. From the start of the war, disastrous bomber losses to the Luftwaffe had proved the necessity of long-range fighter escort.

Even with their mass of rapid-firing armament, the Fortresses were no match for the searing speed and maneuverability of the German fighters. Huge and agonizingly slow with their heavy gas and bomb loads, the B-17s were relatively easy prey for the expert enemy pilots. By late 1943, the Germans had adapted the American cowboys' method of cutting into the bomber formations with a dead-on massed attack, then sweeping in and singling out individual planes for concentrated assaults. The Fortresses' defense lay in dense numbers, tight formations with each plane's guns laying down a protective, cross-patterned curtain of fire-power.

Because of their individual vulnerability to fighter attack, each B-17 pilot was aware that if he dropped out of formation—for any reason—engine trouble, or crippled by enemy gunfire—he was on his own. The formation would tighten up, another plane slipping into the wounded bomber's slot. To do otherwise would be to risk the entire flight for the lives of ten men.

The Dutch coast loomed ahead. Smith caught sight of the fighter escorts, P-51 Mustangs, vectoring on the formation from the south. They were late—but welcome. The Germans had no doubt been tracking the bomber stream both visually and on radar. From the moment the formation edged into Holland, Smith knew they could expect a 400-mile corridor of flak and fighter attacks. When they reached the German border, he was also aware of an additional enemy: the German civilians.

The German people were demoralized. As the Allied raids mounted in intensity and range, a numbing awareness took hold that the Nazi high command was lying; they were not winning on all fronts; the stark evidence of ravaged cities and starving populations proved the lie. Hitler's war had come home. Faced with possible mutiny throughout the country, Joseph Goebbels, the Minister of Propaganda, had issued a nationwide "kill order"—all Allied pilots and crew members were to be considered fair game for the civilian population. If Goebbels could not satisfy his countrymen's hopes for battlefield victories, he could at least provide an outlet for their rage and suffering. At Glatton, Smith had heard stories from escaped airmen of German mobs stoning captured pilots; of farmers shooting or pitchforking to death wounded crews. For all the obvious reasons, Smith hoped that he wouldn't be shot down. If he was, the .45 weighing heavily on his left shoulder would be of little use; he was still a lousy shot.

Again, as he had done on his first observation flight, he found himself wondering where the enemy was hiding. They were almost four hours into the mission and not a single German fighter had come up to challenge them. Flak over Holland and on their penetration into Germany had been light and ineffective. Smith's navigator had called out the target dead ahead, the airfield at Lippstadt. The ship's airspeed fell off as the bomb-bay doors opened, creating drag. The bombardier was about to begin his run. Even through the tension, Smith felt let down. He hadn't come this far only to have his first mission turn into a "milk run."

"Wolves . . . four o'clock!"

The tail gunner's voice was drowned out over the intercom by a deafening burst of gunfire almost directly under Smith's legs. He felt the plane shudder as the navigator opened up with the twin .50s in the nose turret. Smith still had not seen the enemy fighters.

The thirty-odd FW-190s had been lingering in a cloud layer several thousand feet below the formation, keeping pace with them, waiting for the bombers to begin their run on the target. From long experience, the German pilots knew that once the B-17s had begun their bomb runs, they were ducks in a gallery. The pilots were committed to stay unswervingly on course. No evasive action would be taken.

"Jesus! . . . Four coming up your side!" Smith recognized the radio operator's voice as he shouted from his position on the right side of the plane.

The entire aircraft was shivering under the pounding hammer blows of thirteen heavy machine guns firing simultaneously. A gray blur swept across Smith's windshield. He barely caught sight of the black Iron Cross outlined with white on the fuselage of the 190.

The sky was filled with twisting, diving fighters as the Mustangs set up a protective rim about the bombers.

"Bombardier to pilot . . . commencing the run."

A flak burst exploded directly in front of the plane. Another rocked the ship under the left wing. The ground gunners were beginning to find the range. Smith felt a tug on the control yoke. He released his grip.

In the nose, the bombardier was hunched over his Norden, both of his hands making delicate adjustments to the knobs on either side of the bombsight. Until he gave control back to Smith, he would be flying the aircraft. For three minutes, the length of time needed to bring the plane directly over the target and release the bombs, the lives of everyone in the ship were in his hands. Through a gyroscope linked to the automatic-pilot control, the bombardier, his eye glued to the sight, slipped the plane a shade to the right. The airfield came into focus, the runways and oil tanks sliding directly between the cross hairs. He jabbed the release trigger . . . once . . . twice.

"Bombs away!"

Smith felt the plane surge upward as the twelve bombs fell free. Throughout the formation, one after another, each plane salvoed its explosives.

"Bombardier to pilot . . . giving her back to you."

Smith took hold of the control yoke and trounced on the right rudder. His gunners were still firing short, savage bursts at the waves of 190s. But it was the flak Smith was worried about. He had just seen two of his bombers hit by ground fire. One had plummeted down in a twisting spiral. Only two chutes had come out before the Fortress tore apart. The other, with one engine knocked out and its rudder shredded, was losing altitude. Smith saw two Mustangs fall in on either side of the crippled plane, giving cover as it falteringly turned west, back toward the Channel.

The mission had been a success. Smith had led his men on their first combat assignment with unerring accuracy and with a bare minimum of loss. He, and they, had been blooded.

*   *   *

The missions mounted.

Berlin, 6 March '44 . . . Lead Pilot, Smith.

Bac-Queriette, 13 March '44 . . . Lead Pilot, Smith.

Frankfurt, 20 March '44 . . . Lead Pilot, Smith.

Berlin, 22 March '44 . . . Air Commander, Smith.

Rahmel . . . Schweinfurt . . . Hamm . . . Lyon . . . Luxembourg . . .

It had become routine to him by then, the pre-dawn briefings, fogbound takeoffs, the eight- to ten-hour missions, the deck-level flights homeward across the Channel in search of Glatton, perpetually hidden by rain and mist. Smith was now a major, and with the promotion came the leadership of the 750th Squadron.

The men were exhausted. All were frightened. And some were terrified, like the tail gunner in Smith's squadron who walked into the spinning blades of a warming Fortress rather than crawl into his Plexiglas cocoon one more time.

Smith was frightened; but unlike most of his comrades, who blandly stated the facts, or expanded reality, he remained, for the most part, silent. Yet, attached to that quiet was an air of total self-assurance. Nowhere did it assert itself more than in his dress. The demon mud, scourge of men and machines at Glatton, somehow never seemed to attach itself to Smith. Whether in his flight suit or in dress uniform at a local pub, Smith was immaculate. With his swagger stick, shoes spit-polished by Bolton, and razor-trimmed mustache, he seemed perfect—uncomfortably close to the image Lorenz Hart conjured when he wrote "Too Good for the Average Man."

Many of his fellow officers sought release in drinking and making rounds of off-limits establishments such as Mrs. Brady's, but Smith was content with a rubber of bridge now and then. He shared an occasional scotch or beer, but excused himself when the bull session turned to dirty jokes. Since childhood, Smith had loathed off-color humor. And cursing. Even under the most extreme pressure, Bill Smith had never been heard to utter a swear word. Given these principles, it was inevitable that a subtle difference would evolve between the deep respect the officers and men felt for him and the close warmth they shared among themselves. Smith's separate housing, his "batman," his preference for fellow West Pointers, and his disciplined pursuit of career visibly set him apart from the rank and file.

In July and in October of 1944, two momentous events occurred in Smith's life.

Having just returned from a week's holiday in Scotland, Smith was seated at the evening mess when the loudspeaker demanded the officers' attention. Groans went up, the men certain that in minutes they would be scrambling to their planes, bound for the Channel. Instead, a musical fanfare trumpeted, and Colonel Luper announced that word had just been received: Major Smith was the proud father of a baby boy born the day before. As if by magic, bottles of scotch and champagne appeared on each table. For one of the few times in his life, Bill Smith got smashed. That night he sent $100 to his mother-in-law, instructing her to keep Martha's room filled with flowers for a week.

The second occurrence brought Harris Rogner into Bill Smith's life. While flying as air commander on the October 6 raid on Politz, Luper's lead plane was hit by devastating ground fire. The crew was seen to bail out over the small town in eastern Germany. Word came back to Glatton a few days later that Luper had been taken prisoner. The 457th was to have a new commander.

Rogner had been graduated from the Point in 1938, the year Smith had entered as a plebe. His career had been meteoric. A full colonel, he had been deputy commander of the 94th Combat Wing, a distinguished pilot and air commander. On October 11, he arrived at Glatton to assume command of the 457th.

Where Luper had been outgoing, with charm and a sense of showmanship, Rogner was all business. Quiet and reserved, he made it quickly known that he was not available for base social events or after-dinner poker games. He had a single goal: to make the 457th the most outstanding unit in the Eighth Air Force. In a matter of weeks, intensive raids over Cologne, Hamburg, and Merseburg left gaps in Rogner's chain of command. Smith's record of combat expertise and strong discipline, attributes Rogner admired most, made him the natural choice for the post of Group Operations Officer. A short time later Smith gave up the tent to share quarters with Rogner.

Mannheim . . . Harburg . . . Kassel . . . Koblenz . . . Gemund . . . Cologne . . . Aschaffenburg . . .

On a moonless night over Dresden, as Smith's lead bomber dropped its load of incendiaries, he slid open his panel window and tossed out a pair of his son's baby shoes.

It was for luck, he explained to Martha in the letter asking for them. All the boys do it. Sort of a superstition.

Ellingen...Recklinghausen...Seddin...

April 20, 1945. His war was over. Smith had flown the 457th's first, hundredth, and last mission. He was now a lieutenant colonel, deputy commander of the bomb group, rewarded with medals and a service record which assured him a full colonelcy within months.

He had flown more than five hundred combat hours through forests of flak, against slashing fighter attacks, in blinding snowstorms and concrete fogs. He had brought his fortess in over the flat, unobstructed English countryside at full throttle, letting wheels and flaps down 10 miles from the base. Not once, but fifty times his aircraft had been sieved with shrapnel, punctured by enemy machine-gun bullets and cannon fire. His windshield had been blown out, control cables shredded, wings and tail surfaces ravaged by fires and exploding engines.

That he had never lost an aircraft was a dual tribute to both his experience and the B-17. In those five-hundred-odd hours Smith had gazed at, pulled, gripped, tapped, pushed, yanked, turned, pressed, and twisted each of its gauges, controls, and switches thousands of times. He had trusted it with his life.

*   *   *

"Navy eight one four two on course at seven thousand. Request final approach into Floyd Bennett."

"Roger, Navy eight one—you have a go-ahead."

"United one zero one headed west at six thousand."

"United one zero one...you're cleared to twenty-five west of Phillipsburg. Climb to nine and maintain on route."

Smith had tuned in the New York Airway Traffic Control Center's frequency a few minutes ago. Twice now, as he approached Bridgeport, he had attempted to transmit. But breaking into the heavy tower talk had proved frustrating; he was a Contact flight, and the center's attention at the moment was concentrated on Instument traffic entering and leaving the New York area. The foul weather was playing havoc with both commercial and military flights. Smith had been asked to stay off the air until he, with his request for local weather conditions, approached La Guardia.

The fog banks were now moving in layered sheets, on a diagonal from the sound into the shoreline. Bridgeport sat under an undulating carpet of gray, forcing the bomber down to 900 feet. Smith checked his panel: oil temperature, 120.5 . . . manifold pressure, 26.5 . . . cowl flaps, half-open.

Ahead, through the rising vapor, he saw the sound as it curved in a sweeping arc to the left. Short of its terminus was Stamford, his swing-point for crossing into New York.

Army 0577 was moving along the Connecticut shoreline at 225 miles per hour. It would reach Stamford in less than four minutes.

CHAPTER IX

9:35—The Building

THE WALK FROM THE SUBWAY EXIT to the Empire State Building left seventy-three-year-old George Witten slightly sodden and winded.

Normally, the two-block distance would have been made in a leisurely stroll, with frequent stops to peruse the merchandise displayed in the building's ground-floor shop windows. But this morning the rain had forced him to quicken his pace. His cheeks flushed from the unaccustomed exercise, Witten hurried into the lobby and shook the moisture off his hat before entering the elevator.

"What's the big shots eating today, George—franks and beans or corned beef and cabbage?" the operator asked with a laugh. It was a standing joke between them, but this morning Witten shook his head and sighed morosely. "I wish I had thought of that," he said with a lingering trace of a German accent. The veal roast he had ordered prepared for today's important business luncheon had been on his mind all during the subway ride. The war had made everything uncertain, especially veal. By the time the elevator halted at the 37th floor he was positive that he had made a big mistake. "Hey, George—save me enough for a sandwich," the operator called out as Witten plodded down the corridor to the Schenley Distillers suite of offices. Fitting his key in an unmarked door, the executive maître d' entered the seventeenth century.

119

He was standing in an oak-paneled chamber that had once been the library of an English manor house. It had recently been shipped over piece by piece—hand-carved chairs, pegged tables, stained-glass windows and twin fireplaces—to serve as the company's executive dining room. Witten had come out of retirement to oversee the kitchen and serving staff.

The aroma of roasting veal reached him from the kitchen. His brows arched in surprise. Promising—quite promising. He crossed the Aubusson rug and pulled open the heavy velvet drapes covering the stained-glass windows. The Palisades across the Hudson River were shrouded in a misty fog. Both the towering view of New Jersey and his presence in the ancient room never failed to amaze him. Where else but in America could a man begin and end his career on a single piece of real estate, only to pick it up again—this time thirty-seven stories higher!

Forty-eight years before Witten had been a busboy, and then a waiter, in the Waldorf-Astoria Hotel, when it stood on the site where the Empire State Building now soared.

From the moment of its opening, in 1897, the Waldorf-Astoria was *the* hotel in America. Royalty paraded before the world's rich in its famous "Peacock Alley." Edward, Prince of Wales, nodded hello to King Carol of Rumania, before sitting down to supper with Kitchener of Khartoum. Teddy Roosevelt hosted an intimate luncheon for ninety in honor of the King and Queen of Belgium, while in an adjoining private dining room glasses were being raised to celebrate the forming of the United States Steel Corporation. It was in a suite of rooms above the opulent mahogany-and-marble lobby that engineers and international money men drew plans to dig a canal through Panama.

The Waldorf-Astoria was the first hotel to install room telephones. Mail was delivered to the upper floors by pneumatic tubes, and each floor had its own pantry and kitchen to provide instant room service to the pampered guests. On any given day the desk register read like a global *Who's Who:* Prince Henry of Prussia might be down the corridor from Buffalo Bill; Li Hung-chang, the famous Governor General of China, across the hall from Lillian Russell.

In 1799, John Thompson, a farmer, paid the city $2,600 for a 20-acre parcel of land, for which in the not-too-distant future boundaries would be fixed to the south and north by 33rd and 36th Streets, and to the west and the east by Broadway and Madison Avenue. Sunfish Creek, crystal-clear, fast-moving, and deep enough for several varieties of fish to thrive, traversed the property in a channel that would become the intersection of Fifth Avenue and 34th Street.

While Thompson was clearing the land to build his frame house and barn, he undoubtedly cursed each and every rusting cannon ball and musket shot his plow blade found hidden in the tall grass. In those moments it is highly doubtful that Thompson gave serious thought to the major Revolutionary battle that was fought within the boundaries of his farm. The artillery had been fired by the British on September 15, 1776, at the retreating colonial army. Thompson's farm was alive with ragtag militia men racing across Sunfish Creek as the redcoats shot at them from Kips Bay, just south at the foot of the East River. Watching the rout, first with despair and then in a raging anger, General George Washington, positioned on a grassy knoll at Fifth Avenue and 42nd Street, spurred his horse and charged at his men, turning them back into the fight by laying his cane over their shoulders. The colonists managed to break through a small group of redcoats who had arrived in advance of the main force, and made their way safely along the Bloomingdale Road to lower Manhattan.

But it was on the neighboring farm, owned by Robert Murray, that a drama of far greater importance to the Revolution was taking place. British Generals Howe, Clinton, and Cornwallis, accompanied by New York Governor William Tryon, rode up from Kips Bay and stopped at the Murray farm to pay their respects. Legend has it that Mrs. Murray knew that at that very moment General Israel Putnam and his infantry were on a forced march, heading south along the Bloomingdale Road in a desperate effort to rescue Washington's army.

While Mary Murray fed the Englishmen tea and cakes, Putnam's troops passed within a half-mile of the lavishly furnished house. Had they been captured, historians agree, New Yorkers might never have had the opportunity to develop their unique accent.

Whether Mrs. Murray actually knew of Putnam's movements is questionable; but legends die hard, and in 1938, Mayor La Guardia christened a new Staten Island ferry the *Mary Murray*.

By 1825, Thompson sold the farm, giving his reason in an advertisement: "Circumstances require removal to the City." The property brought $10,000. Two years later the new owners, Thomas and Margaret Lawton, doubled their money by selling the farm to one of the city's richest young men, William Blackhouse Astor.

William B., the second of "robber baron" John Jacob Astor's sons, purchased the property as an investment for the future—fitting it in his bulging portfolio of other New York investments, which included brothels, opium dens, and blocks of paupers' shanties. Although luck played a back-row part in any of the Astors' business ventures, the future dropped in William's lap sooner than even he had a right to expect. Within a short time of his acquiring the farm, the city took title to the Fifth Avenue road rights as far north as 129th Street. By then, a thoroughfare had already been cut through 34th Street, from the East River to the Hudson.

To the delight of quarry owners and stonemasons, the rich discovered Fifth Avenue. Beginning with Henry C. Brevoort, the ruling king of the social lions, one prominent family after another built palatial mansions and town houses on land that only a few years before was graveyards and sheep meadows. William Astor sat content in his downtown mansion until his older brother, John Jacob, Jr., decided that he too should live on the new Millionaire's Row. In 1859, J.J.'s four-story brownstone mansion went up on the corner of Fifth Avenue and 33rd Street. Not to be outdone, a few years later William built an exact duplicate of his brother's house on the southwest corner of Fifth Avenue and 34th Street.

The mansions were twins, but there the resemblance between the two Astor families ended. John Jacob, Jr., was married to a Philadelphia heiress, Charlotte Gibbs. She was a gracious and well-traveled woman who spent at least part of her time dabbling in philanthropy. He, if his father's assessment can be taken at face value, was an idiot in an elephant's body. True or not, the elder Astor left the bulk of his vast fortune to young William, who married the lady destined to become "the" Mrs. Astor. She was born Caroline Schermerhorn, the product of an old Dutch family who left her in possession of $50,000,000, and little in beauty or brains. But she was determined to become New York's leading socialite. Her black wig in place—she was totally bald—Mrs. William Astor set about spending $2,250,000 on her mansion, where every year, on the third Monday in January, she gave a ball, restricting the guest list to four hundred of New York's elite.

For decades, "the" Mrs. Astor ruled Fifth Avenue society. Not even the coming of horse trolleys careening up and down 34th Street, nor the invasion of commercial business along Sixth Avenue and on Broadway, diminished the splendor of Millionaire's Row. It took nothing less than the death of John Jacob, Jr., to signal the end of Mrs. Astor's monarchy.

Enter William Waldorf Astor, who inherited not only his father's house but an active dislike for his Aunt Caroline, who lived next door. With a single sentence announcing his intention to tear down the mansion and in its place build America's grandest hotel, he gave *the* Mrs. Astor a fit. How could she, or any of her prestigious neighbors, possibly live beside a *hotel*! She would sue. They would sue. One *lived* on Fifth Avenue—business had no business there. Deaf to the cries of outrage, Astor filed plans with the Building Department and his mansion came down. Two years later, in March 1893, the Waldorf Hotel opened on the corner of Fifth Avenue and 33rd Street.

The hotel, named after the small German town which spawned the Astors, was a 450-room red-brick-and-sandstone structure in the German Renaissance style. That it cost $5,000,000 could hardly be doubted. Opening-night guests at a

charity concert were given a tour of the eight private dining
rooms, one an exact replica of the dining room in the old Astor
mansion. They saw suites decorated with antique canopied
beds and Persian carpets, and a grand salon copied line for line
and mural for mural from a French palace. The gold-and-
burgundy Empire Room, a treasure house of rococo, was
draped with the finest European velvets and flocked wall
coverings.

The "400" quickly overcame their indignation and
poured into the Waldorf to attend extravagant costume balls
and bacchanalian feasts. Even the dowager Astor succumbed,
and while grumbling, she forced herself to enter her nephew's
"tavern down the street" for fear that the social scene would
pass her by.

Recognizing that the Waldorf was a tremendous financial success, old William Blackhouse Astor shrewdly
swung his wife to the idea of moving out of the declining
neighborhood—and making a pile for their trouble. Like their
upstart nephew, they would build a hotel right next to his and
call it the Astoria, after the town in Oregon founded by his
father. It would be bigger and more posh, and like "the" Mrs.
Astor, it would be "the" hotel. Nephew William quickly got in
touch with Uncle William, and after much heated negotiation
they agreed to a partnership—with one stipulation insisted
upon by Mrs. Astor: the new hotel must be constructed in such
a way that it could be separated from the Waldorf if family got
in the way of business. The building went up with provisions
made for sealing up the doorways that joined the two
structures.

If the Waldorf-Astoria was a magnet for New York's
society, the area in and around Fifth Avenue and 34th Street
quickly developed into the market place of the people.
Department stores such as Bonwit Teller, McCreery's, B.
Altman, and Best and Company moved onto the avenue as the
rich fled farther uptown. Macy's built on Sixth Avenue and
Herald Square, Pennsylvania Station went up on Seventh
Avenue, and the city's largest post office sprawled over much of
Eighth Avenue and 33rd Street. The millinery, textile, and

garment industries poured into the area, settling into the new tall buildings that were shooting up on the crest of the mid-'20s building boom.

"New" money was taking over Millionaire's Row, and the venerable Waldorf-Astoria had become an expensive anachronism. While its prestige and volume of business remained great, taxes and huge operating costs forced the board of directors to the unhappy conclusion that the property could be put to more profitable use. The days of cavernous lobbies and public rooms sprinkled with potted palms and priceless oriental rugs no longer fitted into the economic or cultural needs of the Jazz Age. Rumors began to circulate that the hotel was going to be sold. Why not? What better time to move into the future? Republican Herbert Hoover was President, even the most conservative Wall Streeter was predicting still-higher profits, and with Fifth Avenue land more precious than titanium, any sensible real-estate man would give his eyeteeth to develop the Waldorf property. It was December 1928, and New York's future, not to mention the country's, never looked brighter.

While real-estate syndicates were thrown together to make offers on the property and newspapers raced into print with premature announcements of its sale, a Horatio Alger millionaire named John Jacob Raskob was quietly solidifying plans to erect the world's tallest building on the site of the Waldorf-Astoria.

Raskob, who had climbed out of the slums of Hell's Kitchen to co-found General Motors, had long harbored a dream of building the tallest structure on earth. What he lacked, until the Waldorf property went on the market, was the right location. With the Du Pont brothers as partners, and former New York Governor Alfred E. Smith as front man, Raskob wrote out a check for $16,000,000 to buy the Waldorf-Astoria and the two acres upon which it stood. On August 29, 1929, the New York *Times* broke the story that the Empire State Building would soon begin construction. The cost, including the land, was put at $60,000,000—an astronomical sum, but not all that mind-boggling at a time when ticker tapes were grinding out paper fortunes daily.

Any doubt that Raskob meant business was put to rest when a demolition crew's truck drove through the Waldorf's front door a few days after the *Times* story appeared. By then, the former owners had removed several loads of furnishings which would eventually grace the new Waldorf-Astoria on Park Avenue. The truck continued on to the far end of the lobby and turned into the columned Peacock Alley. Raskob had staked out three of the graceful marble pillars for use in his Maryland country home and had instructed his crew to remove them before the actual demolition began. Using hand saws so as not to injure the delicately veined stone, the workmen started to cut into one of the columns. White powder sprinkled out. The columns were ordinary plaster, artfully painted to look like ancient marble. If Raskob had a philosophical turn of mind, that decorator's deception in a hall which once echoed with the sounds of power and wealth was prophetic. Within two months the world was reeling under the shock of the Great Depression.

While Wall Street was littered with plummeting stocks and brokers, Raskob and his partners found themselves scrambling to protect their enormous investment. Wheeling and dealing in the shattered money market, a $27,000,000 loan was finally negotiated with the Metropolitan Life Insurance Company and the project was rescued. By the end of December, the last of the stone-and-steel framework of the Waldorf was hauled out to sea on barges, and dumped five miles beyond Sandy Hook, New Jersey. Only the foundations of the old hotel remained.

As workmen were clearing the site, a padlocked steel door was uncovered on the 34th Street side. Breaking it open, they discovered a long-forgotten wine cellar that had been in the sub-basement of "the" Astor mansion. Much to Raskob's delight, it contained five huge hogsheads of whiskey, each barrel dating from the Spanish-American War, and over a hundred cases of rare French wines and champagne: an ample reward for his disappointment over the plaster columns.

* * *

Midtown Manhattan rests on a sunken and glacially eroded mountain ridge: three deep layers of metamorphic rock older than a billion years. The first known earthquake to send shivers through this dense bedrock was recorded in 1663. By 1930, there had been so few quakes, and those of such small consequence, that fear of earth tremors was the least of architect William Lamb's problems in designing the Empire State Building.

For six months prior to the Waldorf's razing, Lamb had struggled with the puzzle of how to fit a 100-story, 36,000,000-cubic-foot building onto an acre of land. Although Raskob had bought two full acres, the city building code set rigid guidelines on the height-to-land ratio of skyscrapers, forcing designers and builders to progressively narrow their structures as they rose beyond a certain elevation. Lamb was also haunted by other problems: time and money. Calculating the soaring interest rates to the penny, Raskob's accountants informed the architect that he would have eighteen months to complete the building, from the final plans to the opening-day ceremony.

Just the incredibly short timelock would have frightened off most architects, especially men like Lamb with unblemished reputations to protect. A Scotsman by descent, Lamb was both methodical and creative. Weighing the fixed conditions of space, time, and money against the intangibles of weather and delivery of materials, he agreed to take on the assignment —on one condition: in addition to the landlord's needs, the building had to be beautiful.

"What do you have in mind?" Raskob asked, thinking Lamb would offer as an example one of the city's multi-tiered wedding-cake-style skyscrapers.

The architect reached across his desk and without a word, held up a pencil. Raskob studied the spare, clean lines of the slender object for a long moment, and then nodded his approval. He had hired the right man to design the world's tallest building.

While Lamb was rooted to his drafting table revising one plan after another, an army of engineering and design experts were preparing for what literally would be an assault on Fifth

Avenue. Time was the enemy. Lamb had agreed to a seemingly meager span of days to erect a building so immense its interior could shelter a city of eighty thousand people.

In quarries from France to Italy, American stone artisans handpicked an entire year's output of the finest marbles for the elevator lobbies and office corridors. More than 300,000 square feet were ordered, the contracts calling for each quarry to deliver the marble cut to exact dimensions, polished and ready for installation.

Steel mills in Pittsburgh were handed structural plans so detailed that the exact number of rivets needed to join the massive skeleton had already been predetermined. Orders were placed for more than 60,000 tons of steel, enough to lay a railroad track from New York to Miami. Each girder was given a code number that tied it to a delivery date. Eighty hours from the moment molten steel poured into a specific mold, the girder would be in the hands of the riveters on Fifth Avenue.

Glass factories worked double shifts to turn out five acres of precut glass for the 6,500 windows. Legions of bricklayers were hired to set the ten million bricks needed for the building's interior walls. Stonemasons readied themselves for the Herculean task of facing the structure with over 200,000 cubic feet of Indiana limestone.

In the factory of John A. Roebling, the man who had designed and built the Brooklyn Bridge, more than 1,000 miles of steel wire were being braided for the wrist-thick cables that would shoot the sixty-seven elevators up and down seven miles of shafts.

Throughout the country, from hardware factories in New England to the lumber mills of the Pacific Northwest, industry veterans, Depression-desperate as they were for Raskob's business, ran incredulous eyes over figures they were being asked to copy down on their order sheets. Time and again, purchasing agents for the building's contractors were forced to repeat the six- and nine-digit totals for items such as door knobs, water faucets, light switches, locks, radiators, and hinges. The Bell Telephone Company diverted dozens of its New York staff to work on the planning and installation of

15,000,000 feet of phone cable that would connect 3,000 office switchboard trunklines to more than 15,000 phones. To feed the building with power and light, over 2,000,000 feet of electrical wire would be run through hundreds of miles of conduit tubing.

To offer the public some idea of the immensity of the project, Lamb used a graphic illustration. If every single piece of material needed to construct the building arrived on a train in one shipment, the number of boxcars required would stretch 57 miles; with the locomotivve stopped in Grand Central Station, the rear caboose would be left standing on the outskirts of Bridgeport, Connecticut.

Above Lamb's desk was an artist's rendering of the building, and in large letters the promised date of completion—May 1, 1931. With the skill and ingenuity of a neurologist tracing the pathways of a million nerve endings, he had planned the project down to the most minute detail. Scale models of the building in varying sizes and detail filled his office—along with a picture of the Chrysler Building, then just nearing completion.

Before the Empire State Building had been announced, the Chrysler structure was being heralded as the world's tallest building. A pet project of automobile manufacturer Walter Chrysler, the building on Lexington Avenue had been designed to dominate the New York skyline, topping by 40 feet the Bank of Manhattan's 927 feet—a respectable, yet not ostentatious, outdistancing. But even as his monument was under construction, Chrysler's title to owning the tallest building was challenged by Raskob's dream. Competitive as he was rich, Chrysler had an elaborate Art Deco spire secretly constructed inside the building and elevated through the dome. At 1,046 feet, Chrysler had one-upped the Eiffel Tower by 62 feet, and his designers assured him that though Raskob's pride might be hurt, he was a businessman first and last; to force the Empire State Building higher would be economic suicide.

The Chrysler Building's surprise finish threw Raskob and Lamb into a moment of panic. Although their building had three times the volume of the Chrysler Building, they had fixed

the height of the Empire State at slightly under 1,050 feet—
eighty-five floors of office space topped by an observation
deck. To add more stories at a time when money was tight and
the future uncertain was indeed bad business. And yet, Raskob
refused to give up his goal of making the Empire State
Building the world's tallest structure. Ego was not the sole
reason; the real-estate man was certain that tenants would flock
to the building for the prestige factor alone. One suggestion
after another to make the building taller was rejected as being
either too costly, or frivolous; Raskob wanted height, but not at
the expense of the building's integrity. One afternoon while
examining the scale models, Raskob suddenly whirled around
and shouted at Lamb, "A hat! That's what this building
needs—a hat!"

What he meant was a mooring mast for dirigibles—a
soaring tower where giant airships like the *Graf Zeppelin*
could land their passengers after a transatlantic crossing. Not
only would the tower instantly become the world's most
unusual passenger terminal, but the 200-foot mast would also
serve a practical purpose; by landing a quarter of a mile above
Fifth Avenue, airship passengers would be saved the long trip
back to Manhattan from the dirigible station at Lakehurst,
New Jersey.

In one inspired stroke Raskob had not only solved the
problem of how to add profitable height to the building, but he
had fired the public's imagination by focusing attention on
what aviation experts were claiming would be the future
method of international travel. Within a week of announcing
the mooring mast, Al Smith was conferring with Navy
dirigible experts and officials of the Goodyear Zeppelin
Corporation. They not only assured him that the mast was
structurally feasible, but left little doubt that it would return
the building's owners a handsome profit in landing fees.

By January 1930, the country was beginning to feel the
first symptoms of the Depression. A leveling grimness had
settled in. The future seemed stagnant; reality became
something to be bartered for a few hours in a movie theater
watching Harlow and Fairbanks make the world right again.

This is the last photograph taken of Bill and Martha Smith.

West Point Cadet William Franklin Smith, Jr., as an upperclassman.

An outstanding athlete, Smith was elected to the All-American lacrosse team in his senior year at West Point.

The Smiths were married at the Most Holy Trinity Chapel at West Point the day after his graduation. After a weekend honeymoon, Smith began his flight training.

Martha holding William Franklin Smith III, age six months.

Bill Smith and "Willie Three." The photo was taken during Smith's last visit with his wife and son.

Lieutenant Colonel William Franklin Smith, Jr. on the day his Bomb Group, the 457th, was leaving Glatton Airdrome in England for home. During the year and a half he spent overseas he acquired the British officers' tradition of carrying a swagger stick.

After a raid over Berlin, Smith poses with his lead crew.

Inspecting his B-17, *BigTime Operator*, Smith carries his ever-present swagger stick.

Eighth Air Force's General William Lacey congratulates Bill Smith on the 457th Bomb Group's 100th mission.

Bill Smith and his driver and "batman," Roy Bolton, at Glatton Airdrome, England. Smith picked Bolton out of the motor pool because of his deep Southern drawl.

Pilots flying over enemy territory carried small photos of themselves taken in civilian clothes. The pictures were for use on forged documents to be provided by the Underground if they were shot down.

Lieutenant Colonel William Franklin Smith, Jr., the pilot. A highly decorated combat veteran of the European war, he was about to be redeployed to the Pacific.

Staff Sergeant Christopher Domitrovich, the plane's crew chief. Four months before the crash, Domitrovich had escaped from the Germans after being shot down over Holland.

Aviation Machinist's Mate Second Class Albert Perna. The twenty-year-old sailor had hitchhiked a ride on the B-25 to console his parents after learning that his brother had been killed in the Pacific.

A	OPERATIONS OFFICE BEDFORD ARMY AIR BASE—BEDFORD FIELD			DATE JULY 28, 45
	ADDRESS BEDFORD, MASSACHUSETTS		CONFIDENTIAL	

CONFIDENTIAL

B	PILOT'S NAME SMITH, V.F.	RANK LT.COL	HOME STATION SFAAB	ORGANIZATION 457 BOMB GR	AIRCRAFT NUMBER 0577
	NAME, INITIALS, RANK, HOME STATION OF OTHER OCCUPANTS W.F. SMITH JR. LT COL. SFAAB			I CERTIFY THAT THE WEIGHT AND BALANCE OF B-25 TYPE AIRCRAFT, SER	
	T. L. Hall A CERTIFIED TRUE COPY			NO 0577 IS IDENTICAL WITH THAT SHOWN ON FORM "F" FILED AT SIOUX FALLS ON JULY 1ST	
	T.L.HALL CAPT. AIR CORES			/S/ W.F. SMITH, JR. PILOT'S SIGNATURE	

LIST ADDITIONAL PASSENGERS ON SEPARATE SHEET

C	WEATHER DATA		EXISTING LOCAL				ALTIMETER SETTINGS
	EXISTING ROUTE						LOCAL
	LG	0730E	D150 15	67/62	NE15/995		DESTINATION
	DESTINATION (LATEST) NK	0730E	7021/16	66/60	NE18/994		29.95 ETA
	ALTERNATE (LATEST) SW	0730E	A180/012	65/53	N/10/998		28.99 ETA
	FORECASTS (ESTIMATED FLIGHT TIME PLUS 2 HOURS) 7/10 STRATOCUMULUS						RESET ALTIMETER BEFORE APPROACH
	ROUTE AT 1000 FT LIFTING TO 1500 FT. MSL BEYOND PROVIDENCE						
	WITH TOPS 2000 FT VISIBILITY 6 MILES						
	DESTINATION 7/10 STRATOCUMULUS AT 1500 FT VISIBILITY 4 MILES NORTHWESTERLY WINDS 10 MPH						
	ALTERNATE 8/10 STRATOCUMULUS AT 1800 FT VISIBILITY 15 MILES.						
	WINDS ALOFT GIVE ALT DIR VEL AS PILOT REQUESTS 1000 FT		15 MPH.				
	AAF FORM 23A REQUIRED ☐	NOT REQUIRED ☐	FORECASTER /S/ MAJOR J.G. MURPHY			TIME 0820E	

D	FLIGHT PLAN (PILOT COMPLETES) 1000	RADIO CALLS 0577	TYPE OF AIRCRAFT B-25	PILOT (LAST NAME ONLY) SMITH	POINT OF DEPARTURE BEDFORD
	1 ALT DIRECT ☐ CFR ROUTE NEWARK ☐ IFR TO	2 ALT ☐ CFR ROUTE ☐ IFR TO	3 ALT ☐ CFR ROUTE ☐ IFR TO	4 ALT ☐ CFR ROUTE ☐ IFR TO	
	AIRPORT OF FIRST INTENDED LANDING LG	TRUE AIR SPEED 230	4495 TRANSMITTING FREQUENCIES RC RC		RECEIVER ONLY ☐ NO RADIO ☐
	PROPOSED TAKE OFF TIME 0845	EST. TIME ENROUTE 1 HR	ALTERNATE AIRPORT STEWART	HOURS OF FUEL 7 HOURS	INSTRUMENT RATING TYPE WHITE	FLIGHT PRIORITY 3-2
	REMARKS: SHOW FIXES WHICH WILL BE REPORTED WHILE ON INSTRUMENT FLIGHT.				013
				PILOT'S SIGNATURE /S/W.F. SMITH, JR	
	TOWER FREQUENCIES 395 RC	ALTERNATE RC	WEATHER CODE RECEIVED ☐ YES ☐ NO	MILEAGE 200	DEST. TO ALTERNATE	☐ COMMAND PILOT ☐ SENIOR PILOT ☐ CONTRACT PILOT ☐ CARGO AIRCRAFT ☐ PILOT

E	FLIGHT CLEARANCE AUTHORIZATION			
	SUBMITTED TO	TIME	BY	OPERATIONS IDENTIFICATION NO.
	TIME APPROVAL RECEIVED	CONTROL INSTRUCTIONS RECEIVED	CLEARING AUTHORITY C.L. WRIGHT, LT.COL.A.C. COMDG.	
	I HAVE OFFICIAL BUSINESS WITH THE 1338th BU AT LG. I AM FAMILIAR WITH THE DANGER AREAS IN MY LINE OF FLIGHT. /S/ W.F. SMITH, JR.	INSTRUCTIONS AND APPROVAL TRANSMITTED TO	ACTUAL TAKE-OFF TIME	/S/ WM.B. CURTIS, 1 LT. CLEARANCE OFFICER

F	PILOT COMPLETE FIRST LINE BELOW PRESENT TO LINE CREWMAN BEFORE TAKE-OFF	DEPARTURE RECORD			LINE CREWMAN WILL COMPLETE SECOND LINE AND DELIVER TO OPERATIONS OFFICE
	PILOT (LAST NAME ONLY)	AIRCRAFT TYPE	AIRCRAFT NUMBER	ACTUAL FUEL	GROSS WEIGHT
	DATE OF DEPARTURE	TIME	NUMBER PERSONS ON BOARD	LINE CREWMAN'S SIGNATURE	

CONFIDENTIAL

Aircraft Clearance Form
A copy of the original aircraft clearance form Smith signed at Bedford Field on the morning of July 28. This copy, prepared for the official Army inquest investigating the crash, is still classified "Confidential" by the Air Force 32 years after the incident.

B-25 "Billy Mitchell" bombers in varying stages of construction at North American's Kansas City assembly plant. *Old John Feather Merchant*, the B-25D model that crashed into the Empire State Building, was built here in 1943.

Two photos of the B-52 D-type model of the "Billy Mitchell" bomber flown by Lieutenant Colonel Smith on his flight into New York City. In the top photo the plane is painted in military-combat olive-drab. The bottom picture shows the bomber in its bare metal state as it came from the North American assembly plant in Kansas City.

The B-25's cockpit as shown in the pilot's flight manual issued by North American. Lieutenant Colonel Smith piloted the plane from the left seat. The upper set of levers in the control pedestal are for throttle and propeller pitch adjustment, the lower levers for fuel mixture and engine cooling.

Fig. 93 PILOT'S COMPARTMENT — GENERAL FORWARD VIEW

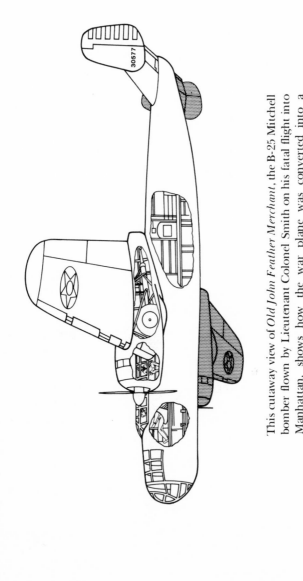

This cutaway view of *Old John Feather Merchant*, the B-25 Mitchell bomber flown by Lieutenant Colonel Smith on his fatal flight into Manhattan, shows how the war plane was converted into a passenger craft. Smith piloted from the lefthand seat, staff Sergeant Christopher Domitrovich, his crew chief, occupied the copilot's position. Albert Perna, the young sailor who had hitchhiked a last-minute ride to New York, was seated in a small jump seat just behind Domitrovich. Wooden benches on either side of the plane were installed, replacing the compartments formerly housing the radio operator and navigator.

The Fifth Avenue entrance to the building. Taking up the entire block between 3rd and 4th streets, the building's vast interior can accommodate 80,000 persons.

The Empire State Building lobby as seen from the Fifth Avenue entrance. More than 300,000 square feet of marble was used in the lobby and corridors, each section cut to exact dimentions and polished before being shipped from quarries throughout Europe.

The Empire State Building was constructed on a site rich in historical lore. Formerly occupied by the Waldorf-Astoria Hotel, the 2-acre plot fronting Fifth Avenue between 33rd and 34th streets was a farm during the Revolution. Freshwater streams and Sunfish Pond were used by early Dutch and English settlers who moved north from the tip of Manhattan Island during the late 1600's. Before their encroachment, more than a half-million Algonquin Indians roamed the woods and meadows, hunting a variety of game that included bears and wolves.

Construction workers, many of them Mohawk Indians noted for their fearless agility on high steelwork, set building records still unequalled today. At the peak of construction the building rose more than a story a day. Fourteen workers lost their lives erecting the Empire State.

The German dirigible *Graf Zepplin* sails close to the nearly completed building on the New York leg of its maiden voyage. The builders captured the public's attention by announcing that dirigibles would provide door-to-door service by mooring to the building's 200-foot mast. After two unsuccessful experimental attempts, the idea was given up as impractical.

The 102nd-floor observation tower. The RCA experimental television antenna on top replaced the dirigible mooring mast in 1934. By 1945, WNBT, the National Broadcasting Company's New York television station, was broadcasting regularly scheduled programs, to more than 12,000 television sets in the New York area.

Former New York Governor Al Smith dedicates the opening of the Empire State Building as its first president.

Army Air Service Major Fiorello La Guardia while on leave in Rome during World War I. His early passion for flying carried over to peacetime. As New York's mayor, he copiloted one of the first DC-3s delivered to United Airlines. La Guardia was an outspoken critic of the government's lax regulation of civilian and military flying.

La Guardia in 1942, as he took delivery of a police squad car to replace the gas-consuming limousine he had used prior to the war. The mayor sped to the crash site in this car, lights flashing, siren wailing. The box on top of the roof flashed "Mayor" when he was racing to an emergency.
ABC

Mayor Fiorello La Guardia's interest in flying began before World War I, when he took flying lessons from a friend. During the war he saw action as a major in the Air Service, piloting a bomber. As a result of his efforts to make New York City the hub of commercial air travel, the city renamed North Beach Air Terminal in his honor in 1939.

The control tower above the administration building, where La Guardia chief tower controller Victor Barden, was in radio contact with Colonel Smith as he circled the field before crossing into Manhattan.

Colonel Harris Rogner, Smith's commanding officer (top left), Lieutenant Colonel Carl Hinkle, Jr. (top right), and Lieutenant Colonel William Garland were about to leave for Newark Field to await Smith's arrival when the crash occurred.

Empire State Building elevator operator Betty Lou Oliver. She had just started down from the 79th floor when one of the plane's engines severed her car's cables. She plunged 1,000 feet to the sub-basement.

Paul Dearing, director of public relations for the Catholic War Relief Services.

Margaret Mullins, bookkeeper, Catholic War Relief Services.

Ellen Lowe, secretary, Catholic War Relief Services.

Patricia O'Connor, secretary, Catholic War Relief Services.

Donald Molony, seventeen-year-old Coast Guard hospital
apprentice. He was standing opposite the Empire State Building
watching the cloud formations swirl about the observatory when he
heard the crash.

Mary Scannell

Ed Cummings, field supervisor for the Catholic charity, wearing a volunteer uniform provided by the Army for an overseas inspection tour.

Receptionist Lucile Bath had planned to spend the day with her husband, but an early morning phone call asking her to fill in for an ill co-worker brought her to the Catholic War Relief Services office.

Anne Gerlach, secretary, Catholic War Relief Services.

Therese Fortier, secretary, Catholic War Relief Services.

A building project was about the last thing economists and sociologists would have counted on to divert the nation's attention. But as newspapers across the country reported that excavation for the Empire State Building had started, the people quickly identified with the enormous undertaking. That in a dark and unsettled time men would so audaciously challenge nature and science seemed symbolically right. What had started out as a New York City real-estate venture soon became an example of courage and hope for millions who had lost both.

The daily crowd of "sidewalk superintendents"—mostly out-of-work men and women—who watched the excavation through windows cut into the wooden fencing around the site were amazed when the chugging steam shovels quit clawing at the earth only 33 feet below the sidewalk. They had reached bedrock. Into this exposed hump of the earth's backbone engineers drove the steel-and-concrete footings that would support the building's 365,000 tons of steel, stone, and glass. That even bedrock could withstand such massive, concentrated weight staggered the imagination; yet the engineers' report showed that the weight of the earth and stone excavated was equal to three-quarters of the weight of the building itself. The Empire State would be to the earth little more than a flea on an elephant's back.

On St. Patrick's Day, March 17, 1930, Al Smith officially declared the start of the building's construction. While newsreel cameras rolled, the first steel piers were sunk in place. From that moment to the completion of the building, construction records were set that have yet to be equaled. The steel skeleton, weighing 57,000 tons, was erected in just twenty-three weeks. Using a network of railroad tracks running from the sub-basement to the street level, flatcars transported the huge steel girders to cranes operating on military-type schedules. Each girder was hoisted to one of the thirty-eight riveting gangs, who set it in place in a matter of minutes.

Working seven days a week, including holidays, more than three thousand men clambered over the rising building. Bricklayers and stonemasons followed close behind the steelworkers, who in turn were often working only a few hours ahead of the pipefitters and electricians. The building was growing a story a day. In one ten-day period it leapt fourteen floors.

The intersection of Fifth Avenue and 34th Street is one of the busiest in the world. Each day during construction of the building over 40,000 cars and some 200,000 pedestrians moved past the site. From start to finish, there was not a single traffic tie-up, or an injury to a passerby. Even during one peak eight-hour period, when five hundred separate loads of material and equipment arrived, the preset schedule functioned as smoothly on the job as it had on paper.

Each week newspapers reported another construction record had been broken. The steel skeleton was completed twelve days ahead of schedule; the flooring, four days ahead; the exterior metalwork, thirty-five days ahead; the exterior stonework, seventeen days ahead. The thousands of workers, many newly arrived immigrants, had become a fraternity, sharing the common goal of creating the world's tallest building. The phenomenal construction records they set transcended hours and wages. Each of them knew that this job was unique, that they were building for history.

It had taken seven million man-hours, and cost the lives of fourteen workers, but one year and forty-five days after steel first pierced bedrock the Empire State Building was completed. It soared 1,250 feet over Fifth Avenue. On May 1, 1931, Al Smith presided over the opening-day ceremonies.

In the Oval Office in Washington, D.C., President Herbert Hoover pressed a button. In the rose-colored marble lobby of 350 Fifth Avenue, the Empire State Building's lights flashed on. With Smith leading the way, New York Governor Franklin Delano Roosevelt, Mayor Jimmy Walker, and over three hundred invited guests toured the building. Newsreel cameras and radio stations WEAF and WOR recorded each step of the sightseeing party, as Smith rattled off a raft of numbing facts and figures about the building's construction.

As the guests were whisked up to the 86th floor for a buffet luncheon, one of the less visible but most attentive members of

the party was Fire Captain Patrick Walsh, who was there on a
final inspection tour of the building's fire-prevention system.
As part of his early training he had studied some of the city's
more spectacular fires, including New York's first skyscraper
blaze in the sixteen-story Home Life Insurance Building back
in the winter of 1898. The building, located on Broadway
across from City Hall Park, had burned to the ground because
firemen were unable to pump water above the 8th floor.

By the time Walsh had joined the Fire Department,
buildings were being constructed with fireproofing materials
and adequate water-pressure systems. The record for the
world's highest fire was held by the 1929 blaze on the 55th floor
of New York's Woolworth Building. It had been put out
quickly with a minimum of damage. Walsh, like most of the
city's firemen, had fought dozens of fires in Manhattan's tall
buildings.

But the Empire State, at least from the Fire Department's
point of view, presented not one, but two unique problems.
For the first time in the city's history the threat of an air crash
into a skyscraper became something more than an idle worry.
The government had set 1,000 feet as the minimum altitude
for planes crossing Manhattan. That seemed adequate—until
the Empire State's 1,250 feet was thrust into the sky. The Fire
Department's second concern was not only how to fight a
resulting fire, but of equal importance, how to evacuate the
building's occupants efficiently and safely. Walsh himself had
just heard Al Smith boast that on any given business day there
would be an average of 35,000 people in the building.

The builders had begun to tackle this problem from the
first set of interior plans. Working with the New York City Fire
Department and the Bureau of Fire Prevention, Lamb had
created the most modern and sophisticated fire-protection
system ever installed in an office structure.

Throughout the building there were four hundred fire-
hose connections, each of them tied into an eight-inch
standpipe system. From street level, the height of the building
required a pressure of 542 pounds per square inch to raise water
to the top of the mooring-mast tower. Less ingenious

designers, Walsh recognized, would have planned the building's firefighting capability around a series of pumps dependent on the city's water supply. But the Fire Department captain had just finished inspecting six huge steel water tanks housed on various levels of the building, from the 101st floor down to the sub-basement. Their combined capacity of more than 60,000 gallons gave the Empire State an instantly available water supply independent of the city's system. A series of back-up pumps were built into each tank, so that if the main system failed for any reason, the second would automatically take over.

Throughout the building was a sprinkler system with an automatic alarm connected directly to the Central Fire Station. Telephones placed in strategic locations were set aside exclusively for Fire Department use, with many of the lines attached to exterior outlets so that firemen inside the building could remain in constant touch with outside units. In addition to these built-in safeguards, the building maintained its own full-time fire brigade, composed of retired city firemen who made daily checks of the emergency equipment.

But Walsh knew the key to any building's safety lay not in after-the-fact protective devices, but rather in the basic integrity of its structure. On that basis the Empire State Building was virtually fireproof. With the exception of the dirigible tower and the 86th-floor observation deck, the entire building was sheathed with solid blocks of limestone backed by eight inches of brick. The floors were solid cement poured over a thick bed of steel and reinforced concrete. The elevator shafts were housed in steel and brick, and faced with fireproof white tiles. Each of the elevators' seven lifting cables had been mummified in a thick blanket of rubber and then wrapped with fire-resistant asbestos material.

The building of itself, empty of tenants and furnishings, would not burn. But Captain Walsh was aware that within a matter of days the building's first occupants would be moving in. The Empire State was already 28 percent rented; a faceless figure that nevertheless represented several thousand human beings occupying offices on all levels of the building.

Throughout the week he had personally walked each of the 1,860 steps encased in the smokeproof stairwell leading up to the 102nd-floor tower. These central stairs, and the public stairways, plus the sixty-seven high-speed elevators, were the vital links to any evacuation plan for the building's occupants. Walsh and his superiors not only were greatly impressed with the building's safety, but felt secure that in the event of a high fire, they could handle it efficiently, with a minimum of panic or loss of life.

Which of the guests at that opening-day ceremony could foresee that Patrick Walsh would become New York City's fire commissioner? Or that his sanguine judgment made that sparkling clear afternoon in 1931 would, on a foggy Saturday morning fourteen years in the future, be put to the severest test?

*   *   *

From 800 feet the Long Island Sound steamer *Mayflower*, bound for Bridgeport, looked like a child's toy as it churned under the B-25's left wing.

Smith was holding a light left rudder, banking the plane in a shallow turn away from the Connecticut shore. Within the past few minutes, as if a gauzy theater curtain had been suddenly drawn, the Long Island shoreline had dissolved behind a rising ground fog. Above the bomber an unbroken layer of dark stratocumulus clouds stretched from Stamford deep into southern Westchester.

Leveling out, Smith held his course to 130 degrees. The flight plan plotted on his sectional map called for a diagonal run across the sound to the jutting promontory of Kings Point. From there, he would head due south until he made a westerly swing across Queens to La Guardia Field.

He had smiled when he had told Lieutenant Curtis that he thought it was a lousy flight plan; all the jogging Boston Air Traffic Control insisted on not only made his navigation more difficult, but took him miles out of his way. But the air controller had been adamant; Smith's Contact flight, once he reached the New York area, had to steer clear of all Instrument traffic taking off or coming into the congested air space. Planes from the four major airfields located in the metropolitan area—La Guardia, Mitchell Field, Floyd Bennett Field, and Newark—made for a crowded sky.

Ahead, stabbing out through the fog into the sound, were two jagged reaches of land. The closest, shaped like a crooked finger, was Sands Point; the second, separated by Manhasset Bay, was Kings Point. Smith scanned the leaden overcast surrounding the bomber. He was now approaching the area the air controller had cautioned him about. Somewhere above him, or to his right or left, unseen aircraft were being guided by radio. Until he reached La Guardia, he was on his own.

CHAPTER X

The City

A HEAD, OFF THE PORT BEAM, THE
Statue of Liberty loomed like an apparition out of the dense
mist shrouding the harbor. Now, more than an hour after his
troop transport, *Winnipeg*, had cleared the Ambrose
Lightship stationed off the Narrows, Major Jean Mayer felt his
first real tinge of excitement. As the two thousand combat-
weary troops crowding the deck began to cheer wildly, the
young officer wearing the uniform of the Free French Forces
pressed his way to the starboard rail.

Ignoring the chill of the open harbor and the light rain
that again had begun to fall, Mayer offered a silent prayer of
thanks for being allowed to keep a promise he had made three
years ago. In 1942, recently graduated from the University of
Paris and on a military mission to the United States, the
Frenchman had met and married an American girl. Twenty-
four hours after the ceremony he was on his way back to De
Gaulle's forces in Tunisia—leaving behind a promise to his
bride that not only would he return safe and sound, but on that
day he would pick her out of the dockside crowd and blow her a
kiss.

Mayer glanced impatiently at his watch. As an artillery
commander awarded the highest decorations, he had fought
for five grueling years to free his homeland. A dozen times,

from Egypt, through the Normandy invasion, to the border of Germany, he had come scathingly close to certain death. Through it all, Mayer had not been nearly so nervous as he was at this moment. The ship seemed to be almost standing still in the channel, barely making steerageway. He peered through the swirling fog, scanning the shoreline for a familiar landmark. In the distance, all but obscured by banks of fog and clouds, he caught a fleeting glimpse of the Empire State Building. Mayer smiled. The ship's berth, and his wife, were waiting only a few blocks uptown from the world's tallest building.

*   *   *

Waiting for the light to change at Fifth Avenue and 35th Street, Rabbi Avrum Blotner felt naked; stripped of the tieless, starched white shirt whose buttoned collar was cutting into his neck; of the brown suit his wife had so carefully pressed early yesterday for the Friday-night service; of the black raincoat his daughter had given him for a birthday present last month; and finally, of the yarmulke hidden beneath his brown felt hat. he felt naked because he felt guilty. He was certain that everyone on the street was aware of his intended crime—that they had already judged and sentenced him. The light changed. Rabbi Blotner, eyes downcast, joined the stream of pedestrians with a hunched, stiff-jointed gait that made him seem older than his fifty-eight years.

That he should be doing business on *Shabbas*! No matter how noble or selfless the reason, or how necessary, even vital, it was to his congregation's well-being, Blotner knew that there was no possible excuse for this almost blatant affront to his faith. For an Orthodox Jew even to think about money on the Sabbath, much less *carry* it, was the sin of sins. And yet here he was, about to enter a temple of commerce for the express purpose of buying heating fuel from a black marketeer. The two crimes!—compound felonies against God and country.

Since yesterday afternoon, when his brother-in-law had told him that he had found a "source" willing to sell the tightly rationed oil for cash under the table, the rabbi had been locked in a Talmudic battle. On the one hand he was clearly breaking God's Law; of that he had not an instant's doubt. But on the other hand, as his elderly congregation's leader, wasn't it his duty to protect their health as fervently as their souls? Did he not have an inescapable obligation to prevent them, this rapidly approaching winter, from freezing to death in the ancient, draft-ridden synagogue? He had spent a sleepless night, each hand arguing with the ferocity and cunning of a *dybbuk*. In the end Blotner's pragmatism won out; for God to lose his devoted followers to pneumonia seemed an impractical solution.

Lost in thought, the rabbi almost walked past the Empire State Building's revolving door. He stopped and peered through the glass. Somewhere in the cavernous lobby was a cigar stand where the *momser* was waiting to collect his blood sacrifice. Involuntarily, Blotner patted the wallet nesting over his heart. Even through the layers of clothing he could feel the three $20 dollar bills radiating vengeful heat. Aware that in another moment his hesitation would force him to flee, the rabbi planted his hand resolutely against the door and pushed.

*   *   *

Standing in the doorway of a millinery store on Fifth Avenue directly opposite the building, Donald Molony was surprised to see the gray clouds scudding past the upper floors of the Empire State suddenly change direction.

For the past few minutes the seventeen-year-old Coast Guardsman had been transfixed by the dazzling aerial display. Through breaks in the lower layer of stagnant haze, Molony had watched as a fast-moving bank of oddly-shaped clouds encountered the tower and pressed against its limestone bulk, and then in a melting gesture, seemed to drip down the sides of the structure. The clouds had been moving toward the west, but now, quite suddenly, the slim, red-headed youngster watched them halt momentarily, then sideslip and cling to the north face of the building.

Molony, a hospital apprentice second class, had arrived in the city an hour ago from his training base at Groton,

Connecticut. Tucked in the waistband of his blue bellbottoms was his wallet, holding a forty-eight-hour pass and $55 painstakingly saved for this weekend vacation.

Although he had been in the city several times before, this was the Detroit youngster's first trip alone; each previous visit had been made in the company of fellow trainees, most of whom had women, not sightseeing, on their minds. This time Molony had promised himself a typical tourist's feast of New York. First on his agenda was the Empire State Building.

But now, at 9:40, it seemed certain that Molony would be forced to revise his plans. Even with the shift in wind direction, the observation deck was still lost in a heavy cloud cover. Had this been just another weekend leave, the young Coast Guardsman would have shrugged off the weather as so much bad luck and moved on. But his eight-month medical-training course was almost over, and it was only a matter of weeks before Molony was due to be transferred to a permanent shipboard assignment. This weekend would most likely be the last chance he would have to tour the city for a long time to come.

The weather had fouled up his plans to see the town not only from the top of the Empire State, but also from the water. After the observation deck, Molony had planned to take a sightseeing boat ride around Manhattan. But that too had to be ruled out. On his walk down Fifth Avenue he had seen that both the East and the Hudson Rivers were blanketed by a hovering fog. Reluctantly opening the copy of the *Daily Mirror* he had picked up in Grand Central Station, Molony turned to the entertainment section. Maybe he would catch and early movie, and later have lunch at one of the fancy hotels.

Molony scanned the advertisements, rejecting out of hand films that were not accompanied by a stage show. At the Capitol, Frank Sinatra, Kathryn Grayson, and Gene Kelly were starring in *Anchors Aweigh*. The stage show featured Paul Whiteman and his orchestra, with Lionel Hampton as an added attraction. *Incendiary Blonde*, with Betty Hutton, was playing at the Paramount, and on stage was Phil Spitalny and his All-Girl Orchestra. The Radio City Music Hall was showing *A Bell for Adano*, with Gene Tierney, John Hodiak, and William Bendix. That was the one, Molony decided; anything with William Bendix in it had to be great. He checked his watch. The film started at 10:24; the stage show, featured the Rockettes, let out at 12:45. The timing was perfect. After a leisurely lunch he would play it by ear, keeping the afternoon open just in case the weather made a miraculous recovery.

He spotted an uptown bus stopped for a light. Signaling the driver with his paper, Molony stepped into the light drizzle, glancing up at the building with lingering curiosity as he crossed to the bus stop. Once again the cloud formations had shifted, the wind now sweeping them away from the uptown side of the building like powder snow whipping off a mountainside. The young seaman frowned, torn by this latest development in the weather 1,000 feet overhead. The area where he guessed the observation deck to be seemed virtually free of clouds. Behind him he heard the bus pull into the stop and the doors hiss open. Molony hesitated, then gave the driver an apologetic smile and waved him on. He would gamble a few minutes more to see if the weather held long enough for him to dash up to the observation deck.

Settling back into the doorway, Molony's attention was captured by a pair of flags fluttering languidly over a brownstone building on the northwest corner of 33rd Street. Below the American flag was an Army Navy "E" pennant. The blue-and-gold emblem piqued his curiosity. It seemed to him an ordinary, old-fashioned office building, with no visible sign or window lettering to name the company the government had honored for its war effort. To Molony, the building, dwarfed into obscurity by its massive neighbor, suddenly attained an air of mystery. Who worked behind those oversized windows set beneath the ornately carved roof cornice? Why, in a block of soaring, modern building, did this—he counted the floors— this twelve-story structure still exist?

As the young Coast Guardsman's eye roamed the building he became aware of an elderly woman walking along the edge of the roof. She was wearing what looked to him like a pink housecoat, and in each hand she carried something the distance prevented him from identifying.

*   *   *

Mrs. Oswald Hering set the pots of grape ivy down on the table that had once served as her husband's drafting board. With the exception of the gnarled fig tree, which was too heavy for her to move, all of the more than two dozen plants in her penthouse apartment were now being nourished by the fine drizzle filtering down on the rooftop.

This ritual airing, staunchly observed except during the frigid winter months, was an important part of the seventy-one-year-old widow's weekly schedule. Since her architect husband's recent passing, she had taken over the Saturday-morning chore; but for the thirty-six years they had lived together on top of the Waldorf Building, it had been his job to carry the plants out, water and prune them, while she prepared breakfast in the small kitchen they had decorated in Norman farmhouse style. His gardening done, they would sit down to breakfast under the living-room skylight, accompanied by a recorded concert of Brahms or Mozart. In this hour or two, they would exchange their past week, catching up on each other's lives. Once in a while, more in winter when a wood fire was blazing, they would invite their neighbors in the three other penthouse apartments to join them.

But being alone had radically altered Mrs. Hering's Saturday mornings. Now, instead of enjoying a leisurely breakfast, she hastily clipped off a few of the more visible dead leaves while sipping her second cup of coffee. She had discovered that time was a widow's enemy, and so she contrived to fill her waking hours with a schedule of friends and events that even a woman half her age would be hard pressed to maintain. This morning, after first shopping for a nephew's birthday present around the corner in Macy's, she was meeting a friend for lunch and a matinee performance of *Life with Father*.

Stepping into the kitchen, she spotted the Special Delivery parcel that had come late last night. As routinely happened, it had been delivered to the wrong Hering. Long ago, after the famous sculptor Henry Hering had moved into the penthouse next to hers, she had given up explaining to the postmen that the two Herings were not one and the same, but separate and unrelated—joined only by the coincidence of their last names.

The sculptor had told her yesterday that he was driving up to Westchester to play golf and would be back on Sunday. He had joked about playing hookey from the large commission he was working on, and admitted to feeling somewhat guilty about not working over the weekend. But Mrs. Hering had laughingly begged him to go; one more day and night of hearing his chisel whacking into stone, and she'd go out of her mind.

As if on cue, the yelps of drill presses and lathes tearing metal carried up from the floors below and cut into her thoughts. She grimaced and shook her head. On the rare morning when she wasn't awakened by Hering's mallet tapping its way through her bedroom wall, Joseph Bing and his orchestra and chorus of tool and die makers were certain to correct the oversight.

At times like this, when the factory din of Photo Utilities, Inc., invaded her rooftop aerie, Mrs. Hering did not feel particularly patriotic. It was a selfish failing, she admitted, and not even staring long and hard at Mr. Bing's "E" pennant—he had graciously invited her to the raising ceremony a year ago— did much to dissipate her annoyance at living over a war-production plant. She had often thought of talking to her old friend Vincent Astor, the building's owner, about the racket, but always decided against it; besides having become friendly with Mr. and Mrs. Bing, who had moved into the penthouse directly across from hers, the last thing in life she wanted to be thought of was a crotchety old woman. If she and her husband had survived the construction of the Empire State Building, dynamite blasts and all, she would somehow manage to weather this latest bother.

She closed the kitchen door, then crossed into the living room, turned on the radio, located the morning concert, and raised the volume just enough to overcome the rumbles of industry filtering through the floorboards.

*   *   *

Down in his 12th-floor office, Joseph Bing's knuckles were drained white from pressing the phone against his ear. He swiveled his desk chair to face the window, and with a look approaching terminal frustration, he stared up at the Empire State Building. Lost in the haze was the 53rd floor. The president of Photo Utilities knew that somewhere on that floor, seated at a desk among the sea of desks in the Office of Price Administration, was a clerk who was either certifiably insane or—the thought crossed his mind—an enemy agent.

For the last half-hour, Bing had attempted to wrest a single item of information out of the woman: the price he would be permitted to charge the Navy for a special run of lenses used for aircraft photo reconnaissance. It was a rush order. For the past two weeks more than half of his seventy-five craftsmen had been working overtime to meet the deadline. Now, with thousands of dollars tied up in material and overtime costs, Bing found himself locked in a bureaucratic labyrinth; trapped between a seven-inch-thick manual of rules and regulations created by the OPA, and a snafu caused by a typographical error in the Navy contract.

For three days, calmly at first, then with mounting exasperation, he had contacted one government agency after another, each bucking him along to another, each assuring him that the next bureau or department had the authority to solve his dilemma.

Helplessly, like a moth irreversibly attracted by dew shimmering on a spider's web, Bing was sucked deeper into the regulatory boneyard. Somehow—he had long since lost the route taken—he had been told to contact this division of the OPA.

As the woman droned on, reeling off page-long clauses and subclauses pertaining to rationed commodities, Bing's eyes rolled to his white Civil Defense helmet hanging on the wall next to the fire extinguisher. He was the Waldorf Building's chief warden. Only yesterday morning he had held a practice air-raid drill for his employees. It had gone off like clockwork, thanks to Bing's efficiency; the very same efficiency that had won the firm the Army/Navy "E." Bing prided himself on his attention to detail, so vital in his type of work, where micrometer exactness, total precision with no tolerance for error, was the rule.

And yet, for three solid days he had done nothing but attempt to unravel what he now saw was a hopeless mess. He, Joseph Bing, the very same man who with an unaided eye could measure a handmade tool to within a thousandth of an inch, was being driven mad by an error that *he* had overlooked.

The woman was now suggesting that perhaps her department wasn't the one to deal with the problem after all. In the background Bing heard the all too familiar rustle of pages being thumbed. He hung up the phone as the clerk was in the midst of asking if he had contacted . . .

*   *   *

John Monte chose to ignore the clacking signal. Two could play the same game, the sixty-nine-year-old elevator operator thought as he casually ambled away from his car. Again he heard the starter's wooden castanets echo impatiently across the Empire State's marble lobby. He glanced over his shoulder and gave white-haired Chauncey Humphrey an arch look.

"Is that meant for me, Mr. Humphrey?" Monte asked innocently.

"You know very well it is," the starter answered sternly. "Go up to the eightieth and relieve Gluck."

"My break's coming up," Monte said with a stubborn glare. "Why don't you send one of the girls?"

Carla Haynes stood in the open door of car Number 5 and grinned as the cadaverously thin starter crossed to Monte with quick, angry steps.

The eighteen-year-old operator had been on the job for only three days, but even in that short time she had come to look forward to the running battle between the elderly men. Apparently, the other operators informed her, the feud had been going on for years; if there once had been a solid basis for their constant bickering, it had long since been forgotten by both men. Now, every morning, they circled like fighting cocks, each looking for the merest excuse to open combat.

The starter jabbed his finger into Monte's shoulder.

"Since when did they promote you to starter? Until you get this"—he pointed to the starter's emblem sewn on his sleeve—"and this" he whipped the castanets in front of Monte's face and snapped them victoriously—"I'll tell you when to go up, down—or out!"

Humphrey planted his hands on his hips and rocked on his heels. Monte's face went through the spectrum of anger, then, as Carla had come to expect, somehow managed to settle into a surprisingly beatific expression. No matter that Monte turned and, without a word, headed into his car; once again the contest appeared to end in a draw, each man satisfied that he alone had triumphed.

*   *   *

Looking like a postage stamp, Central Park faded in and out of the clouds swimming past the north windows of the 102nd-floor observation tower.

For the last half-hour, the park had been the only landmark that Lieutenant Allen Aimen and his wife, Betty, had been able to pick out through the heavy overcast. They were the only sightseers in the tower, and had it not been for observation-deck guide Pat Hipwell's seemingly endless font of anecdotes about the building, the young couple would have left long ago. An audience, especially a captive one, was pure bliss to Hipwell. In his fourteen years as a guide he had developed several "acts," as he called his lectures. This morning, because of the weather, the Aimens were being treated to his "killing time" routine—assorted facts "not even Ripley would believe."

Did they know, he asked—relishing the fact that he was about to astonish them—that when the wind currents were just right, you could suspend a paper drinking cup filled with water in midair? The gravity-defying parlor trick worked best in winter, when warm and cold air were racing up and down the sides of the building at equal velocity.

The dirigible mooring mast? Used only twice, Hipwell said with a memoried grin, back in 1931. The wacky, but intriguing, notion was shelved when one of the blimps, after battling gusty winds for more than an hour, managed to wrap its line to the mast—and then in trimming the airship, the captain, of necessity, or from a perverse sense of humor, released a thousand gallons of water ballast over Fifth Avenue. Spectators and pedestrians were drenched for blocks around by the surprise downpour.

No, the Aimens learned, the building didn't sway in high winds as so many had mistakenly come to think, it *bent*; the steel frame was designed with enough elasticity to allow the huge structure to yield a half-inch off center in all directions. Hipwell had been in the tower when the highest recorded gust—it had literally blown out the instruments mounted on the dome—had smacked against the building at 125 miles per hour.

And lightning. The building was the tallest lightning rod in the world, and the safest place in the city to be during an electrical storm. Because the structure was sunk in bedrock, lightning bolts hitting the building were harmlessly discharged into the ground. Cameras mounted on the roofs of nearby tall buildings photographed the Empire State being struck nineteen times during one electrical storm without the slightest harm to people or building.

And talk about winds. One day, Hipwell recounted, he nearly swore off drinking after he saw a gigantic "python" writhing on a cloud not 100 feet from the tower. Fortunately for his sanity if not his liver, another guide standing next to him was also gaping at the lifelike mirage, which they later discovered was caused by high winds splitting around the building. Another adventure with the wind took place as Hipwell was guiding a tour along the 86th-floor observation deck. A strong gust blew his hat off, spiraled it up into the clouds and out of sight. It was returned to him a week later, having been found by a small boy playing near the George Washington Bridge—more than five miles away.

Tactfully as possible, while Hipwell launched into one of his favorite anecdotes—when members of the 1932 Polish Olympic ski team ran up the stairs from the lobby to the 102nd floor as a publicity stunt—Betty Aimen glanced out the north

windows. Where moments before a mass of solid gray vapor
had hugged the tower, she now saw a strikingly clear vista of
open sky. The guide followed her gaze and broke into a broad
smile.

"Hey, looks like you're in luck. Give it another ten or
fifteen minutes," Hipwell judged with a mariner's squint,
"and we should be in the clear."

The twenty-three-year-old pilot and his wife moved to the
windows as Hipwell began pointing out some of the famous
skyscrapers squatting below the tower, their spires and tarred
rooftops poking giraffelike through a corrugated field of
clouds.

*   *   *

For the forty-odd people down in the 86th-floor
observation lounge, the piped-in medley of Strauss waltzes
was small consolation for the zero viewing conditions. Only
minutes ago a sudden downdraft had locked the observation
deck inside a dismal confusion of clouds and fog.

Leaning against the rain-spattered glass doors leading
to the outside deck, tower manager Frank Powell and guard
Louis Petly were doing their best to keep a half-dozen small
children amused with stories and word games. With the
exception of the souvenir-stand owner and the snack-bar
counterman, who were happily ringing up sales, gloom
pervaded the brightly decorated lounge. For the most part the
disappointed tourists were seated next to the windows,
morosely sipping coffee as they stared into the overcast.

It was not by casual whim that Powell had ordered Sam
Watkinson to lock the double doors to the outside deck before
leaving on his break. In his fourteen years of working the
observation deck, Powell had gained an astute firsthand
knowledge of human behavior. More than a million people a
year visited the viewing stations. So far, twelve of them had
used the 86th-floor deck as a diving platform; Powell had
personally witnessed four of the suicides. In each case the man
or woman had chosen to end life on just such a day as this, as if
nature in its primal brooding mirrored their anguish. It

became instinct for the observation-deck personnel to take precautionary note of every person entering the tower; extra attention was paid on holidays, especially Christmas and New Year's Day, traditional times for leapers, or when the weather was bad.

Aside from screening sightseers for obvious telltales— beagle-eyed depression or skittish exhilaration—the tower staff made a point of not overlooking those who appeared perfectly normal: mothers and fathers with children in tow, or, a more recent target for scrutiny, servicemen. Earlier this morning, Powell and Petly had discussed an item in the papers about a San Francisco war vet who had taken his six-year-old daughter out for a drive, had stopped in the middle of the Golden Gate Bridge, and with the child's hand grasped in his had plunged into the bay.

Perhaps it was the news story, all the more stark because it was void of details, that caused Petly to focus attention on the graying, pale-faced Infantry major across the lounge.

For the past fifteen minutes the guard had been keeping an eye on the officer as he moved about the lounge, noting his stoically barren expression as he tested each step first with his cane before putting weight on the wounded leg. Since entering the lounge the soldier had made one complete circuit, absently glancing out the windows in all directions. Now, reversing his steps, he had begun another circumnavigation.

He seemed to Petly restless, glancing too often at his watch. An appointment to keep? Boredom—or was it anxiety? And why did he keep glancing from the windows toward the elevator? Petly asked himself. The man didn't look healthy; his skin had a rheumy pallor, and his body was too rigid, the movements too harp-wire taut, for Petly's liking.

The guard decided to wait until the officer came closer before he struck up a conversation.

Shifting the cane to his other hand, Major Bert Woodstock checked his watch. Almost 9:45. His appointment back at the First Army hospital on Governor's Island wasn't until two. Four hours . . . might as well be four years, he thought, as the pain seared through his leg. He'd been a damn fool to come into the city without his codeine; four pills scavenged over weeks from his daily dosage, saved for just such an emergency as this, and now lying useless in his footlocker on the island.

A half-hour ago, as Woodstock was entering the Empire State, he had lost his footing on the rain-slicked marble and had fallen heavily on his shattered left leg. The wires and stainless-steel pin that held his kneecap together felt as if they had exploded—the pain not a millimeter less excruciating than when the mortar shrapnel had done the original damage. For some maddening reason born of the embarrassing moment, Woodstock had assured the corporal, assigned by the hospital as his aide, that he was perfectly all right; the youngster could take off and see his girl friend for an hour while he went up to the observation deck. By the time he reached the 86th floor the major had known he was in trouble. His knee had swelled considerably, and the waves of pain, surprisingly worse when he sat or kept the leg immobile, were nauseating him.

He could kick himself (how in hell's name, he thought— with one leg?) for not thinking to ask the corporal where he could be reached. Now he was stuck here, 1,000 feet in the air, until the kid came to collect him. Even the weather was conspiring against him—the grayness, the bored faces of the people around him, and those damn waltzes they kept playing.

He caught himself before his depression could edge deeper. He was on guard these days, constantly monitoring his moods now that he understood the reason for his irritability since returning from Italy. Post-combat depression, the doctor explained, prevalent in combat commanders who were no longer called on to make life-and-death decisions. The diagnosis made sense to Woodstock; his authority as well as his responsibility to anyone but himself had been stripped away the moment they had loaded him on the hospital ship. Back in the States he was just another of the walking wounded, and the battle stars studding his chest served as a reminder more of loss than of deed—of a present emptiness that dwelling on the past made even more hollow. He reached into his pocket and took out a pack of cigarettes, shook one loose, and began searching for a match.

Flicking the lighter open, Louis Petly gave the major a friendly smile as he held the flame up to his cigarette.

*   *   *

During business hours, Monday to Friday, an average of 15,000 tenants and employees and 35,000 visitors occupied the Empire State Building.

But this Saturday morning, shortly before 10:00 a.m., a generous outside guess could place no more than 2,000 persons working or visiting. The combination of a half workday and the rain had drastically cut down the building's population.

On the 85th floor, directly below the observation deck, the National Broadcasting Company's television transmitting studios were dark. The four technicians who would be broadcasting the afternoon baseball game between the Brooklyn Dodgers and the Boston Braves were scheduled to arrive at 10:30 to warm up the transmitter.

As he dragged two 10-gallon paint cans across the canvas tarp, laborer William Sharp avoided looking out of the 78th-floor window.

Heights made him break out in a sick sweat. For years he had avoided any work that might conceivably take him above ground level, but a long stretch of unemployment because of illness had forced him to take the first available job. For the past two weeks he had started off each morning with a dizzying elevator ride up to the unoccupied 78th floor, which was being redecorated for a new tenant.

Having placed the cans of paint next to a drum of turpentine left by the painting contractor, Sharp began rolling up the canvas. This morning he and another man were to start cleaning and polishing the newly laid linoleum. Nearing the windows on his hands and knees, Sharp was suddenly seized with an overpowering urge to take a peek. His palms clam-cold, the laborer eased his head above the windowsill and stared straight out. He found himself peering into a swirling mass of fog. Screwing up his courage, he edged his body higher, and with fingers clamping the sill in a death grip, he

looked down. Across 34th Street he could make out dots of
people standing under McCreery's awning. The department
store's large display windows were brightly lighted, making
the dark wet pavement glisten invitingly. Sharp closed his eyes
quickly and backed away from the window.

Christ! he muttered. How in God's name could anyone
volunteer to work this high up! Rubbing his sweating palms
on the front of his overalls, Sharp opened the stairwell door
and started down to the 73rd floor to pick up his helper.

Of the twenty men and women at work in the Catholic
War Relief Services office on the 79th floor, none was more
relaxed than Ed Cummings.

Feet up on his desk, the thirty-four-year-old Brooklynite
was deeply engrossed in the *Herald Tribune* crossword puzzle.

Normally, Cummings would have finished the puzzle
before his subway ride ended, but this morning he had used the
time to clean up some paperwork needed by Father
Swanstrom for their meeting at the British Consulate. He and
Jack McCloskey, the balding, heavy-set man seated at the next
desk, were accompanying Swanstrom to Europe on Tuesday.
Both men were in charge of setting up vocational and recreational programs in prisoner-of-war camps throughout the
country. Their mission to Europe was to set up similar
programs in camps scattered throughout France, Germany,
and Italy.

For the past half-hour, Cummings—whose face still held
a deep, healthy tan from a recent tour of POW camps in Texas
and Colorado—had been fending off envious digs from his
fellow workers.

"Is the chairman of the board comfortable?" asked Kay
O'Connor with an acid-sweet smile as she dropped a stack of
mail on his desk.

"I'd check the weather over there, Ed," Joe Fountain
called out from his office across the aisle. "Sure would be a
shame to let that tan fade."

Outwardly Cummings fielded the jibes with equal good
humor, but he still had difficulty assuaging his guilt. He felt
less for not having spent the war years fighting rather than

dealing with the results. A former New York State parole officer, he had tried to enlist, but his age and poor eyesight kept him in the civilian ranks. Wanting to be of some effective use to the war effort, Cummings had quit his Civil Service position two years ago and joined the War Relief Services.

Given the circumstances, it had turned out to be a comfortable and gratifying choice. Like Cummings, the staff were all staunch, practicing Catholics of lower-middle-class backgrounds; their attitudes about life in general and the war specifically were in total concert with his. Unlike most business organizations, the charity's payroll carried no soapbox malcontents or stockroom Lotharios. Of the nineteen men and women sharing the office this morning with Cummings, none offered surprises: there were no hidden pasts to be kept secret from all but confessors, no skeletons tensed to spring out of family closets, no eyebrow-raising excesses of flesh or spirit to justify whispers over the water cooler. They were a predictable lot, decent people content to pluck or receive small pleasures from lives orbiting about family, service, and duty.

If any came close to the colorful stereotype of a Manhattan officeworker, it was Anne Gerlach.

Balancing her plump frame against the desk with one hand, the forty-four-year-old secretary exchanged her new white high heels for the brown loafers she kept in her bottom drawer. Pausing only long enough to voice a loud sigh of relief as her swollen feet spread in freedom, Anne returned her attention to the two young women snared only moments before.

"You above all, Maureen, should be putting *something*— fifty cents or a dollar—away from every paycheck. Why haven't you been doing it?"

Like a child trapped by a teacher's unexpected question, Maureen Maguire cast her blue eyes on the floor and shrugged. The twenty-two-year-old bookkeeper had just returned from her honeymoon. Until Anne's chiding lecture, she had spent the early part of the morning reveling in her married status, exchanging in giggling whispers all but the most intimate details of the past week with several of the younger women. But now, under fire from "Mother Hen" Gerlach, as the staff dubbed her, Maureen felt not only shamefully immature, but guilty for being a millstone about her Merchant Marine husband's neck.

"Mark my words, if you get pregnant," Anne said with a stern, doomsday look, "you'll have to stop working—and there goes your nest egg!"

Knowing she was to be the next target of opportunity, Patricia O'Connor quickly dissolved the knowing grin she had been sharing across the aisle with Mary Louise Taylor and presented Anne with a serious, alert expression

"Did you show your father that insurance brochure, Pat?"

"He says I'm already covered under his policy."

Fixing the slender, brown-haired girl with a doubting look, Anne shook her head in slow, theatrically sweeping arcs.

"Tell him to take another look. Now that you've turned twenty-one, I'll bet you're not covered for accident or sickness. Most family policies only cover minors. If anything happened to you, God forbid, you could end up costing your folks a fortune in hospital bills."

Anne was aware of the girls' stifled giggles as she moved off toward the bank of file cabinets lining the far wall.

She knew that most of the staff, especially the younger ones, thought her a busybody; they more tolerated than respected her for the concern she showed. And yet, in her own defense, she was certain that even if most of her questions were misconstrued as prying, in the long run the staff benefited from her advice and generosity. Every office needed a confidant, a crying towel, and who could serve better in that capacity than she, she rationalized; unmarried, living with her sister and brother-in-law and their children, she was in the perfect, objective position to view and comment on their pleasures and pains. They could trust her, she knew, because she asked for nothing in return. A little thank you now and then was sufficient payment for making them family.

Halting his dictation to relight his pipe, John Judge stole a glance at the delicately pretty woman seated across his desk.

Even through the haze of smoke he could tell Jeanne Sozzi had once again spent a better part of the early morning crying.

Since a week ago, when he had pressed Paul Dearing, the forty-year-old secretary's boss, for an explanation for her depression, Judge had felt burdened with the knowledge. Swearing him to secrecy, Dearing had told him that a man Jeanne was about to become engaged to had suddenly died. The life had gone out of her. Once open and vivacious, she now moved about like an automaton, her dark Italian eyes vacant and unsmiling. She had confessed to Dearing that she could no longer attend Mass in her neighborhood church because she became hysterical, embarrassing not only herself, but the other communicants.

Through a tear in the cloud cover hanging outside his window, Judge focused on the Chrysler Building's lancelike spire. He was thinking of the years he'd spent in the Church as a Christian Brother working among the poor. That leveling experience, he felt, should have presented him with an attitude, if not the exact words, with which to comfort Jeanne. But for the past few days he had found himself brooding as much over his surprising inability as the woman's tragic situation.

Until joining the War Relief Services as director of the seamen's project, providing religious and recreational articles for American and British merchantmen, he had led a somewhat cloistered, introspective life. He had married a woman much like himself, and rather late in life fathered two children. But within the past year, since spending his days in close association with the charity's staff, John Judge had become more aware of life's complexities. Basically still a hard-working loner, he was nevertheless exposed to the office gossip. Surface judgments, before sanguinely taken at face value, had, with rumor or fact, altered and deepened his view of human beings and their relationships.

Canting his head toward the west side of the office, Judge caught a glimpse of Margaret Mullins tearing a ribbon of paper out of her adding machine.

Until just the other day he had hardly given the matronly-looking bookkeeper a passing thought. In her mid-thirties, although appearing older because of her choice of clothes and hairdo, Margaret had always seemed to him self-sufficient, quietly pleased with herself. How the rumor got started, based on what facts or suppositions, he had no idea; but now Judge found himself wondering at odd moments in the day what kind of man her Marine husband was. Why—if there was any truth to the rumor—did he write to her from overseas asking for a divorce? If true, how heartbreakingly sad for her to learn of his discontent by opening an eagerly awaited envelope. If false, how did such a malicious lie take flight? Why would someone, especially someone in *this* office, choose to create pain for a fellow human?

Placing his pipe in the silver ashtray his wife had just given him for his fortieth birthday, Judge glanced at his watch. Another ten minutes should wrap up the report. If he hurried, he could catch the 10:25 out of Penn Station and be home in time to play with the kids before their nap.

*   *   *

Behind the central reception area in the south section of the office, Anna Regan was quietly having a fit.

Moments ago, as the short, gray-haired personnel manager was reaching across her desk for a file folder, she had upended the inkwell. Jabbing a fistful of tissues at the puddles of black fluid spreading across her records, she dared a quick look through the glass cubicle to the secretaries in the pool area. With relief she saw that they were unaware of her clumsiness. Not five minutes before she had chewed out her secretary, Theresa Scarpelli, for keeping her files like a broom closet. To make present matters potentially more embarrassing, she had offered her own surgically neat office as an example of the professional standard she insisted her girls maintain. Sloppy desks and files, she had cautioned Theresa, make for sloppy minds and work habits.

Tucking the Rorschach-blotted files safely in her desk drawer, Anna Regan slipped unobtrusively out of the office to wash the ink stains from her hands.

Charlotte Deegan said, "Thank God it's Friday!" as she located the file folder that had been eluding her search.

"It's Saturday," said Ellen Lowe, without turning from the letter in her typewriter.

"What did you say, Ellen?"

"I said it's Saturday, not Friday."

Charlotte turned from the file cabinet and stared blankly at Ellen's back, then broke into a laugh. "I must've been talking to myself again." The thirty-year-old secretary shook her head in mock sorrow. "I really must be losing my marbles. That's the third time this morning."

Ellen exchanged a sly smile with Therese Fortier, seated at the desk across from hers. Both young women had pretty much gotten used to Charlotte's conversations with herself, but this morning, even by her own admission, she was in rare form. From the moment she had come into the office, she had kept up a running dialogue complete with questions and answers. For the most part the talk was in fragments, bits and snatches about the work she was doing, or had to do, or didn't want to do. Twice she had misplaced letters awaiting signing by her boss, Father Swanstrom, causing the girls to drop what they were doing and join in the search.

"It's the weather," Charlotte explained with a shrug. "I knew this was going to be one of those days the minute I got up."

Munching like a squirrel, Lucille Bath swallowed the mouthful of Hershey bar before plugging in the switchboard cable.

"Good morning, Catholic War Relief Services." Involuntarily, she slid her elbows off the console and sat bolt straight in the chair. "Hello, Father Swanstrom . . . yes, I'm still on vacation, but Frances Taylor called in sick. I came in to take over for her. Uh huh, Mr. McCloskey's here, Father."

Selecting a cable, she fitted it into the board and depressed a lever. "Mr. McCloskey? . . . Father Swanstrom's calling."

She leaned back, balancing the chair on the two rear rollers, and heaved a sigh of boredom. For the nineteen-year-old receptionist the morning was standing still. Her eyes drifted to the wall clock. About now, she guessed, her husband would be in their new apartment. They had planned to spend the morning painting the living room, then take in a movie. She had even put together a picnic lunch last night to christen their new home, overruling Charlie's preference for beer by packing the special bottle of wine she had saved from their wedding reception for just such an occasion. But then Anna Regan's call came, asking her to help out. She'd leave exactly at noon, she promised him, and go directly to the apartment. It suddenly hit her—the wine! She'd forgotten to pack a corkscrew—and after making such a fuss about it. Reaching for a message slip, she scribbled a note to herself to stop at the liquor store and pick one up before going on to the apartment.

Holding the phone loosely against his ear, Jack McCloskey leaned over and closely examined his brown shoes. There was no getting around it, he decided; even with a fresh shine they were scruffy. The time had come to buy a new pair. After they were done at the consulate he'd drop in at the Florsheim's on Fifth Avenue and take advantage of the sale they were having.

"Sure, Father, no problem. See you in a couple of minutes." He hung up and swiveled his chair to face Ed Cummings at the next desk.

"Swanstrom's still at the barber's. He wants us to meet him there."

Cummings looked up from his crossword puzzle and scowled. "I've got just a couple left. Give me a few minutes." He settled back in his chair, recrossed his feet on top of the desk, and concentrated on the puzzle. Grinning, McCloskey shifted his cigar to the corner of his mouth, stood up, and with a sudden move swept Cummings' feet off the desk.

"Come on, you lazy bugger—put your ass in gear. We're supposed to be at the consulate at ten."

Cummings sighed, lifted himself and stretched, then turned to the window behind his desk and peered out. "I can't see through this damned fog. You think it's still raining?" McCloskey reached for their raincoats hanging on the coat tree between the desk, and tossed Cummings his. "If it isn't now, it'll start the minute we get out of the building," McCloskey said with a fatalistic glance at the weather. Shrugging his bulk into the coat, McCloskey turned toward Paul Dearing, seated behind his desk in the corner office.

"Hey, Paul," he boomed in his Brooklyn accent. "In case King George should happen to be having tea at the consulate, you want his autograph?"

Dearing looked up from his typewriter and laughed. McCloskey was always ribbing him about his autograph collection, some of which was attractively framed and hanging in his office. "Sure, Churchill's too, if you bump into him." McCloskey stuck the cigar in the middle of his mouth and gave Dearing the V sign, then, mimicking Churchill's hunched walk, he took Cummings' arm and led him toward the reception area.

Turning back to the yellow sheet of copy paper in his typewriter, Dearing hunt-and-pecked out the end of a sentence. He was writing a feature story for the Buffalo *Courier-Express* on a group of hometown boys returning from overseas. Two of the troop ships he was to meet today, the *Sea Robin* and the *Winnipeg*, were scheduled to dock at 11:00. He glanced out his window at the thick bed of clouds and fog moving in from the north and cursed his luck. If the fog got any worse the dockings would probably be delayed by an hour or more; he'd miss his deadline to teletype the story to Buffalo from the Associated Press office.

Of course, he could always cheat. Lying on his desk was a folder of press releases put out by the Army Information Office, short biographical sketches of each of the men he was to interview, mostly background, short on battle color and personal experiences. But as so many other stringers did by rote, never moving from their desks, Dearing could fill in their heroics with quotes pratically guaranteeing the men keys to the city. It was a tempting thought; no hanging around in the rain hunting for a few familiar faces among the more than 6,000 troops that would be pouring off the ships. He could take what he'd already written, cab it to the AP office in Rockefeller Center, and bang out the rest of the piece directly on the teletype. He'd be dry and make his deadline, with no one the wiser.

Allowing a small grin at the transparent game he was playing with himself, Dearing glanced at his note pad and began hammering at the keys, leaving sufficient blank spaces to be filled in later with the quotes he would get from the men at dockside.

*   *   *

"American 301 off at nine-forty-three."

"Roger, Newark, American 301 cleared to twenty-five southwest of Philadelphia to climb to eight thousand on the Newark Radio Range before proceeding on course."

"New York, this is Mitchell. How about clearance for Navy cargo nine five four to Elmira? He's holding at four thousand."

"New York Radio to Mitchell. No release for Navy nine five four until we get that Colonial DC-3 into La Guardia. He's coming in at two thousand on final instrument approach. I'll let you know when he's down."

"You're a good man, Tommy."

The chatter in his earphones was constant as Smith eased the bomber down through a solid bank of stratocumulus.

For the past minute, since *Old John Feather Merchant* had cleared the scalloped shoreline of Kings Point, the ceiling had continued to fall off sharply. Smith was locked inside the cloud layer, flying blind at 900 feet north of Little Neck Bay on his approach to Queens.

This was English soup, viscous-thick, impenetrable—and as the tower controllers' cross-talk from the various airfields warned him, a dangerous atmosphere for him to remain hidden in too long.

Since tuning in the New York Airway Traffic Control Center's frequency, Smith had given up hope of keeping track of the number and type of aircraft moving in his area. Between the military and the commercial airline flights, there were no less than six or seven planes taking off, landing, or being guided to altitude and course at any given minute by the

Traffic Control Center located at La Guardia Field. All were being directed by radio—either by voice command or range beacon signals. Their every move had been fixed by a flight plan filed prior to takeoff, and now, relying solely on their instruments because of the poor visibility, the pilots were being monitored by dozens of men on the ground; invisible hands and eyes sharing their cockpits, clearing safe passage through the concrete overcast.

Smith was a man alone—traveling at 225 miles an hour through a sea of gray-white vapor that clung to his windshield, blinding him not only to the outside world, but worse, concealing Army 0577 from those in the air as well as on the ground. His earphones crackled alive.

"Go ahead, La Guardia."

"We still can't get a fix on Navy two one seven one. He was reported over Bendix at zero nine three nine at two thousand descending and ordered to change over to two zero nine kilocycles. Have you heard from him?"

"Negative, La Guardia. We haven't any word on Navy two one seven one. Did you clear him for approach?"

"Say last part again, New York."

"Did you clear Navy two one seven one for landing approach?"

"Affirmative, New York. We've been trying to raise him continuously with no luck. Will you give it a go?"

"Roger, La Guardia. We'll try and get a fix on two one seven one and report back to you."

Pulling his eyes from the altimeter, Smith glanced past Domitrovich through the starboard window. Somewhere off the right side of his aircraft, either in the clear or, like him, snubbed in the overcast, there was a plane on the loose—one that might be heading in his direction. How close and at what altitude, he had no idea. One thing was certain—he was going to make Army 0577 very visible, very quickly.

Pressing •the wheel forward, Smith put the B-25 into a shallow dive. The altimeter needle fell below 850 feet, its revolutions sweeping the dial faster as the plane picked up speed. 825 . . . 800 . . . the cloud was thicker than he had first judged . . . 750 . . . 725 . . . there was some thinning ahead, wispy trailings of vapor breaking apart the center . . . 700 . . .

He was suddenly in the clear, the dead-green calm of Little Neck Bay sprawling in front of his windshield. He leveled out at 650 feet.

Glancing from the sectional map to the window, Domitrovich tapped Smith's shoulder.

"Looks like the Bronx Whitestone Bridge, colonel." He was pointing through the sodden haze to an angle off the right wing. Smith checked the map and nodded, then shifted his gaze southwesterly, past the barely visible twin towers of the suspension bridge toward the area where the map positioned La Guardia. The rain had picked up, splattering the windshield with tropical-sized drops. He switched on the wipers. Faintly curtained behind the rising water vapor and industrial smoke curling up from factories and power plants, Smith caught a fleeting glimpse of two airfields.

"Hold that map up, willya, Chris?"

Domitrovich angled the sectional, his finger pinpointing the smaller airfield closest to their position. "I make the one this side of us Flushing Airport. They show two runways."

Smith's eyes lingered on the map for a brief moment, then he nodded in agreement. La Guardia, separated by the narrow reach of Flushing Bay, was directly west of the civilian field. Dead ahead, lying flat and crowded with small houses rimming the shore, was the community of Bayside, Queens, due east of the airfield.

Reaching to the right of the control column, Smith cranked the radio to 392 kilocycles, the La Guardia tower frequency. Rogner had been right: New York was a mess to fly into or out of—a crazy-quilt of fractured waterways and densely populated, continent-sized land masses. Not only were the airways dangerously overcrowded, he thought, but the concentration of so many major airfields within the metropolitan area created confusion for the uninitiated pilot.

The cross-country trip from Sioux Falls had strikingly brought home to Smith the differences between flying by military rules in a combat zone and using the Stateside civilian airways.

In England, regulations had been pared to the bone; only those rules vital to the safety of the airspace over and around an airfield, or the vectoring of formations by strict adherence to detailed flight plans and radio range signals, were considered inviolate, never to be broken or even slightly bent except under the most extreme emergency. Every combat pilot had spent mind-dulling hours memorizing landing and take-off patterns, aircraft to control tower procedures, navigation to and from bomb targets by reliance solely on blind trust in radio compass and instruments.

Beyond these regulations handcuffing Smith and his fellow pilots to the protective custody of the ground controllers, the basic, if unwritten, rule was every man for himself. Once over the English Channel, pilots whose aircraft had avoided mortal wounds raced like soapbox-derby competitors back to their fields—screaming in low over the chalk cliffs, exuberantly hedge-hopping farms and manor houses with wheels and flaps down, throttles wide open.

The limpers, ships with engines shot out, control surfaces useless, or worse, a hindrance, came in any way they could; for them prayers were substituted for the rule book; any approach to the airfield, upwind, downwind, crosswind, however they could put the plane on the ground, was the right way. As Smith had discovered a dozen or more times in his year and a half of combat flying, in an emergency there was precious little time for rules and regulations; necessity overtook procedure. Fifty times, in sunshine and freezing fogs, he had lifted off from Glatton Airdrome and miraculously returned. Confidence, by subtle osmosis, was converted into instinct. Behind the controls of a war plane a man stayed alive by unconscious reflex. If at the end, like Smith, he was not only alive but had come through whole, unmarked by killing metal or corrosive nightsweats, then he was right; his way had been the best. Such a man does not question his instinct, or easily transfer faith.

But things were different here.

Flying as Rogner's copilot on the flight east from Sioux Falls, Lieutenant Colonel Smith came up against the harsh reality that civilians, not the military, controlled the air.

These men, anonymous voices reaching up from unseen towers and range stations, ordered—*demanded*—not only his attention, but his absolute compliance to their regulations. Following their flight plan to the letter, Smith had worked the radios at least a dozen times to announce 0577's reaching or leaving altitudes, or with requests to alter course to skirt rain east of Cleveland, or for weather information en route to Newark. He had quickly discovered two facts: the civilian ground personnel were not impressed by the military and gave no priority, showed no special courtesy to a man who had flown more than five hundred hours overseas without their help; secondly, as he had learned at Newark Field while awaiting clearance from the tower to depart for Boston, at civilian fields scheduled airline flights came and went by the clock. Unless a military flight had an emergency clearance, they sat on the ground, as Smith had done, waiting for the traffic controller to complete his airline business.

None of this came as a complete surprise to him. Before leaving England for home, Smith and the other pilots of the 457th Bomb Group had attended a three-hour orientation lecture on civil flying regulations in the U.S. But the session was held three weeks prior to his departure; in between, the days had been filled with his duties as deputy commander of a unit that was being phased out upon its return to the states. The lecture, too short and cursory, had been all but forgotten in the press of paperwork and the mounting exhilaration of returning home.

He would have plenty of time, Smith had reasoned, to pick up the procedures once he reached his Stateside duty station. But at Sioux Falls he and Rogner found themselves still bogged down with the red tape of reprocessing; in the first few weeks of their return there had been no time for flying. This past Thursday, seated in the copilot's position in an aircraft he'd never flown before, Bill Smith had his first taste of flying by a new set of rules—one that did not recognize, much less appreciate, the individual.

At 650 feet the bomber was barely under the cloud cover as it edged over Bayside.

Scanning the instruments, Smith halted at the panel clock. It read 9:45. His position was now exactly parallel to La Guardia Field, approximately 15 miles to the east. It was time for a decision: Newark or La Guardia?

The ceiling was lowering rapidly. Where just a minute ago large patches of the east-west runways at La Guardia had been visible through breaks in the cloud layer, now the field had all but disappeared behind haze and fog moving in from Flushing Bay.

Smith shifted his gaze over the B-25's starboard engine, to the general area southwest where the map indicated Newark Field. The 30-mile distance to the New Jersey airport was filled with a sullen, impenetrable overcast. It was impossible for him to tell if the cloud cover was localized, or extended beyond the Jersey shore.

Pressuring the right rudder, Smith put the plane into a shallow bank to the west. He would play it safe; by the book. He would leave the decision of 0577's destination to the men who made the rules.

He reached for the microphone.

CHAPTER XI

9:45—The Final Leg

LA GUARDIA CHIEF TOWER CONTROL-
ler Victor Barden abruptly rolled his chair back from the radio
console and stood with the microphone grasped in his hand.
Without taking his eyes off the northwest section of the field,
he flipped the "transmit" switch on the panel.

"Newark Airways—this is La Guardia." His deep voice
had an uncharacteristically taut ring.

"Go ahead, La Guardia—this is Newark Airways."

"I'm getting pretty concerned about Navy two one seven
one. New York control can't raise him. They've been calling
continuously for a couple of minutes. The last report we had
was that he was over Bendix at zero nine three nine heading
east at two thousand descending."

The loudspeaker mounted above the banks of radio
equipment crackled in silence for a few seconds, then screeched
a loud transmission tone broken by bursts of static. Barden
snapped an impatient glance at the speaker.

"Say again, Newark—we've got some breakup here."

"How do you read now, La Guardia?"

"That's better. What about Navy two one seven one?"

*We cleared him to Bendix at zero nine three seven and
instructed him to report after clearing the range station. He
hasn't called in?"*

"Negative, Newark—not here or to New York Traffic. We've got American seven-fifty next up holding on instrument final. I don't want to bring him in until I get some word on that Navy ship. Will you check with Bendix and the range station on his position and altitude?"

"Roger, La Guardia. Will do on Navy two one seven one."

Barden ran a thick hand across his crew-cut as he gave the overcast shrouding the far edge of the field a last probing sweep. Across the Hudson River, running on a northwesterly diagonal from the tower, was New Jersey's Bendix Airport, used by the military and the airlines as a navigational range station for vectoring planes in and out of the New York area. Unless the Navy transport was having mechanical problems, or had strayed off course, the plane should have appeared over the north section of the field minutes ago.

This stray was creating a problem. Within a 25-mile radius of La Guardia, seven commercial airliners were stacked up in holding patterns waiting for clearance to land; three were over Coney Island, off the southern tip of Brooklyn; four were to the north, circling Port Chester at 1,000-foot separations. All were flying blind, being guided through the weather by radio beacon signals.

For the thirty-eight-year-old Barden, the situation was hardly unique. In his five years as chief tower controller for the New York Municipal Airport, and for ten years previously spent with the Army Signal Corps performing the same duties, he had handled hundreds of similar problems. It was not at all unusual for aircraft to stray off course. In theory, flying had been honed to a science; but as Barden and every other ground controller knew, the science was only as predictable as the humans employing it. Errors in judgment or a foul-up in communications quickly pivoted the science into an art—a technique vulnerable to interpretation and individual choice.

But for that one elusive factor, Barden was a man happy in his work. His days were filled with a pride that comes to those who make life-balancing decisions based on knowledge digested from experience. As chief controller in one of the country's busiest towers, his judgment was inviolate; pilots, their passengers, and those living their lives on the ground under the airspace he controlled paid him the ultimate respect of unquestioned trust.

Unlike a movie star or a hero athlete who thrives on fame, a tower operator's measure of competence, his expertise, is reflected by his anonymity; a mistake by his hand calls attention to him. Daily success, the unruffled, uneventful, safe passage of aircraft from one point to another, depended upon a personality void of drama; suspense, the minutest trace of a desire to taste the unknown, must be alien to the occupation.

If a mold for the job existed, it had been cast from Victor Herbert Barden. Named by his musician father after the famous composer of popular operettas, who was a close family friend, Barden had immersed his life in a pursuit of precision. Over the years he had collected an impressive number of patents for devices to monitor and control aircraft electronically. He had also invented an electronic method of tuning pianos. More as a hobby than as a source of additional income, he worked at this exacting craft in his spare moments.

Therefore, personality as much as job dedication was making Barden uneasy over the missing Navy plane; aside from the obvious danger of an uncontrolled aircraft, the situation clearly pointed up the sloppy, unscientific aspects still attached to flying.

"La Guardia Tower, this is Army 0577," the speaker blared.

Instinctively, Barden swiveled his chair and glanced to his left at the large scheduling board. There was no Army 0577 chalked in on the Instruments arrivals list. Turning back to the console, Barden snapped the "transmit" switch.

"Army 0577, this is La Guardia Tower. What is your position and altitude?"

Smith's southern drawl resonated loudly through the speaker above the muffled sound of his engines.

"About fifteen miles southeast of you at six-fifty, Contact. I'd like the current Newark weather."

Barden frowned. It was getting to be epidemic, military pilots calling in on the tower frequency for local weather and routing information.

Either the Army Flight Service Center's existence was being kept a deep government secret, or more likely, he suspected, these boys were just too damn lazy to follow the regulations. In the past month Barden had noticed a sharp rise in the number of weather requests he was receiving from pilots fresh from overseas. The government had set up the Flight Service Center not only to provide up-to-the-minute weather and routing information across the country, but to reduce the amount of military transmissions to civilian towers and control centers.

With the war in Europe over, more combat pilots were using—or misusing—the civil airways. Two weeks ago, in a report to the Civil Aeronautics Administration, Barden had made a formal complaint that insufficient transition training was being given military pilots before their return home.

His concern was based partly on an incident that had taken place a month before, involving three military aircraft he had cleared for a flight to Newark Field. The pilots, all young, recent combat veterans, had been clearly instructed to overfly Central Park at a 2,500-foot altitude before turning south into New Jersey. They had been warned to stay well north of the midtown Manhattan area because of heavy commercial airline and cargo traffic using that airspace. Instead, the pilots made a diagonal run across the East River, and for a hair-raising five minutes played ring-around-the-rosy about the Empire State Building's observation tower before continuing on to Newark Field. That the offenders were immediately arrested and were now facing court-martial did little to weaken Barden's argument; unless regulations were strictly enforced, his report ended, a major air disaster involving military aircraft over a civilian population was very likely.

But this morning Barden had too much on his mind to lecture this Southerner. He wanted him out of his hair. Fifteen miles southeast would put the Army ship closer to Newark than La Guardia.

"Army 0577," he called with clipped detachment, "contact Newark Tower on three four one kilocycles for Newark weather, or Army Flight Service Center. Over."

Domitrovich watched Smith hesitate, then lower the microphone from his mouth. They had leveled out of the banking turn and were now lined up with the southeastern section of the airfield.

The sergeant reached for the radio. "Do you want the Newark frequency, colonel?"

His gaze locked on the rapidly nearing field, Smith was weighing his alternatives. If he called the Newark Tower requesting weather information he would have to identify himself. As he had already been informed by the Boston controller, Newark Field was closed to him as a Contact flight; and if he attempted to land there unannounced he would be in direct violation of his flight plan. His eyes shifted to the altimeter. As it was, at 650 feet, he was well below the minimum for a CFR flight—but not if he intended to land at La Guardia.

Smith shook his head. "Leave it on the La Guardia frequency," he cautioned the sergeant softly.

He had promised Rogner that he would pick him up at Newark no later than 10:00. He glanced at the panel clock. If his plan worked, Army 0577 should roll to a halt in front of his commanding officer precisely on the button.

Victor Barden stared incredulously at Gerard Aide, the controller working the interphone communications slot next to him.

"What the hell's he doing way over there?"

Aide hung up the phone and swiveled to the scheduling board. "Apparently his radios went out when he was crossing the range station," Aide said, as he erased Navy 2171 from the arrivals list. "Newark Tower has him in sight circling the west side of the field at five hundred. They're clearing all traffic to bring him in now."

The tension in Barden's face visibly drained. He leaned close to the microphone.

"New York Airways—this is La Guardia."

"Go ahead, La Guardia."

"We've located Navy two one seven one. His radio's dead. At the present time he's circling the west section of Newark Field at five hundred feet. They're going to land him now."

"Roger, La Guardia. I'm releasing American seven-fifty for an unrestricted approach from the southwest. You can release United eighteen-twenty and Colonial seven-forty for departure at your discretion. Please report their off times."

"Roger, American seven-fifty will be up next, cleared on a southwest approach. United and Colonial for departure."

"That's correct. I'll give you a release for TWA nine-eleven in about five minutes."

The bomber was now less than a mile from the field. Easing the throttles back a hair, Smith watched his rpm needle fall off to 1,800. He was moving through a scattered layer of clouds and thick haze at 200 miles per hour.

He reached across to the radios and turned up the volume on the receiver tuned to the La Guardia frequency. The transmissions entering his earphones from the tower were breaking up with loud, crackling pops, like sap bubbling out of a burning log.

"Tower—United eighteen-twenty ready to go."

"Roger, eighteen-twenty, you're cleared for takeoff. Colonial seven-forty, you're go for taxi and hold at runway three six. Wind north-northeast at twelve."

Below him, Smith watched the result of the tower's instructions as a twin-engine DC-3 raced down a runway and lifted off the northernmost portion of the airfield. Within a matter of seconds he lost sight of the airline as it entered a hovering bank of fog over the East River.

Directly under his left wing Smith saw the chain-link fence marking the field's outer perimeter. Just beyond the fence was a series of single-story buildings and a row of corrugated metal quonset huts. Painted in large white letters on top of one of the buildings was the legend "U.S.AAF 1338th Base Unit— La Guardia Field." Off to his right, on the periphery of the hangars and passenger terminals, the control tower rose from the roof of the administration building. He was now well within the boundaries of the field.

Responding to a light rudder, the B-25 began a sweeping turn to the right that would carry it across the tower's line of sight.

"Traffic, this is La Guardia Tower. United eighteen-twenty's off time is zero nine forty-seven . . . Colonial seven-forty off at zero nine forty-eight. Do you have position and altitude for American seven-fifty?"

"*Roger, Tower. American seven-fifty reported leaving four thousand descending to Bendix at forty-seven. He'll report on reaching two thousand five hundred over Bendix. Stand by on a release for TWA nine-eleven in about a minute or two.*"

"Roger, thank you," Barden said. He pushed himself back from the console and glanced appraisingly at the horizon. From his position facing west he saw that the ceiling had lowered even more since his last check a few minutes ago. He judged the canopy of clouds intermixed with smoke and haze to be no more than 700 feet over the field. To his right, Riker's Island, squatting like a giant turtle in the middle of the East River off Hunts Point, faded elusively in and out of the rising mist. For a brief instant he caught sight of the factorylike penitentiary complex on the western edge of the island; then just as suddenly, the gray structures were swallowed, leaving only ghostly tracings of the gun towers and water tanks floating above the vapor. Still farther north, across College Point, the Bronx Whitestone Bridge was all but obliterated by a barley-colored ground fog.

Turning to his left, Barden noticed that the light drizzle was holding the smoke streaming out of the Consolidated Edison power-plant stacks in a muddy suspension over Bowery Bay. In a sweeping, 180-degree survey through the tower windows he estimated the forward visibility to be under three miles, and falling off rapidly.

Both men saw the B-25 at the same time. Aide turned to Barden with a look bordering on shock.

"Who in Christ's name is *that*!"

Barden, stonefaced, didn't answer. He was following the banking trajectory of the silver bomber as it arced across the field toward the north. With his eyes riveted to the plane, he groped for and located his binoculars resting on the console ledge. He drew the glasses to his eyes and sharp-focused as he stood.

The bomber's twin tail was partially hidden by clouds.

"I can't get his serial number in the clear," he said in a voice strained with control. Barden lowered the glasses and with eyes narrowed in anger, watched as the B-25 reached the far edge of the field, then banked left. Using his thumb, the controller jerked the switch to "transmit" as he picked up the microphone.

"This is La Guardia Tower calling the B-25 circling left over the field. Please call in and identify yourself on three nine two kilocycles."

His hunch had been right. The Southerner's voice rumbled mellifluously over the loudspeaker. *"Tower . . . this is Army 0577."*

"What's that silly bastard doing?" Aide's attention was frozen on the bomber as it circled over the runways, at moments half-lost, the silver body merging into the cloud cover.

"We'll find out once he's down," Barden said tautly. He brought the microphone close to his mouth. "Tower to Army 0577—wind northeasterly at twelve. Use runway three-six. Are you familiar with the traffic pattern? Over."

If Smith had caught the undertone of command in Barden's landing instructions his voice gave no indication. *"I'd rather land at Newark, Tower. What's the weather over there, please?"*

"Incongruous" was the word that flashed through the controller's mind—both the situation and the pilot's patronizing manner. His offhanded, breezy disregard or ignorance of his frightfully dangerous actions left Barden momentarily speechless. He caught himself staring dumbly at the loudspeaker.

"Tower to 0577 . . . you are out of bounds," Barden said icily, punching each word into unmistakable italics. "You are in active airspace—these runways are in use. Move to the extreme southeast section of the field and fly a left holding position, Contact. Over."

The pilot's voice carried no trace of surprise or apology. *"Roger, Tower, will do."* There was an audible click as the transmission ended, then abruptly, the speaker hummed and again carried the engines' drone into the tower: *"Tower—I have official business at Newark at ten hundred. I would appreciate as little delay here as possible."*

Barden watched the B-25 bank out of the turn and head across the field. He turned to Aide. "Get Airways on the line. Tell them we've got an Army ship in here under a condition of violation, that I want him down. Remind Traffic that we've got American seven-fifty due on southwest final."

Aide picked up the interphone. "What's that ship's number?"

Barden had already turned to his left and was following the bomber through his binoculars. "0577—and tell them he claims to have official business at Newark, that he requested Newark weather."

Smith edged the wheel a shade more left and increased pressure on the rudder. He was using a parkway overpass just outside the field as the pivot point for his holding pattern. The panel clock read almost 9:50. He looked across to Domitrovich and broke into a grin at the sergeant's doubting look.

"He sounded kinda put out, colonel," Domitrovich said.

Smith shook his head and chuckled. "Just your imagination, Chris. Why in the world would that fella be angry at me?" He patted Domitrovich's knee comfortingly, and turned and glanced over his shoulder toward Perna.

"How're you doin' back there, sailor?"

The young seaman wasn't doing well at all. Tucked in the small jump seat behind the cockpit, hemmed in by the flanking oxygen tanks, Perna was getting airsick from the steep, banking turns. The same queasiness had happened on his first and only flight a month ago. Because of heavy traffic, the pilot had been instructed to hold over this same section of La Guardia Field for what seemed to Albert an eternity. Then, as now, he had attempted to tamp down the nausea by fixing his attention on a point east of the field where he guessed his father's small furniture factory was located. He had never seen

Elmhurst from the air, but from the angle the airliners came over the factory on their approach to the field, he judged the single-story building to be on the far side of the Long Island Railroad tracks.

As the plane dipped low to the left, Perna shifted his gaze from the cockpit window to the colonel. "I'm doing fine, sir, thanks," he said, managing a bilious smile. Then, as an afterthought, he asked, "How long do you think they'll keep us circling?"

Smith read the sailor's pasty coloring and offered him a confident grin. "Oh, not too much longer. It's a case of mutual necessity—they don't want us here any more than we do." Leveling out of the turn, he glanced down at the tower. Unless he overshot his guess, they would be contacting him with an instrument clearance to Newark in the next minute or two.

*   *   *

On the top floor of the administration building, directly below the tower, the New York Airway Traffic Control Center was a hushed maelstrom of activity.

The room bristled with radio equipment and wall-sized plotting maps. A dozen men were in constant motion, issuing crisp orders into headset microphones, their hands giving or receiving teletyped weather reports or moving magnetized blocks of wood representing incoming or outgoing aircraft from one air corridor to another on the maps. To a visitor sensing the pressure the men worked under—the unrelenting flow of verbal information that poured in and necessitated instant decisions—the activity would appear insanely random: a modern-day Tower of Babel, so haphazard its purpose was . doomed by design. But there was an ordered rhythm to the movement. Each man was responsible for a fixed number of aircraft within rigid boundaries. The movement and safety of any one plane was a shared venture, the controllers passing the ship from one territory to the next with familial discharge. Fathers guiding favored sons.

The man in charge of this ordered chaos, Chief Airway Controller Allen Morrissey, picked up the flashing phone marked "LG-TWR." The instant he lifted the receiver a

Webcor wire recorder sitting next to the phone was automatically triggered into motion.

"Go ahead, La Guardia."

The spinning thread of metal picked up Aide's terse announcement.

"We've got an Army ship in here CFR—number zero five seven seven. He's just under the stuff holding southeast at about six-fifty at the present time."

Morrissey poised his pencil over a note pad. "What was that Army number again?"

"Zero five seven seven. He wants clearance to Newark. We have American seven-fifty on at approximately zero nine fifty-three from the southwest, unrestricted."

Jotting the number down on the pad, Morrissey shot a glance at the radio console clock, then elevated his eyes to the schedule board. A quick scan reported no IFR flight plan had been filed for Army 0577. "What's the present ceiling at La Guardia?" he asked.

"Just around seven hundred, variable," Aide answered. "He came in here without authorization and didn't identify himself until the tower called. Tower wants him down on a condition of violation."

"Keep him where he is. I'll get right back to you." Morrissey hung up and pulled the clipboard holding the teletype weather reports close to him. The 8:30 Newark sequence showed 600 feet overcast, with light rain, smoke, and haze cutting visibility to 2½ miles. He picked up the phone.

"La Guardia—this is Control. Is that Army ship still CFR over the field?"

"Roger," Aide confirmed. "He's getting itchy. He just called the tower requesting an Instrument clearance to Newark at a thousand feet, or CFR direct. He says he has important official business with the Newark Base Unit at ten hundred."

Morrissey scowled and shook his head. "Negative on both requests. Instrument into Newark will be heavy until 1300. The Newark sequence for zero eight-thirty shows 600 feet overcast, visibility under CFR minimums."

There was a pause on the line, as Morrissey heard a muffled conversation between Aide and Barden.

"Tower wants authorization to land him," Aide said finally.

Morrissey had anticipated Barden's request; it was the normal precaution he would have taken had he been in charge of the civilian tower. At least a half-dozen times during the war the military and civilian authorities had clashed over jurisdictional procedure at the field. The Army Flight Service Center claimed king-of-the-mountain status whenever a question arose over a military flight. Although there was no clear-cut official order separating their powers, the avalanche of red tape resulting from past arguments had given the civilian sector reason to be gun shy. It had become routine to check with the Army before making a decision affecting one of its aircraft.

"Contact zero five seven seven and tell him to maintain his position, CFR. Advise him that American seven-fifty is making a standard instrument approach from the southwest. I'll have Army Flight Service contact you." Morrissey replaced the Tower receiver and reached for a phone marked "AFS Center."

Not twenty feet down the console board from Morrissey, Captain Charles Esterlein, Jr., was sweating out a thorny dilemma. The commanding officer of the Army Flight Service Center was on the radio to Mitchell Field Tower, attempting to placate an Air Corps general who insisted on landing with "Five Star Priority" over an emergency Air Evacuation aircraft that had already been given clearance.

Seated next to Esterlein, Captain George Miller snatched up the flashing interphone.

"Army Flight Service, Miller."

His eyes focused on the spinning wire-recorder reels as Morrissey gave him a rundown on Army 0577, ending with a request for authorization for the tower to bring the aircraft down.

Miller glanced over to his commanding officer. Esterlein was still engrossed in his problem but Miller decided the immediacy of the situation required his attention.

"Hold on, Airways," he said into the phone, then turned to Esterlein and tapped the officer's shoulder. Esterlein turned with an exasperated look.

Miller held the receiver up by way of explanation. "It's Airways—they want authorization to land an Army ship pending a condition of violation."

Esterlein sighed wearily, then turned to the microphone. "Hold on, Mitchell, be right back to you." He swiveled his chair to face Miller. "What's the problem?"

"This ship came in CFR, unauthorized, and didn't identify himself until the tower called him. He's requested Newark weather and clearance to the field. Both the tower and Airways want us to order him down."

Esterlein shook his head impatiently. "Didn't you tell Airways we don't have authority to bring him in?"

Miller hesitated. "No, I thought under the circumstances you might want to handle it directly with the pilot."

"It's up to them if they want to file a violation. Give the pilot the latest Newark weather and ask him to advise his intentions to Airways," Esterlein said, dismissing Miller by turning back to the radio. Miller motioned to the corporal manning the teletype machine.

"Have we gotten the 9:30 weather?"

"Yes, sir." The corporal pulled the sheet out of his clipboard and handed it to the officer.

Barden took the interphone from Aide, his pencil poised above the memo pad.

"Newark sequence zero nine-thirty," he repeated, then quickly jotted down the figures Miller was feeding him. "One thousand feet variable overcast . . . two and a quarter miles visibility . . . light rain . . . light smoke and haze." The tower controller straightened and pivoted his chair around to the left, glancing out at the circling bomber. "Yeah, he's still CFR. Roger, I'll have Airways advise his intentions. Thanks," he added dryly, then passed the receiver back to Aide.

Aide read Barden's troubled look. "They won't bring him down?" The tower controller shook his head. "Nope. They claim they don't have the authority," he said derisively. He turned back to the console and picked up the Airways interphone.

"This is La Guardia. Flight Service refuses to file a violation on 0577 or order him to land." He was tracking the bomber as he talked, his head turning with the plane's flight path as it dipped in and out of the lowering layer of broken clouds. "Has American seven-fifty reported over Bendix yet?"

Morrissey's eyes were darting over the La Guardia plotting map, pausing at the block of wood bearing "AA7/50" inked on a plastic card. A controller was just pushing it into a new position. "Roger, seven-fifty has reported leaving two thousand five hundred over the Bendix range station and descending on the southwest leg," he reported to Barden. His glance trailed to the clock, a gesture he was certain the tower controller was duplicating simultaneously. As much for the record as to express his concern, he added, "He should have the field CFR in a little over a minute."

The situation was perfectly clear to both controllers; if any violation was to be registered against the Army ship it would have to come through them, not the military—and it would have to be done immediately. Not only had the B-25 broken the CAA rules for entering an airfield's traffic pattern, but the plane's unannounced arrival was creating a hazard. With the imminent approach of the American Airlines DC-3, the circling Mitchell bomber was—under the Contact weather conditions—a potential time bomb; a false move by either aircraft, a misread altimeter or a random turn, could shunt the planes onto a collision course. And then there was the red tape. The reams of Army and CAA forms Barden and Morrissey would be required to fill out, the hours of testimony they would have to give to the military and civilian examiners; and ultimately, the entire process repeated again when the pilot filed his automatically expected appeal.

"The decision's yours, Tower," Morrissey said accurately, but not without relief. Barden, as chief tower controller, was in complete charge of sending off and bringing down aircraft into

La Guardia Field. At this moment, his word was the ultimate law.

Standing at the console, Barden was studying the Newark weather figures—or rather his eyes were fixed on the pencil markings; his mind was functioning like a camera obscura, a blackened box isolating himself and the silver bomber circling overhead from the rest of the world.

Army 0577 was an errant ship; a violator of time and space.

The weather, here at La Guardia and across the Hudson to Newark, was clearly below CFR minimums—grounding conditions for flights of proven necessity, much less unsubstantiated urgency.

And yet the military refused to discipline one of their own; ignored the fact that 0577 was an infection in an otherwise healthy, smoothly functioning body.

If they were not responsible, who was? Himself? The pilot?

The console clock read 9:52. Barden looked across the field toward the southwest, searching the overcast for first signs of the incoming airliner, a glimmer of wing lights or a parting of cloud cover. There was nothing. He knew the airline captain would call once he had the field in sight.

The drone of the bomber's engine pulled his attention. The plane was close to the tower, too close, almost overhead. The Army ship was straying from its holding pattern, moving deeper into the field. Barden turned with the sound and caught a shrouded glimpse of the plane as it banked into a cloud. He grabbed up the microphone.

Smith reached over and adjusted the radio's volume, then depressed the microphone button. "Say that last part again, Tower."

Barden leaned hard on each word, pausing briefly for separation. *"Ceiling one thousand . . . variable . . . lower broken . . . visibility two and one quarter miles. Advise intentions."*   •

Left wing low, Smith broke out of the cloud. He glanced to his right in the general direction of Newark Field.

"Roger, Tower . . . one thousand . . . visibility two to three."

The controller's impatience was unmistakable. *"Negative, 0577 . . . visibility two and one quarter miles! Advise intentions!"*

"I'd like to try it to Newark, Tower," Smith said evenly. He was approaching the southeast edge of the field, the tower directly below. He turned the wheel, dipping the bomber into a right banking turn.

"The decision is at your discretion, 0577 . . .," Barden said with cold detachment. *"Advise your intentions."*

Old John Feather Merchant leveled out, moving now on a southwesterly heading toward the East River. "I'll go CFR for Newark, Tower."

Barden stared through the tower windows as the B-25, without his releasing it from the holding pattern, started across the field. He shook his head angrily, eyes darting off toward the gray horizon where American 7/50 would be letting down through the solid overcast.

"0577," Barden called, "maintain three miles—repeat, three miles—visibility. If unable to maintain three miles visibility return to La Guardia Field immediately. American seven-fifty is making a standard instrument approach from the southwest. Over."

Smith's drawl came in laconically. *"Roger, will do."*

Watching the bomber skate through a patch of dense haze and fog, Barden had a sudden thought. His eyes drifted an inch south of the plane's position to a point on Manhattan Island he often used as a fixed weather vane—a ceiling marker for aircraft flying into Newark Field because the structure, six miles distant, was exactly in line with the airfield. He lifted the microphone, then flinched, as the loudspeaker took him by surprise.

"La Guardia Tower—this is American seven-fifty."

The tower controller shot a glance to his left. Almost imperceptibly two pinpoints of light stabbed through the overcast. Barden snapped the "transmit" switch.

"American seven-fifty—stand by, please," he said, racing the words into a solid block like a tobacco auctioneer. He turned his attention back to the bomber. It had just cleared the field, edging now over Bowery Bay on a direct run toward the Hell Gate Bridge.

"Tower to Army zero five seven seven."

The loudspeaker crackled. Barden stared up at it expectantly.

"Go ahead, Tower," Smith answered. He sounded slightly annoyed at the tether Barden was holding.

"At the present time I can't see the top of the Empire State Building. Over."

The speaker remained silent for several seconds, then Smith's voice, low, tinged with an air of boredom, came on. *"Roger, Tower, thank you."* There was a loud click, like the snapping of a rifle bolt as the pilot ended his transmission. Barden watched the bomber submerge into a cloud. A moment later he was issuing landing instructions to the airliner as it broke through the overcast into the clear.

CHAPTER XII

9:55—The Moment
of Impact

IT HAD WORKED. AT 9:52 BILL SMITH
glanced down through his left window and saw the last of
the airfield's perimeter slip under the wing. The bomber was
now heading west, over the rippled scoop of Bowery Bay. For
the second time in a little over a month he had bulldozed his
way through the bramble of regulations to get where he was
going.

Flying his B-17 back from England, Smith had crossed the
Atlantic on instruments, letting down to refuel first at
Greenland, then at Newfoundland. His navigation had been
textbook-precise; the radio calls to the range stations and
military airfields had been made with the exactness of a combat
commander who had demanded nothing less of his own men.
But on the last leg of the wearying journey home, as the Flying
Fortress neared the coast of Maine, a radically different Bill
Smith was behind the controls.

With Colonel Rogner in the copilot's seat, Smith had
astonished his navigator by waving off the course he had
plotted to their destination, Bradley Field, Connecticut.
Instead, and with Rogner's wholehearted approval, Smith
exuberantly announced that he could locate the field "with
his eyes closed." Whooping and horsing around like a busload
of teenagers on a school outing, the crew and passengers

grabbed for handholds as Smith shot full-throttle, tree-level passes at six or seven airfields before locating Bradley. From Maine, through New Hampshire, down into Massachusetts and Connecticut, Smith left in his wake tower operators radioing ignored demands for the barnstorming B-17 to identify itself.

He had failed to follow his flight plan filed with the Air Transport Command in Newfoundland; disregarded his scheduled calls to range stations along the route; played roulette with the airspace around and over military and civilian fields. For one of the rare times in his life, Bill Smith raised hell. He was home, and probably for the last time flying the plane that had carried him safely through the war. At that moment it seemed perfectly natural for him to bring in his ship the way he had so many times back in England—wide-open, scooting the deck, engines screaming his joy at being alive and in command. It felt right; an allowable, if not strictly innocent, final act of bravado.

But this morning was different. Everything was estranged. The plane was not his. The weather, though foggy and rainy as it had been in England, looked and even smelled alien; the vapor formations drenched with a yellow-brown sulfurous smoke, gritty and acrid as it filtered into the cockpit. And the terrain, his surroundings, was as to a stranger. England had been palm-sized, comfortably flat; its horizon, in fog or moonless night, assured the pilots of no man-made or natural surprises. Smith had found it a human and forgiving geography.

New York was another story.

As a cadet he had traveled down from the Point on a dozen weekends, booking a room at the Barclay or staying at a classmate's apartment. No matter how often he was in Manhattan he felt a trespasser. He was a country boy used to natural contours; the rightness of a hill slope or the squirming of a river settling into a new bed were expectations he'd never been denied.

But New York was constructed to startle. It reached for you, he said. It was too big, on an island too small to have such dimension. And he was sensitive to the city's aggression—the chest-pounding power of the stone-and-glass skyscrapers; the background hum of tension that constantly played under the excitement of the bigness. No man could find his full height, stand really straight, in the city, he thought, without making comparisons—and having once made them, being diminished.

He would feel a lot easier once Manhattan was behind him.

The bomber was speeding toward the lip of Astoria Park. Smith switched on the wipers to rid the windshield of a film of soot sprayed on by the power plant's smokestacks. Just off to his right, lying under a bleak mass of fog, he caught sight of two bridges spanning a large island.

While circling La Guardia he had double-checked the map for the route he'd fly into Newark. He made a mental fix that Ward's Island, with the Triborough and Hell Gate bridges straddling the East River channel, should be to his right. He held the B-25 on course, waiting the few seconds it would take to make positive identification of the landmark. The visibility had fallen off as he approached the East River. The ground fog was climbing to a height of several hundred feet, leaving just a narrow corridor of forward vision below the pressing clouds. With a feather touch he eased the wheel forward. The bomber's nose sank. Smith peered down to his right, across the propeller's blur, to the island less than a half-mile distant. Through the scattered cloud layer he could make out lanes of cars moving along the Triborough's roadways, the traffic emptying out onto a ramp cutting through the park directly below him.

It was Ward's Island. His left foot pressured the rudder. The B-25 dipped into a turn toward Hallets Point, a bulbous spit of land jutting a portion of Astoria into the East River. Smith watched the compass rotate as he held the plane in a banking arc to the south-southwest.

Once over the East River he would run a diagonal across Manhattan on a 240-degree heading. The flight path would take him over the Hudson River, across Jersey City, beyond Newark Bay, and into Newark Field.

The bomber leveled out of the turn and started across Hallets Point. The panel clock read just shy of 9:53.

*   *   *

Standing on the bow of the Erie Railroad tug *Celia C*, Dominick Mazzuco cursed the weather as he took off his glasses and began to dry them on his oil-stained sweater.

For the past few minutes, as the stubby green-and-black boat beat its way through the heavy fog along the shore of Welfare Island, Mazzuco had been on the lookout for the flashing beacon of Mill Rock Light, off Hallets Point. The tug was cautiously moving at quarter-speed up the west channel of the East River, nearing the tip of the cigar-shaped island. The deckhand glanced to his right. Between the clinging water haze and the higher layer of fog blanketing the island, he could barely see the century-old buildings of Metropolitan Hospital.

The harsh drone of an approaching plane caught his attention. It sounded low; in fact, Mazzuco could feel the deck vibrating in rhythm with its engines. He looked across the island toward Hallets Point. The sound grew louder, carrying from behind a wall of dark clouds. He slipped his glasses on just as the silver plane nosed through a break in the layer. It *was* low; maybe 400, certainly not higher than 500 feet above the east channel, and moving on a diagonal toward the tugboat. Transfixed by the thunder of its engines, Mazzuco watched as the forward section of the plane dissolved into a fog bank levitating over the east side of the island. A moment later it reappeared.

To his atonishment he saw that the plane's landing gear was being lowered.

Brushing aside a momentary fear, Mazzuco followed the bomber as it raced across the island. The pilot must know what he was doing, he thought; why else would he be flying so low into Manhattan?

*   *   *

Watching the panel indicator, Smith saw that the wheels were coming down smoothly. He felt the plane shudder and the airspeed fall off slightly as the tricycle gear locked into place. Reaching across the control pedestal, he adjusted the throttles to maintain his 200-mph airspeed.

Moments before, as he had cleared Hallets Point and started across the river, Smith had spotted a land mass half-hidden under a thick cover of fog and haze. Large clusters of buildings set around a landscaped park fleetingly revealed themselves on the northern edge of the island. Farther south were more buildings, and what appeared to be a large factory with several towering smokestacks. The twin peaks of a steel bridge pushed through the fog near the island's midsection.

For several reasons, Smith thought that Welfare Island was Manhattan.

As he approached the river Smith had found himself locked in a dense bank of fog. The airspace surrounding the bomber formed a solid sheet of white. He had no visual reference to the ground, yet it was of little concern; as long as he kept his heading steady on 240 degrees, he would be on course.

But fog often acts like a prism, distorting objects, disorienting even the most experienced pilots. Through thinning patches or breaks in the fog bank Smith had caught glimpses of an island. The sightings were disjointed—snatches of land crowded with large, industrial-type buildings set around a park here, factory structures and more cosmopolitan-looking buildings there; a bridge stretching ethereally into a shrouding haze.

The island lay directly between what he mistakenly took to be two distinctly separate bodies of water: the river below him, running to the left of the island, he knew was the East River; the one on the far side, to the west, therefore had to be the Hudson.

Memory and the map conspired with the distorting fog and haze to enlarge the narrow land mass; Smith saw the Metropolitan Hospital complex as taller, more densely grouped, than it was in reality. The grim overcast, the rain beading the windshield, the scattered reflections from the river's surface—all acted as a magnifying lens to swell the less-than-two-mile-long island sitting in the middle of the East River into gargantuan size.

It was Manhattan not Welfare Island because Smith wanted it to be.

Topography, landmarks, time, and distance were redrawn from his memory of weekends in the city to fit the immediate desire to put New York behind him. The Queensboro Bridge, ghosting black and directionless above the fog blanketing 59th Street, could logically, in Smith's mind, be either the Brooklyn or Manhattan Bridge—structures his experience told him were located much farther south, near the tip of Manhattan. But the partnership of weather and anxiety pushed Smith to accept a shifting geography. Instinct, and the vague outline of what he took to be the New Jersey shore lying behind the island, had guided his hand to the landing-gear lever. Once past Manhattan he knew that it was only six or seven miles to Newark Field.

He was flying at 500 feet as he began his letdown over the East River. Ahead, through the milky vapor whipping across the windshield, Smith saw the tall apartment buildings lining Sutton Place. The panel clock was edging toward 9:54 as the bomber cut over the center span of the Queensboro Bridge at 59th Street. Smith began to relax. Within seconds now he would be crossing into what he was convinced was Jersey City. Straining to see beyond the masking fog, he attempted to locate Newark Bay.

*   *   *

In her top-floor apartment on York Avenue and 61st Street, Elise Anderson was stirring milk into a steaming pot of oatmeal. Suddenly the entire kitchen seemed to explode with a deafening rumble. Pots and pans hanging on a rack over the stove began to clang like steeple bells. The frying pan danced off the burner, splattering the floor with a half-dozen basted eggs. The sheet of glass in the window facing the Queensboro Bridge rattled like a machine gun.

"My God!" she exclaimed. "It's working!" The startled reference was to the marijuana cigarette she had smoked a half-hour earlier with several fellow art students who were in the living room awaiting breakfast. Until this trembling upheaval, Elise, who had never tried the narcotic before, had thought its powers were highly overrated. She hadn't hallucinated and was feeling only the slightest bit giddy. Or so she had thought. Out of the corner of her eye she caught an object moving past the window. She turned and watched the silver plane shoot over the bridge, heading on a diagonal toward Rockefeller Center. Its wheels were down, and it looked so close that for an instant, had the window been open, she thought she probably could have reached out and grabbed its wing. Mesmerized, she stared after the retreating bomber, trying to remember if she had seen anything in the newspapers about an airport having been built on top of one of the skyscrapers. It seemed to her that she had.

*   *   *

Walking his beat on Lexington Avenue, Patrolman Albert Schneider had reached the corner of 56th Street when he heard a thunderous roar overhead. He, and an elderly deliveryman dragging a cash register on a dolly, looked up as the B-25 moved through a scattered layer of fog and clouds. They glimpsed only pieces of the plane as it traversed the avenue to the southwest. The old fellow winced at the echoing racket and shook his head.

"It's a wonder they don't hit one of these buildings," he said to Schneider with a nervous laugh. "I guess they must teach those guys pretty good."

"Not *that* good!" the policeman said. His eyes fixed to the overcast, Schneider was tracking the sound of the plane's engines. He lived close to La Guardia Field, and had developed an ability to determine an aircraft's distance, altitude, and direction just by its sound.

"That ship's in trouble if he doesn't get higher," he told the deliveryman. "He's heading straight for Radio City"— Schneider slapped his nightstick into his palm for emphasis— "and he ain't gonna make it!"

*   *   *

Something was wrong.

Even as he had crossed the bridge Smith had noticed that the buildings facing the river seemed too high, too massed together, for Jersey City. And the docks crowded with freighters and barges. And the railroad yards with their tracks running spur lines onto the piers. *Where were they?* Could he have missed them in the fog? He had a sinking feeling that he hadn't. Twice before, when he had landed at Newark Field from Sioux Falls, and again when he had taken off for Boston, he had seen the flat industrial town from the air. It lay to the northeast of Newark Field, sprawling unmistakably between the Hudson and Newark Bay. At the speed he was traveling he should have spotted the large island waterway by now.

His eyes were darting from the windshield to the cockpit's side windows. The fog was thickening. His only visibility was straight down through the left window, and even then he had just veiled sightings of rooftops and streets, an impression of a city.

"What's that?" Domitrovich was jabbing Smith's shoulder with his left hand, his right pointing directly ahead. The sergeant's voice sounded more awed than startled.

Smith drew his attention from the ground to the windshield. A point off the bomber's nose he saw the bulk of a towering object waiting behind the fog. It loomed gray and massive.

"It's a building." Smith said it as a fact, crisply, in a dead calm.

It was almost a relief to have the sighting. The skyscraper confirmed his intuition. He was somewhere over Manhattan. His left hand and foot were coordinating the bomber into a climbing left bank as he grasped the throttles with his right hand. The engines surged with increased power. He pulled his eyes from the windshield to make certain his hand had moved to the correct levers to change the prop pitch. He slammed the ganged knobs into the locked position. The changeover made the engines sound angry as the propellers took chomping bites of the air. He flicked a glance down to his right as he grasped the landing-gear lever and snapped it into the up position. He heard the hydraulics grind and begin to draw the wheels up into the fuselage. He desperately needed to be free of their drag *now*, but he knew that it would take an agonizing twenty seconds before they were sucked into place.

The building was starting to fall away to the right. He increased the bank. His eyes jumped to the altimeter. The needle was climbing past 550 feet. He tore his glance away from the dial and searched the control pedestal for the supercharger blowers. He located the levers and jerked them into the high position, then pushed the arms opening the oil-cooler shutters and the engine cowl flaps. His mind had been racing to remember the B-25's hastily learned technical orders. But now he became aware of a pounding sound coming from somewhere behind the cockpit bulkhead.

It was Perna shouting. "Look out! Look out!" as he slammed his fist against the steel partition separating him from the flight deck. He was arched forward, the safety harness cutting into his stomach as he stared through the windshield. Another building was catapulting out of the fog. It seemed less than 100 feet away, its roof level with the bomber.

Reacting to the terror in Perna's voice, Smith hauled back on the control column even before he saw the granite tower.

*   *   *

In her 12th-floor office at 485 Madison Avenue, Adele Halpern was conscious of the plane drawing closer. For the past half-minute the lettering pens and ink pots on her drafting table had been vibrating with its approach.

She was used to planes flying low over midtown, but this one sounded *too* low. The thought flashed through her mind that maybe it was in trouble. Lost in the fog or having mechanical problems. Diving toward her building! With a panicked urgency she swung off the high stool and started out of the partitioned cubicle. Sheets of art work thumbtacked to a bulletin board sailed to the floor as the plane roared directly overhead. Instinctively, she ducked her head, then, realizing the danger had passed, she ran to the window and looked out across to Fifth Avenue.

For an instant she glimpsed the plane through a hazy patch in the overcast. It was pivoting on its left wing as it veered over 51st Street. Horrified, yet incapable of tearing herself away from the window, she waited for the plane to crash into the top of the International Building in Rockefeller Center.

*   *   *

Jan King had raced out of the lunch bar on the roof of the RCA Building. Pressing against the east parapet sixty-nine stories above Rockefeller Center, he felt totally helpless peering into the swirling fog obscuring Fifth Avenue.

A former radio operator for Delta Airlines, King had known the ship was in trouble the instant he'd heard the props change pitch. Risking balance, he leaned farther over the low wall. The fog was impenetrable. The hammering engines grasping for altitude reminded him of a locomotive hurtling through a tunnel.

"Pull up! ... Pull up! ... Pull up! ... " King continued the shouted cadence as he caught sight of the plane. It was no more than 50 feet distant and about 100 feet below him as it banked directly over the International Building's rooftop garden. The propellers cut a swath through the overcast, allowing him to see the bomber clear the building by less than 25 feet. Within a blink the fog closed in behind it.

*   *   *

The pulsing sound of the plane's engines had carried down to Park Avenue and 34th Street. From his bathroom window on the top floor of the Vanderbilt Hotel, David McKay was startled to see a B-25 swing out of a fog bank over the RCA Building and head down Fifth Avenue.

While shaving he had been studying the clouds and fog rolling across the midtown area. From his vantage point almost a mile to the south he saw that the overcast was scattered; portions of the city were lying under a filmy haze, while in other areas heavy fog obliterated entire groups of skyscrapers. Looking toward 42nd Street, he could clearly see the Chrysler Building's chromed spire, yet almost directly in front of his window the top third of the Empire State was invisible behind a leaden field of clouds. The area where the bomber was moving into had the lowest ceiling, less than 600 feet, McKay judged. But the airspace directly below the plane was only slightly hazy. If he could easily pick out the twin peaks of St. Patrick's Cathedral, surely the pilot could. Why, then, he asked himself with mounting apprehension, was the plane flying so low among the towering buildings?

The phone in the bedroom rang. Startled, McKay turned toward the sound, then instantly jerked his attention back to the plane. It was gone. He heard its engines coming from behind an opaque layer of clouds.

*   *   *

"Six twenty-five . . . six thirty-five . . . six forty-five . . . " Domitrovich was calling out the altimeter reading.

Smith eased the wheel a hair more to the right. He was cautiously, blindly leveling out of the banking left turn. "Where's the gear?" He didn't dare pull his eyes from the windshield.

The sergeant shot a look at the dial in front of him. "A third up!" Slow. Too slow. The drag was anchoring their rate of climb. He started to glance out his window.

Smith caught the movement out of the corner of his eye. "Altimeter!" he snapped. Every foot was precious.

"Six sixty . . . six seventy . . . " Domitrovich was shouting to overcome the howling engines as Smith added more throttle. "Coming through seven hundred, colonel!"

Seven hundred feet above *where*? Smith demanded of himself. Altitude was not enough. The fog wrapping itself around the plane was hiding all landmarks. He was smack in the center of Manhattan—that and only that much was certain. He gambled a fleeting look at the compass. South. Maybe a trace west of due south. The fact was useless by itself, meaningless without another reference. What was he north of? What was the fog concealing to his left or right? His eyes dropped to the airspeed indicator. The needle was quivering on 250. Another dismembered fact. Was 250 miles per hour too slow or breakneck fast for his blind flight path? The building he had just missed by a whisper was over 600 feet high. The structure directly behind it had been taller still, its top buried in the fog. Was he moving deeper into the canyons of skyscrapers, or had he already miraculously, with sheer dumb luck, passed over the city's tallest buildings? Were they clustered together, all jammed into a dense mass as he had thought on those weekend vacations from the Point? Or could they actually have been spaced farther apart, separated by channels of open air that would offer a safe passage through the aerial minefield?

He was scavenging his memory for the map he knew was imprinted in its recesses. Disjointed impressions were flashing on and off like lights on a busy switchboard. The Radio City Music Hall. Times Square. The Camel cigarette sign with the man blowing tire-sized smoke rings. Central Park. There were tall buildings, hotels, facing the park. He had stayed once at the Sherry-Netherland. Too low. The buildings around him were much higher. Forty-second Street had tall buildings, near Grand Central Station. The Chrysler Building. The Empire State.

"At the present time I can't see the top of the Empire State Building."

The message had been meaningless when the La Guardia tower operator had given him the information; isolating the landmark had had no relevance to his situation then. He had gone to the top, the 102nd floor, with his roommate, Skip Young. That was when? . . . four or five years ago. They had looked *down* on the Chrysler Building—on the entire city. The largest buildings looked like Monopoly-set pieces. Where was it? Could he have passed it?

"Wheels half up!" Domitrovich shouted. "Seven ten feet!"

*   *   *

"Bloody idiot!" Captain Thorolf Ingall muttered as the plane thundered overhead. The British Intelligence officer dropped the report he was reading and swiveled his chair to the window behind him. The fog and cloud layer had lowered even more than when he had last glanced through his windows on the 36th floor of the British Empire Building. Scanning the overcast across 50th Street, he located the bomber as it emerged from a rolling mass of fog. It was moving crablike to the south, angled toward Sixth Avenue.

His secretary had joined him at the window. "Look at his wheels," he said, tapping the glass. "Seem a bit off, don't they?" The wheel struts were canted inward under each wing. The secretary nodded. "I guess he must be coming in to land somewhere." Ingall watched as the plane's nose seemed to drop in a slight downward glide. Perhaps she's right, he thought. But certainly the pilot had to see that he was heading directly toward the Salmon Tower. The 700-foot building was sitting on the corner of Fifth Avenue and 42nd Street.

*   *   *

The B-25's pounding engines were attracting attention throughout the midtown area. Pedestrians and motorists, officeworkers, hotel guests, and apartment dwellers were staring into the overcast, searching for the source of their sudden apprehension. Manhattanites deaf to the cacophony of subway trains and snarled traffic, born with immunity to unending barrages of demolition and construction, insulated against the unique and unnoticing of the bizarre—all were now listening to the drama unfolding overhead.

Stopped for a light at Fifth Avenue and 45th Street, Stan Lomax, the sports announcer for radio station WOR, glanced up through his rain-spotted windshield and searched the sky. He felt the pavement under his tires shake with the plane's closeness. Even before he spotted the bomber racing toward the Salmon Tower, he was climbing out of the car and jumping onto the running board. He heard himself pleading: "Climb, you damn fool, climb!"

Annette Dutton was having difficulty breathing. Standing in the doorway of the shoe store where she worked on Fifth Avenue and 43rd Street, she watched the silver plane slice above a row of towering office buildings. The turbulent overcast and the menacing engines brought back her memories of the London blitz. For three years she had lived through the firebombings and German rockets. It had been only in the last

few weeks that her nightmares had begun to taper off. "He's
going to hit it sure as hell!" shouted a man standing next to
her. He sounded superior in his safety, a spectator more than
half-hoping to see a fall from the high wire. Annette turned to
him with the thought of overcoming her shyness and telling
him to shut up. Instead, she felt her hand pummeling his face,
saw his glasses shatter and a ribbon of blood start down his
cheek. She found herself screaming exactly as she had in her
nightmares.

In his 16th-floor room in the Hotel Commodore, Mort
Cooper was sitting on the bed fitting a new flint in his lighter.
The Boston Braves pitcher was listening to music, relaxing
before taking a cab to Ebbets Field for his afternoon game
against the Dodgers. He had subconsciously picked up the
drone of the plane when it was still far off, then became
annoyed as the rumbling engines began to echo down 42nd
Street. Now his room was literally quaking, as if an avalanche
were descending. Bolting to the window, Cooper looked up to
his right. He recognized the bomber as a Billy Mitchell.
Through a shifting break in the fog he watched the plane's left
wing dip almost imperceptibly, then the angle deepened
slightly. Thank God! Cooper thought, he's seen the building.
He waited for the plane to heel more to the left. To his horror
he saw the wing abruptly come back up to a level position. The
bomber was moving over 43rd Street.

Coming out of Grand Central Station, Walter Daniels, the
New York *Times* day cable editor, stopped under the canopy to
light his pipe. Suddenly he became aware of a great movement
on both sides of 42nd Street. People were surging toward Fifth
Avenue, their faces turned upward, some pointing off to the
west. Then he heard the plane. The engines had been so loud,
the noise seemingly so close at hand, that he had dismissed it as
normal. Con Edison and the phone company were always
jackhammering the streets. His reporter's instinct triggered, he
fell in with the crowd. "What is it? What's happening?"
Daniels asked a heavy-set woman running alongside. She was
cradling two net shopping bags overflowing with old
newspapers. "I don't know," she puffed. "Somebody said a

plane's gonna crash." Daniels stopped. He watched the woman shove her way through the mass of people racing toward the ominous thunder. He hesitated, then looked up. The plane, appearing to him more like a shadow skimming the fog, was about to collide with the Salmon Building.

*   *   *

Old John Feather Merchant was approaching 42nd Street at four miles a minute. An instant past, over 44th Street, Smith had committed himself to turning east, heading back to La Guardia Field.

With his visibility still totally obscured, he had leveled out of the climb, risking that he had enough altitude to clear any surrounding buildings lurking behind the fog. The left wing had just started to dip when he glimpsed metal suspended in a shallow patch of haze. It had been angled to his left, at eye level. At first he thought it was a reflection off his prop blades. Then, as he deepened the bank, he made another veiled sighting. Stone! and rows of windows! He kicked right rudder, aborting the turn. That path was closed. He would have to find another.

The bomber continued on past the Chrysler Building.

*   *   *

In his 39th Street office, James Jagger slipped a fresh plastic recording disk into the Sound Scriber and continued his dictation. "And so, in conclusion, any encouragement you can give would be greatly appreciated. Sincerely." The civil engineer placed the letter on top of a pile sitting on his desk and picked up another. Settling deeper into his leather chair, he scanned it for a moment, then began: "Letter to Dean Crawford, University of Michigan. Dear Dean Crawford. I have just discovered . . ." The drone which had set his windows vibrating moments ago had suddenly become shockingly loud. With singular concentration Jagger ignored the intrusion and proceeded. " . . . that my schedule precludes the visit I had hoped . . ." It was impossible to continue. As it was, he had caught himself almost shouting into the microphone. Normally unafflicated with curiosity, Jagger rose and crossed to the window, wondering if he should issue a complaint. The

city was noisy enough, he thought, without some fool adding
to it. He looked across toward the Salmon Building. Just as he
had suspected—a plane. A bomber from the look of it. He
watched, his head shaking in disapproval, as the aircraft
seemed to teeter crazily, its wings dipping first to the right,
then to the left as it barely scraped over the top of the buff-
colored building. It continued a boomerang climb over the
42nd Street Library, then leveled out and headed down Fifth
Avenue. It struck Jagger that the pilot would most likely play
the same juvenile game when he reached the Empire State. He
turned back to his dictation.

*   *   *

It was as if the air above the city had become partitioned, a
Byzantine maze. For the three men traveling in the fog, time
and direction ceased to exist. The compass pointed south. The
altimeter registered 725 feet. The artificial horizon indicated
that the aircraft was in a slight climbing attitude. The panel
clock reported seconds less than 9:55. The bomber was closing
the seven-block distance to the Empire State Building at 127
yards per second.

*   *   *

Nanette Morrison had been struggling with the press
release for the last ten minutes. The weather boiling past her
tower windows overlooking Fifth Avenue and 40th Street had
an urgency and beauty far exceeding the description of the
stock venture in her typewriter. The rampaging sound of the
plane's engines gave her new reason to search the sky. Over 41st
Street she saw a cloud tear open and the bomber appeared. It
was startlingly close, its left wing bridging the distance to her
window with a steppingstone gap. Like suction pumps the
propellers dredged the fog clear of the fuselage, allowing her to
see the men in the cockpit. Through his open window, the
pilot was peering toward the ground. She raised her hand in
the start of a wave, then froze. The bomber shot past, creating a
shock wave that toppled a crystal bud vase sitting on her desk to
the floor. Overcoming her numbed horror, she threw the

window open and leaned out, oblivious to her lifelong dread of heights. The plane seemed to be climbing, its twin tail slightly lower than the nose as it crossed 38th Street. The climb was so agonizingly slow that Nanette Morrison felt she might go mad watching the bomber, as if on a cable, being pulled toward the Empire State. At 37th Street she heard the engines suddenly grow louder. The plane seemed to hover momentarily in its climb, then the left wing dropped violently. At 35th Street, too slow, too late, she watched it begin a turn to the east. Her hands intertwined, fingers working like rosary beads, she began to chant a whispered "Oh no . . . Oh no . . .Oh no . . . Oh no . . ."

*   *   *

The claxon blast of the stall-warning horn filled the cockpit as Smith pulled the last inch of the control column into his chest. The bomber's nose was almost vertical now, the right wing vaulted perpendicular to the face of the building. At 975 feet above 34th Street the windshield was being filled with pockmarked blocks of limestone and crome mullions dividing windows. And behind the windows, on the 79th floor of the Empire State Building, the men in the bomber could see people seated at their desks.

*   *   *

Gripping the troopship *Winnipeg*'s bow rail, Major Jean Mayer swept the shoreline for the target of the explosive thud. A split-second before the hollow, crumping sound had carried across the Hudson, Mayer had been watching the fog shrouding the tall buildings around 34th Street. Allowing for the distance and sound-distorting characteristics of water, the major was nevertheless certain that somewhere in the city a bomb had gone off. So were the men around him. Hundreds were pressing the starboard rail, their voices rising in anxiety as they searched the skyline.

In a sudden rush, the clouds that had been secreting the top of the Empire State vanished. With perfect clarity, Mayer saw an arrow of orange flame streak out from the north face of the building—high up, near the observation deck, narrow, rolling outward as if being spit from a chemical flamethrower. There was a second explosion, massive this time, a full four or five seconds after the first. The concussive blast seemed of unmistakable origin to the men on the *Winnipeg*.

"Rockets!" a young GI standing next to Mayer shouted. "The Japs are bombing the city!" His panicked cry raced through the troops massed on the deck. "They're using German V-2s!" yelled another man. Mayer was being crushed against the rail as a wave of bodies pushed onto the bow. The flames had mushroomed over the tower mast, predominantly black now, flecked with splotches of deep, hot orange. As the ship moved past the building, Mayer saw rivers of fire sluicing down the center section, pieces falling off in jellied clumps and dropping down onto 34th Street. Throughout the harbor, ships were sounding their horns and whistles in emergency blasts. Tearing his attention away from the holocaust, the major looked off toward the dock where his wife was waiting. He thanked God that so far none of the rockets had fallen in that area.

*   *   *

For seconds after the bomber crashed an eerie silence surrounded the building. In contrast to the ear-shattering roar of the plane's approach, the sound of the impact had been curiously muffled.

To Patrolman Harold Voelbel, directing traffic at the intersection of 34th Street and Fifth Avenue, it had been a distant door slam; in fact, at first Voelbel thought the plane had missed the building, that the hollow boom had been an echo of its engines. For Theodore Eusebi, parking his car on the south side of 34th Street directly beneath the building, the crash was not unlike the sound of a tire running over a tin can, a sudden metallic flattening. Emerging from McCreery's, where he had just finished washing the inside of the large display windows, Horace Walters had the impression of a thunderclap rumbling across from New Jersey. On an inspection tour along Fifth Avenue, Fire Lieutenant William

Murphy had just reached Alarm Box 681 when he heard what he took to be an auto accident, the crunching grind of fenders suddenly meeting.

*   *   *

Reaching the door of the barber shop on 33rd Street, Ed Cummings and Jack McCloskey had heard a dull, scraping sound echo under the engines' thunder. Cummings turned and looked across Park Avenue to the Empire State. At that instant he saw the clouds surrounding the tower blown away. A gusher of flame was shooting out of the north face, just beneath the 86th-floor observation deck. McCloskey had opened the door and was starting inside. Cummings gripped his arm. "Oh, my God, Jack—look!" McCloskey turned and peered off in the direction of Cummings' outstretched arm. Within the moment it took for him to grasp that the building was on fire, McCloskey's normally florid face had drained white. "Holy Mother of . . . " he started. An explosion, unbridled, from deep within the flaming section, cut him short. The men saw large, odd-shaped chunks of debris hurled with volcanic fury into the space over 34th Street. Rivulets of molten fire were running down the northeast corner of the structure.

Coatless, bearing traces of shaving cream on his face, Father Swanstrom pushed past the men and stared up at the building. As if attempting to mask the damage, the clouds and fog had again settled over the tower area. With grim urgency, the priest was silently reckoning the stories below the charred billows of smoke that poured through the cloud layer. "Do you think its our offices, Father?" Cummings asked quietly. He was shaking. Swanstrom continued to stare at the building, certain that if answered immediately he'd burst into tears. "Whoever's they are," he finally managed, "they'll need help." He turned to Cummings. "Go to St. Francis. Ask them to send over as many priests as they can. Tell them to bring their holy oils." Without waiting for McCloskey, Swanstrom took off on a dead run for the building.

*   *   *

In the time between the bomber's impact and the second
explosion, a yellow-and-red Desoto Skyview cab had entered
the intersection commanded by Patrolman Voelbel. Behind
the wheel, Raphael Gomez was watching the traffic officer
perform a series of startling maneuvers. With his hands raised
over his head, Voelbel was bent at the waist, his feet making
small, shuffling hops around a manhole cover like a Navajo
rain dancer. Then, spinning around, he straightened and
turned his face to the sky. One of his white-gloved hands was
thrust out in a shielding gesture. Gomez started to laugh, his
eyes darting to the rear-view mirror. "Hey, you see that?" he
asked his passenger. "What's that crazy guy doing?" The taxi's
forward motion was suddenly diverted into a sickening skid as
a flaming bar of metal cleaved the hood. The rear end of the
cab jumped inches with the impact. Gomez was fighting the
wheel, flooring the brake pedal, as the vehicle, its wheels
locked, slid like an ice boat across Fifth Avenue. It leaped the
curb at precisely the moment of the second explosion and came
to a jarring halt against a fire hydrant. The blast deafened
Gomez; he thought his cab had been squarely hit by an artillery
shell. Recalling his days in Havana when Batista had taken
over the government, Gomez scrambled from the taxi and,
wild-eyed, raced off shouting, "Madre mia! La Revolución!"

For at least five hundred people, the intersection had taken
on the terror of a battlefield. Chunks of stone and flaming
metal rained down on the four corners bordering Fifth Avenue.
Skeletal sections of the plane—wing ribs, fuel tanks, a 58-
pound piece of the tail structure, a 109-pound portion of the
landing gear—crashed down in an area hundreds of yards in all
directions. Jagged shards of glass shattered against the
sidewalks, trickled along the gutters; miniature lakes erupted
exploding like grenade shrapnel on the roofs of passing cars.
Like a biblical rain of fire, hundreds of gallons of blazing
gasoline showered down from the blackened sky. Puddles of
reddish high-octane fuel formed in the streets, on the
sidewalks trickled along the gutters; miniature lakes erupted

into flaming islands as burning drops of fuel set them off in a chain reaction.

About to begin washing the outside of McCreery's display windows, Horace Walters set his long-handled brush into the bucket of soapy water. The second blast knocked him off balance. Startled, still thinking the tremendous roar was thunder, he looked over his shoulder to the clouds above the Empire State. He never saw the hurtling slab of wing flap that exploded the 10-foot-square sheet of glass less than two yards to his left. He felt a stabbing pain in his right hand.

Dodging the falling debris, Voelbel began evacuating the screaming, panicked pedestrians from the area. He herded a woman whose cheek had been flayed open by glass into a doorway. An elderly man, wailing incoherently, refused to get off the sidewalk, where he had been dropped by a shaft of metal lancing his leg. Voelbel picked him up with a scooping motion and deposited him in the doorway of Altman's department store. A woman standing on the northwest corner was screaming that she couldn't see. A man was rolling on the pavement in front of the Oppenheim Collins store, his suit jacket still smoking from burning fuel. Like a performer in a ballet written by Dante, Voelbel was leaping across patches of flaming concrete, running through clouds of oily black smoke, warding off hailstorms of glass in his rescue efforts. In passing, he saw Patrolman Harold Kennedy throw open the police call box in front of McCreery's.

Staring numbly at the streams of liquid fire running down the face of the building, Kennedy heard the desk sergeant's voice come over the phone with a stale "Midtown South— Sergeant Phalen." Kennedy's mind suddenly went blank. He opened his mouth and made a coughing sound. He tried again, with the same result. A third time produced the best and most succinct statement he could muster: "This is Kennedy—Badge 3772. I want to report a very unusual occurrence. I think a plane just hit the Empire State Building." There was a long pause, then the sergeant blandly asked: "Kennedy, where are you?"

*   *   *

Seconds before the crash, Mrs. Oswald Hering had been standing in her penthouse living room in the Waldorf Building, drawing on a pair of white gloves. The approaching plane had set up a series of vibrations through the old structure. The wood floorboards and plaster walls were oscillating in tempo to the quickening thunder. The panes in the skylight overhead joined in with an ominous timbre. At the very peak of the engines' crescendo the elderly widow heard a metallic thump, as if an empty oil drum had tumbled from a distant height. Then silence.

It was the sudden, unexpected silence that caused her to glance through the skylight to the Empire State. *That's ridiculous,* Mrs. Hering thought, *the plane couldn't have possibly hit the building.* She searched the sky on either side of the towering structure, certain that the aircraft would momentarily appear through the fog.

She saw it first as a tiny flicker of orange darting through the clouds obscuring the observatory level. Then, as the gray shroud abruptly lifted, Mrs. Hering saw a section of the building explode open. Massive chunks of masonry were hurtling out of a tunnellike hole just below the 86th floor. Behind the cascading boulders she caught sight of something being catapulted out of the building. The large object was flaming, trailing a plume of oily black smoke as it plunged over 33rd Street, heading directly toward her penthouse.

*   *   *

In his 12th floor office in the Waldorf Building, Joseph Bing gave a startled cry as he was lifted out of his chair and pitched to the floor. The entire building was shuddering under the impact of the bomber's 1,100-pound forward landing gear and a 340-pound section of an engine.

The room seemed to be coming down around him. Slabs of plaster and wooden joists tore loose from the ceiling, threatening to bury him in a choking rubble. The windows had shattered, sending shreds of glass pinging off the walls like snipers' bullets. The room was beginning to fill with smoke, black and heavy with the smell of gasoline. And above the confused shouts of his workers Bing heard Mrs. Hering screaming in the penthouse directly above him. Staggering to his feet, he grabbed the fire extinguisher off the wall and groped his way out of the office. With several workers falling in behind, Bing bolted up the flight of stairs leading to the roof.

He was greeted with utter devastation. Through a suffocating wall of smoke he saw flames raging out of Henry Hering's studio. The skylight and three of the walls had been blasted open, littering the roof with a maze of bricks and timbers. In the very center of the holocaust, rising like a pheonix, was the sculptor's plaster model of his famous statue *Pro Patria*. By some quirk the 22-foot statue had remained standing, virtually untouched. The acrid fumes were searing Bing's lungs as he strained to see throught he smoke to Mrs. Hering's penthouse. The flames roaring out of the studio had ignited a pile timbers and furniture strewn in front of her apartment.

"Mrs. Hering!" Bing shouted. "Are you all right?" There was silence. Handing the extinguisher to one of the men, Bing tied his handkerchief around his nose and mouth and plunged across the roof. Three times he stumbled to his knees over obstacles hidden by the blinding smoke before reaching her door. He pounded on it. "Mrs. Hering! Are you in there?" No answer. Thinking it locked, Bing threw his shoulder against the door. It flew open. Through the smoke pouring in from the shattered skylight he saw the old woman standing rigidly against the far wall. A glance told him that she was in shock, numbed and incapable of moving. As he started toward her, Bing noticed that she was staring blankly at an object lying on the rug in front of her.

"You're safe now, Mrs. Hering," Bing said gently. He took her arm and attempted to lead her toward the door. She stood rooted, resisting his pressure. Her eyes remained fixed on the object. Bing glanced down, then quickly turned away and gagged. It was a woman's hand, torn off at the wrist. A gold wedding band remained firmly on the ring finger. The red nail polish still retained its gloss. Keeping his eyes averted, Bing

took a stronger grip on Mrs. Hering's arm and pulled her out of
the penthouse.

*   *   *

In the minute remaining before the bomber crashed into
the building, the workers on the 79th-floor office of the
Catholic War Relief Services had settled into a well-trod
rhythm.

In the north section Paul Dearing was nearing the end of
his story on the returning war veterans. Moments before he had
called the dock master to check on the arrival times of the
troopships. He was surprised to learn that they were expected
ahead of schedule. If anything, it seemed to him that clouds
and fog cutting off his uptown view of Fifth Avenue had grown
thicker. But experience had cautioned him against the folly of
attempting to judge the weather from his perch 975 feet above
the city. There were days when the sun could be streaming
through his windows, while just a few floors below a layer of
clouds released a deluge on the streets.

"Paul, got time for coffee?" Kay O'Connor asked. She was
leaning into the office, her arms straddling the doorway.
Dearing swung around, glancing at his watch. "Are you
having it sent up?"

She extended her finger toward the floor. "Walgreen's
with Mary. Soon as I finish the mail." Dearing hesitated, then
shook his head. "I don't think so, I've got to wrap this up.
Thanks anyway." She nodded and started off. "Hey, I almost
forgot," Dearing called out. Kay popped her head back in.

"Do you know if Monsignor O'Boyle got around to
checking that press release I left on his desk yesterday
afternoon?"

"Last night, just before quitting time, naturally. I put in a
half hour overtime typing the ditto."

"What did he think of it?" Dearing asked.

"For a reporter, he said you write like Shakespeare."

Dearing threw his hands up in mock helplessness. "That
bad, huh? Well, at least I'm moving up in class. Last week it
was Walter Winchell."

Moving back into the central office, Kay selected two letters from the dwindling stack of mail and crossed to John Judge's desk. He was leaning back in his chair with his eyes closed, dictating to Jeanne Sozzi in a low monotone. Kay dropped the envelope into his "in" basket, then turned and loked across the room toward Mary Kedzierska's office. The čubicle was empty. Through the glass partition she saw a cigarette burning on the lip of an ashtray.

"Where'd Mary disappear to?" she asked Anne Gerlach.

Planting her finger on a line of the report she was reading, Anne looked up with a befuddled expression. "She's right here," she said, pointing to Mary Lou Taylor seated at the next desk.

"She means Mary K., Miss Gerlach," Mary Lou said. "I saw her heading back to the files just a second ago. Do you want me to get her for you, Miss O'Connor?"

Kay shook her head with an appreciative smile. "I'll be going back there in a minute." Since coming to the charity as a summer replacement secretary, Mary Lou had become a favorite of Kay's. Aside from her spontaneity and cheerful outlook on life, Kay found that of all the young girls in the office, Mary Lou was the only one who consistently had the good manners not to address her elders by their first names. For a moment it crossed her mind to invite Mary Lou down to the drugstore for coffee; then she decided against it. Mary Kedzierska was peculiar about fraternizing with anyone on the staff who wasn't an executive. Instead, Kay made a mental note to ask Mary Lou to lunch one day. She was curious to learn why someone so vivacious and attractive had decided to enter a convent at the end of summer.

Joe Fountain was on the phone, peering at the fog eddying past his windows as Kay entered the office. She waved several envelopes to gain his attention, dropped them on the desk, and started out. Fountain snapped his fingers and held his hand up, signaling for her to wait. A few words told her that he was talking to his wife, pregnant with their fifth child and due to give birth any day now.

Fountain was surveying the litter of reports and budget sheets lying on his desk. "I'll be home around four, honey," he said into the phone. "If you feel up to it, maybe we'll get a sitter

and go out for a bite and a movie. See you later." He hung up
and motioned Kay over to the window.

She had already broken into a smile. Fountain was an
inveterate practical joker, a man truly blessed, Kay thought,
with a sense of humor that allowed him to locate the
improbable or incongruous in most situations and translate it
into fun.

He had picked up a coffe mug from the desk and was
offering it to her. "Feel like a drink?" he asked with a sly wink.

A little early, isn't it? What's the occasion?"

He pointed in a direction across Sixth Avenue. "Can't
turn it down when it's on the house."

Through the window Kay saw a huge Four Roses liquor
bottle hovering above the cloud layer just beyond Macy's
department store. It was tilted at a pouring angle, a stream of
golden liquid flowing out of the mouth. The rest of the
billboard and its scaffolding was completely hidden by the
clouds and fog.

"You nut!" Kay laughed, playfully punching Fountain's
arm.

In the reception foyer, Lucille Bath was struggling to
finish the last chapter of *Bugles in Her Heart*, a romantic novel
of frontier days.

It was a toss-up which was more boring—the book or
sitting behind the switchboard. She released a long-suffering
sigh and closed the volume as Kay swept through the wooden
gate.

She read the youngster's morose look and offered a
cheering grin. "Buck up, Lucille, only two more hours till the
cell doors open."

Lucille returned a halfhearted smile. "It sure is dragging
this morning. It must be the weather. Whenever it rains I feel
like staying in bed all day." She loosened another plaintive
sigh, reaching for a cable to quiet the buzzing switchboard. *Ah,
youth,* Kay laughed to herself. Only a teenager like Lucille
could contort boredom into excruciating pain. She suddenly
felt jealous for the memory.

Entering the south portion of the office, Kay spotted Mary Kedzierska at the far end talking to Ellen Lowe and crossed to her.

"I'm done. You ready to go now?" Kay asked.

Mary reached up and adjusted the pearl stickpin in her turban. "Can you wait a couple of minutes? I've just got to check some figures." She turned back to Ellen. "I need the complete Mexican budget, not just the quarterly. Okay?" She flashed the young, blond secretary a smile meant to prepay the act.

Only Ellen's voice, a touch brittle, hinted at her annoyance. "Can I finish this letter? It'll take just a minute or two."

"I really need it now, dear," Mary said, her smile just slightly less generous. She turned to Kay. "If you want to go down, I'll meet you there in about five minutes."

"No problem," Kay said, "I've got some filing that's just screaming to be done."

Ellen waited until Mary was out of earshot. "I swear, that woman must think she runs this place. She's got her own secretary." She pushed her chair back in a miff and started toward the row of wooden file cabinets resting against the opposite wall.

"Mary probably has her drowning in work," Kay said, feeling a need to soften her friend's somewhat officious manner.

Ellen pulled open a drawer and began rummaging through the crowded files. "The least she could've done was waited for it. I'm not her maid, you know."

Kay was listening to the rumbling sound grow louder. She had picked it up seconds before, while it was still a distant, muffled drone. It seemed to come from the north end of the office.

"I wonder what *that* is!" she said. The vibrations shooting through the floor made her voice sound quavery.

Therese Fortier looked up from her typewriter. "Sounds like a subway train, doesn't it?" she said with a startled laugh.

Paul Dearing was the first to see the bomber. It was banking out of a cloud layer in an almost vertical climb less than twenty yards away. He leaped to his feet and started to turn from the desk when the plane hit. The sudden concussion jerked him backward and hurled him through the closed window. His body fell seven floors before coming to rest on the roof of the 72nd-story setback.

At 250 miles per hour, the 12-ton plane was invading the building with astonishing effortlessness. The blunted Plexiglas nose had made the initial entry through a row of windows directly behind John Judge's desk. Both Judge and Jeanne Sozzi were crushed instantly as the fuselage continued to gouge deeper into the office.

Because its left wing was dropped slightly below the 78th floor, the B-25 was tearing through the War Relief Services office at an upward angle. The raised cockpit flattened like an egg carton as it made contact with a 16-inch beam imbedded in the ceiling just behind the windows. The 2,000-pound column of steel, yielding with a memory of its once molten state, arched up into the 80th floor, slicing open the top of the fuselage as it traveled through the widening passage. The right wing, almost perpendicular to the 20-foot hole in the limestone facing, sheared off in sections. The fuel tanks burst open, spewing hundreds of gallons of the pinkish gasoline ahead of the furnace-hot engine.

Until then, there had been no fire.

During the first second of its rampage, the bomber's impact alone had claimed six lives: the three men in the plane, Bill Smith, Christopher Domitrovich, and Albert Perna; and in the office, Paul Dearing, John Judge, and Jeanne Sozzi. But now, as the remaining portion of the right wing slammed into a vertical steel column, the engine exploded from its mounting. Like a bolt of Greek fire, it catapulted through the office in a southerly direction.

Drenched by the shower of fuel while seated at their desks, Mary Lou Taylor, Anne Gerlach, and Patricia O'Connor were just reaching the entrance to the reception foyer when the blazing engine caught up with them. The incinerating geyser of flame was so intense that it melted the glass and metal partition. Hissing smoke rose from the fused elements of flesh and metal. The fire now raced back into the office to consume the unburnt fuel lying ankle-deep on the linoleum.

The six bright yellow oxygen tanks had been hurled from the disintegrating bomber. Two of the canisters had flown on a diagonal trajectory into the cubicle shared by Maureen Maguire and Margret Mullins. An instant before the flames swept through the office, the women had stumbled out of the glass enclosure. Dazed and bleeding from deep cuts inflicted by exploding metal and glass, they saw Mary Kedzierska standing in the doorway of her office.

"Mary!" cried Margret Mullins. She started toward the slim, dark-haired woman just as a wave of flames rolled across the room. Reaching to the ceiling, the fire cascaded over Mary. She remained standing in the doorway for what seemed the longest moment, then slowly, almost casually, as if she had decided to sit on the floor, her body folded onto the ground. Maureen Maguire had time to scream "Oh, my God!" before three of the oxygen tanks lying in the middle of the inferno erupted.

*   *   *

The sudden blast, a thousand times brighter than the sun, created a momentary vacuum in the reception foyer. Halted in midflight only a foot or two from the hallway door, Lucille Bath was sucked backward into the rapidly expanding ball of orange fire.

Some ninety feet south of the bomber's point of entry, Kay O'Connor had just started out of Monsignor O'Boyle's office with a handful of letters. The resulting shock wave knocked her off balance. "Hey!" she yelled with startled surprise. Her feet were carrying her in small, shuffling steps back into the desk. She had become aware of a deafening roar, a terrible wrenching sound of metal tearing apart. And of wood and glass splintering. The small office seemed to be swaying; then Kay realized the sickening motion wasn't confined just to the room. *The entire building was moving!* Yawing off center, trembling with a side-to-side, up-and-down motion.

Earthquakes aren't supposed to happen in New York, she thought. The horrible sound had grown louder. She felt that if it didn't stop instantly, her head would explode.

The jolt had spun Therese Fortier around in her chair. Facing the north portion of the office, she saw the boiling mass of orange flame rolling out of the reception foyer. It was moving directly toward her. She began to scream. For some reason she was unable to get out of the chair. A dead weight seemed to be pressing on her shoulders, anchoring her to the seat.

Occupying the desk to the left of Therese, Theresa Scarpelli was crying hysterically, her eyes clamped shut as she attempted to thrust her ample weight past her coworker. "Fire!" she began to scream over and over. "Fire!" She was leaning across Therese, pushing down on her in a desperate attempt to squeeze past. Charlotte Deegan, standing next to Ellen Lowe at the file cabinets, was watching Theresa's struggles with what appeared to be an amused look. Her hands were clutching her hair on either side of her head, and her mouth was frozen into a horrified grin. She was moaning an "Ohhhhh" sound as she rocked back and forth, her voice rising and falling with the motion like a wailing siren.

Stumbling out of her office, Anna Regan, the personnel manager, seemed unaware of the blood flowing down the right side of her face. She had been gashed by a shard of glass that had flown into her office through the open door. Standing less than twenty feet from the oncoming wall of fire, she glanced first to the five secretaries huddled at the rear of the office, then turned and, in a daze, started moving toward the flames. After a few steps she halted, looked back toward the women, and placed her right hand over her forehead. She hesitated, then continued toward the fire.

"Anna!" screamed Kay O'Connor, "come here!" This way!" There was a sudden rumbling sound, Kay saw a burst of thick, black smoke shoot through the center of the orange flames. For an instant the fire seemed to be halted in its forward movement. Anna turned from the fire and, still holding her forehead, walked toward Kay. Except for the heavy

flow of blood streaming down her face, her skin was colorless.
Kay was certain that she had been mortally wounded, that only
the reflex of shock was forcing her legs to function.

Ellen Lowe shrieked and covered her face with her hands.
In that instant, as Joe Fountain walked out of the raging
flames, she was left with no doubt that they would all die.

He moved slowly, with deliberate steps, as if cautiously
picking his way over uncertain ground. Both of his arms were
raised at shoulder level, the hands dangling limply at the
wrists. The skin on the back of each hand had risen from the
bone structure and was hanging in flaps by bare threads of
tissue. His face was a mass of blood and charred skin, the once
prominent features now all but unrecognizable. He had been
wearing a white shirt and tie when the fire erupted. As he came
through the flames, Ellen had seen only singed patches of cloth
clinging to his bare arms and chest. In that instant sighting she
saw that his entire upper torso had turned an ebony brown.
Small, bright yellow blotches of skin remained on his chest,
just flecks, like the splattering of paint from a brush. But most
of all, it was Fountain's face that she was seeing behind her
closed eyes. His hair had been completely burned off. In its
place a mass of yellow blisters had swelled the skull to
unhuman proportion. Below the narrowed eyes his mouth was
open, the lips pulled back in a gesture of agonized surprise.

"Oh, Joe!" Kay O'Connor cried. "Oh, Christ in Heaven!
Look at what's happened to Joe!"

He continued toward the women, a ghostly somnambulist
exiting the fires of Hell. Kay ran to him and without thinking
placed her hand on his shoulder.

His body went rigid, as if charged with a jolt of electricity.
"Please . . . please don't touch me!" He was begging, the words
forced out in breathless sobs. The horrible pain had seemed to
bring him into focus. "Go into Father Swanstrom's office," he
ordered Kay. The women remained where they were,
unmoving, gaping at him. Suddenly, Theresa Scarpelli burst
past him and ran shrieking into Swanstrom's corner office.
The spell broken, the rest of the secretaries bolted in after her.
With his arms still elevated, Fountain followed them with

small, jerky steps. The flames behind him were now hidden by a curtain of midnight black smoke.

Waiting for Fountain in the office doorway, Kay started to cough as billows of the dense smoke began to fill the rear section of the office. "Shut the door!" Fountain said as he moved into the room. "Get some window open!" How he could walk, how he could take command of the situation— how he was *alive!*—stunned Kay.

Charlotte Deegan was struggling to open one of the windows facing Sixth Avenue. "It's stuck!" she yelled in panic. "I can't get it open—it won't budge!" She began to cry hysterically as she yanked on the window handles. Fountain crossed to the window. "Let me do it," he said in a voice that had taken on a hoarse, bubbling quality. As he pulled up on the window, pieces of charred flesh dropped away from his hands. Anna Regan gasped and fainted.

The small room was rapidly filling with the black, acrid smoke seeping in under the door. The heat, already intense, was rising. Therese Fortier pushed her way to the east window and opened it halfway. A cooling draft of air rushed over her. She stuck her head out and breathed deeply. Ellen Lowe moved in beside her. "Thank God for some air," she said. "I thought I was going to pass out."

"Ladies," Fountain called out, "get hold of yourselves and listen to me." The women turned toward him. He was standing next to the west window, his head propped against the wall. The skin had continued to swell and now it seemed too heavy for his body alone to support. "I don't know what's going to happen to us, whether we'll live or die. But we're all Catholic, and this is the moment the church has prepared us for."

Theresa Scarpelli let out a screech and drummed her fists on Father Swanstrom's desk. "Oh, my God! Oh, Jesus Christ, save me, save me!" she wailed hysterically. Ellen Lowe turned to Theresa and, in pique of anger that surprised even her, shouted: "Shut up! Stop all that damned screaming!" Shocked by the outburst, Theresa quieted down to a sobbing whimper.

Fountain continued. "Let's pray and ask for God's forgiveness. I want all of you to say the Act of Contrition with me."

In a whisper, barely audible above the rumble of flames outside the door, Fountain closed his eyes and made the sign of the cross. "O my God, I am heartily sorry for having offended Thee . . ." One by one, the five women crossed themselves and joined in. ". . . and I detest all my sins, because of Thy just punishments, but most of all because they have offended Thee, my God . . ." Charlotte Deegan began to cry quietly. She raised her face toward the ceiling and dropped to her knees, clasping her hands together. ". . . who art all good and deserving of all my love. I firmly resolve with the help of Thy grace, to sin no more and to avoid the near occasions of sin. Amen."

*   *   *

The lowered forward landing gear and the left wing had torn into the unoccupied 78th floor. The outer section of the wing cleaved off, dropping in a solid piece onto a setback over 34th Street. Relieved of the encumbrance, the 1,100-pound nose wheel and the 2,700-pound engine separated from the fuselage, which was entering the War Relief Services office a floor above.

Spraying hot fuel from the ruptured gas tanks onto the paint cans and canvas tarp William Sharp had left under the window, the engine, sparking as it passed, touched off a blaze. Within seconds the large drum of turpentine exploded, sending a gusher of blackened flames shooting straight up the north face of the building. Hundreds of gallons of aviation fuel raced along the floor in a flaming torrent. At the stairwells it turned left and found entry under the closed doors. The steel stairs, floor by floor below the crash site, became drenched with the high octane fuel and erupted into brilliant orange flames.

Traveling at a speed of more than 200 miles an hour, the landing gear strut, with its 47-inch wheel still attached, rocketed down the center corridor. Impaled on the front of the gear, fused by the enormous force of the impact, were the engine's oil cooler and a large section of the oil tank. Moving on an unswervingly straight line for almost a hundred feet, the flaming mass of metal and rubber blasted through the south wall and began its plunge to the roof of the Waldorf Building on 33rd Street.

The engine took a diagonal route to the right, heading directly toward the G bank of elevators. It struck an eight-inch brick wall enclosing the vent shaft of the fire tower stairwell, skipped across the four-foot shaftway, and cut through another eight-inch brick wall. It's speed was barely diminished as it entered the steel and brick shaft closing elevators 6 and 7.

On the 80th floor, elevator operator Mary Scannell was standing just inside the open doorway of car Number 7. In her rich brogue, larded with a generous amount of dramatic embellishment, she was putting Sam Watkinson into stitches.

Only a few minutes before, she related to the observatory ticket taker, Carla Haines had asked Mary if she could switch cars with her. The starter had assigned the young, inexperienced girl to car Number 7, which had a left-hand control. Carla, pleading helplessness when it came to doing anything with her left hand, had asked Mary if she could take over car Number 2. "Just until my coffee break," Mary mimicked. "Then she said she'd practice up real hard with her left hand and switch back with me!" She slapped Watkinson on the shoulder and broke into a lusty laugh.

"Maybe she should try tying her right hand behind her back for a week," Watkinson said between wheezing chuckles. "Or better still, we could . . ."

Simultaneously with the sound of an explosion somewhere in the shaft beneath her, Mary felt a violent shudder race through the floor of the car. Suddenly, the roof and the rear wall of the cage blew open. An orange mass of flame, driven by hurricane-force air currents in the narrow shaft, catapulted her off her feet. She sailed across the corridor and slammed into the wall. Stunned almost into unconsciousness, she rebounded and stumbled back into the burning car. Molten drops of steel were dripping on her head, setting her hair on fire. Through the flames she saw Watkinson writhing in agony on the corridor floor. His brown uniform pants had been torn away at the knees and blood was gushing from cuts on both of his legs.

Forcing herself to a sitting position in the center of the blazing car, Mary screamed, "Get away from here, Sam! It's going to explode!" *How strange,* the thought raced through her mind, *that I'm not feeling any pain.* Here she was, being burned alive, and yet she felt nothing. Time seemed to have halted. She was aware of everything—minute details, like one of her shoes lying in the corridor burning; a black smear on the opposite wall that reminded her of a globe her teacher had kept on her desk; a light bulb loosened from the ceiling fixture, dangling just by its filament. She saw Sam Watkinson dragging himself along the corridor, away from the burning car, his blackened face contorted with pain.

Flattening her hands on the floor of the car, she felt the molten metal dissolve the skin on her palms. She pushed herself into a half crouch and staggered out of the flames. A few feet across the corridor she saw the Caterpillar Tractor Company office. Screaming hysterically, Mary burst through the glass-paneled door.

The sudden rush of super-heated air instantly wilted a small cactus plant sitting on John Norden's desk. The executive had been knocked to the floor by the bomber's impact. He was just gaining his feet as Mary staggered into the office. Wild with pain, screaming at the top of her lungs, she ran blindly past him into his assistant's office.

Arthur Palmer had also been toppled from his chair to the floor. Still dazed, thinking that the building had been hit by a bolt of lightning, he stared blankly at Mary for a long moment. Then it registered that the woman standing in his doorway had been horribly burned. Her face and bare arms were pouring blood. Large patches of her bright red hair had been burned down to the scalp. The sight triggered Palmer into action. Overcoming her flailing arms, he forced her into a chair, then ran into Norden's office.

"What the hell happened?" he asked Norden. Seeing the older man's ashen face, he suddenly began to shake.

Norden shook his head. "I don't know, but we better get out of here fast." He crossed the hall door and opened it a crack.

Even before he saw the flames raging in the corridor, the blast
of furnace-hot air and black smoke that rushed into the office
told him that they were trapped. He quickly closed the door
and turned to Palmer. "Art, I guess this is the end. There's no
place to go." The two men stared at each other, then Palmer
smiled ruefully. "We could always try the windows."

Feeling strangely calm, Norden laughed and glanced to
his left. For the first time he noticed that all the windows had
been shattered. Waves of thick black smoke were pouring into
the offices. "I wonder which'll get us first, the fire or the
smoke?" As if in answer, Palmer began to cough. He reached
into his pocket and took out his handkerchief. "Maybe if we
wet these and cover our faces, we'll last until the firemen can
reach us." Even as he was crossing to the water cooler, Palmer
had rejected his idea as futile. He went through the motions
anyway, soaking his handkerchief and Norden's. The bottled
water was almost hot as it poured out the spigot.

Mary's screams had risen in pitch and intensity, forcing
the men to remember her presence. "What can we do for her?"
Palmer asked. Norden started to answer, "We're all going to
the morgue, so what's the . . ." He halted in mid-sentence, a
startled look sweeping his face. Without a word, he turned and
ran to the small supply closet at the far end of the office. He tore
the door open and pulled out a claw hammer. "I forgot I put it
in there last week!" he said triumphantly. Palmer studied the
tool doubtfully. "What're we going to do with it?" he asked
with a shrug. Norden was moving toward the south wall of the
office. "Maybe if we bang on the wall loud enough, somebody,
a tenant or . . . somebody, will hear it. It's worth a try," he said.
He raised the hammer and pounded it against the wall. A small
chunk of plaster broke loose with the impact. Palmer watched
his boss deliver a few more blows, then he turned and, with a
resigned look, went into his office. If nothing else, he thought,
he could at least make the elevator operator's last minutes a bit
more comfortable.

Mary was doubled over in pain. The small office had
become filled with the choking smoke. Between cries she was
coughing. Suddenly, she screamed, "I can't breathe!" Before
Palmer could stop her, Mary leaped to her feet and thrust her

body far out the window. Thinking that she was about to jump, Palmer grabbed hold of her waist and hauled her back into the chair. He pulled off the handkerchief covering his nose and mouth and attempted to tie it about her face. Mary whipped her head from side to side, thrusting him away with her burned hands. "Don't touch me!" she pleaded. The pain had become unbearable. Each time the damp, hot cloth came into contact with her raw skin she prayed that she would lose consciousness.

"Art—come here!" Norden shouted. "Get in here and help me!" Palmer hesitated. He was afraid to leave Mary alone. "Don't go near the window," he told her firmly, "understand?" Getting a nod from her, Palmer ran into Norden's office. The smoke had cut the visibility in the room down to near zero. Following the sound of the hammer blows, Palmer located Norden kneeling on the floor.

"Look!" Norden said excitedly.

Palmer bent close to the hole Norden had chopped in the plaster. Behind the jagged two-foot opening he saw shattered pieces of white tile. He was unimpressed. "What about it?" he asked.

"Look closer," Norden ordered. "It isn't brick, it's tile— just a thin layer of fireproofing. Look through here!" Norden jabbed his finger at a small opening in the squares of tile. Palmer pressed his face close to the tile and squinted into the tiny aperture. He found himself looking into another office. It was free of smoke and appeared undamaged. Without a word, he began tearing at the plaster with his hands as Norden hammered away at the tile.

*   *   *

Seconds before the hurtling engine was to tear into the shaft of car Number 6, Betty Lou Oliver glanced at her watch. It read 9:55, five minutes short of her ten o'clock coffee break.

She slowed the car to a halt on the 79th floor and opened the doors for Morris Needleman.

"I'm going to miss you, Betty," the large, gray-haired man said with a serious shake of his head. "Nobody gives me as smooth a ride as you." He hesitated, then awkwardly leaned over and gave her a gentle peck on the cheek.

"I'll miss you too, Mr. Needleman," she said, certain that his broad smile was the result of her sudden blush. She felt ridiculous; here she was, a twenty-year-old married woman, and still she couldn't control her emotions!

"You make sure you come back and say hello now and then," Needleman said as he exited the car. "And bring your sailor boy. Tell him he can pick out any belt in the place." Betty returned his wave and watched him move down the corridor to the Hickock showroom. She pulled the brass handle back, standing to the side as the doors rushed shut.

Moving the handle all the way back, she slid to the floor of the car as it started down. She stretched her legs out, cleared her throat, and in a high-pitched monotone began to sing the "St. Louis Blues." Since her first day on the job, six weeks before, Betty had discovered that an empty elevator was the perfect place to indulge her passion for singing. From childhood on she had self-consciously forced herself into the role of a "listener"—silently mouthing the words to everything from "Happy Birthday" to "Jingle Bells" to avoid the embarrassment of having family and friends laugh at her squeaky, one-note renditions. But in an empty elevator, secure in the metal, high-ceilinged cage, she was free to sing as loud as she liked. Songs that she once had only dared to hum ever so faintly under her breath—"Dancing in the Dark," "Small Hotel," "Don't Sit under the Apple Tree"—now were given daily airings as she shot up and down the thousand-foot shaft. Adding a dash of growling vibrato to the lyrics, she felt a sadness come over her. In two hours she would not only be saying goodbye to her friends on the staff, but from then on she'd never again have the opportunity to belt out a song with such abandon—and privacy—as now.

The car had begun to pick up speed. As it approached the 76th floor, Betty heard a concussive sound echo high in the shaft. The cage lurched, then began rocking from side to side. Startled, she clutched the handle tighter and stared up at the roof of the car.

Thirty feet above car Number 6, the exploding engine had just severed the first of the six braided steel lifting cables attached to the top of the shaft.

Deflected after having slammed into the base of Mary Scannell's car and jamming the massive counterweight into the brake rails, the motor was now traveling horizontally. It sliced through the wrist-thick cables like a rotary buzz saw and rebounded off the steel fire wall. Blazing white-hot like the head of a meteor, the engine began its last journey toward the roof of car Number 6.

She had been pitched to the opposite side of the cage, the handle torn from her grasp as the car skipped from one wall of the shaft to the other. Betty opened her mouth to scream. She discovered it was physically impossible. Her head and stomach were shooting apart at literally breathtaking speed.

Out of the corner of her eye she caught sight of the red lights flashing on the panel indicator. 76 . . . 75 . . . 74 . . . The numbers were running into a vertical blur.

She was pressing her back against the wall in an attempt to stand when the roof caved in with a blinding explosion. The car filled with flaming chunks of metal and acrid, oil-black smoke. With all her strength, Betty pushed herself to a standing position. She was wondering how she could reach the emergency switch, when a burning piece of cable whacked her over the shoulders. She flung herself across the car, raising her hands above her head to ward off the flaming debris that poured through the hole in the roof.

The overhead light flickered and went out. Guided by the flames, she found the emergency switch and jerked it to "Stop." The car continued its plunge. She snapped it back and forth a half-dozen times. If anything, she felt the car moving faster. She couldn't breathe, and now she became aware of a weightless sensation. It was becoming difficult to keep her feet on the floor. Her hand fumbled for a hold and located the telephone receiver. For a reason unattached to the reality of her situation, Betty found herself pulling the phone to her ear and jiggling the hook. The line was dead—and even if it hadn't been, she suddenly realized, what in God's name could the starter down in the lobby do to end her nightmare?

She was going to die. The possibility hadn't occurred to her until now. She dropped the phone and moved to the rear corner of the car, pressing her hands tightly against the walls. The blistering metal seared her palms. She held on a second longer, then let go. As she felt her feet lift off the floor, she started to cry. Slowly, as if caught in a gentle but persistent updraft, her body was being pulled toward the roof of the car. Glancing up, she saw an inferno. Which was quicker, she found herself wondering—death by fire or being crushed?

Two thoughts, one tumbling upon the other, suddenly pushed death out of her mind: her husband Oscar; and the new suit she had bought for his homecoming. A picture flashed before her eyes. Oscar was standing at the rail of his ship, searching the crowded dock for her. He was deeply tanned from the South Pacific sun, and happy, so happy to be home. The image broke apart as she felt herself being sucked up the side of the wall faster. The car was filled with a strange howling sound.

*   *   *

Running across the Empire State lobby, Donald Molony paid scant attention to the howling echo. Between the sirens of the converging fire engines and the panicked shouts of the people pouring out of the building, the unnerving sound had no special meaning to the young Coast Guardsman.

Seconds after the crash Molony had braved the falling debris and darted across Fifth Avenue into the building. He didn't stop to ask directions. A hunch—a sudden sixth sense— led him directly to the ground floor Walgreen's drugstore. drugstore.

The startled clerk behind the pharmaceutical counter, Charles Wilson, found himself instantly obeying the seventeen-year-old's snapped orders. "A first aid kit—the largest and most complete you've got!" Molony had demanded. And sterile bandages, burn ointment, alcohol— "lots of it!"—gauze rolls, cotton, and some adhesive tape!

While the clerk hurried to gather the items, Molony had darted around the counter and rummaged through the small safe in which the narcotics were stored. He snapped open a paper bag and tossed in four vials of morphine, a syringe, and several dozen needles. Then, slinging the pack Wilson had assembled over his shoulder, Molony had headed for the elevators. He was determined to reach the crash site. This was the moment he had spent eight months training for.

As he approached the G bank of elevators he became more aware of the howling echo. It was growing louder. From a vague, indistinct sound that had merged into the background clamor, it now took on a chilling familiarity. The young man felt the hairs on the back of his neck rise in a sudden shiver. It was a human voice! A woman's!

Molony halted and scanned the crowded lobby for the source. Wherever it was coming from, it was close. And getting closer. He spun around and faced the elevators. All of the doors, with the exception of one, were closed. The Coast Guardsman saw an elderly elevator operator standing in the doorway of his car, wondering, as Molony himself was, where the banshee wail was coming from.

At the moment of impact, John Monte and his handful of passengers were unaware that disaster had struck. The car had been somewhere around the 30th floor, the whistling noise of its rapid descent masking the horrific explosion that was taking place far above.

Now Monte was awaiting orders from the starter, Chauncey Humphrey. The elevator staff had been given emergency training. Each man and woman was to remain at his or her car, standing ready for orders from the starters to aid in the orderly evacuation of the building. On the run, Humphrey had shouted at Monte a few seconds earlier to hold tight, not to move from car Number 8 until he checked with the other starters to learn where the most elevators would be needed.

The eerie sound was now coming from just over his head, and to the right. With a sudden start, Monte realized that it was reverberating from the shaft of Number 6. He was about to start out of the car when the world went black.

Molony had been staring at Monte when the anguished howl abruptly ended in a shattering explosion somewhere below him. In the time it took for the shock wave to race through the marble floor beneath his feet, Molony saw John Monte's car suddenly plunge from sight. Black smoke was curling out of the open shaft, and, although unseen, Molony caught the unmistakable odor of an oil fire. He urgently searched the lobby for a way down to the sub-basement. His training had taught him that the first thirty seconds in a chemical fire were the most critical. Deadlier than the flames, smoke and chemical fumes claimed most victims trapped in a disaster such as this. He was moving toward the far end of the lobby, pushing his way through the mass of people who were making frenzied exits from the stairwells.

"Sailor!" The shouted cry brought Molony up short.

He turned and saw a squad of firemen running toward him. Dragging coiled lengths of hose, several of the helmeted men broke off and made for a brass standpipe connection near the elevators. The chief, Arthur Massett of the Seventh Battalion, continued on to Molony. He had caught sight of the first aid kit slung over the seaman's shoulder and correctly guessed that the youngster was a trained medical corpsman.

"Two elevators crashed to the basement!" Molony blurted out. "I think they're both on fire."

Massett turned and waved to a half-dozen of his men. "This way!" he ordered. Grabbing Molony's arm, he guided him through the crowd to a door leading down to the sub-basement.

The elevator shaft compartments under the G bank were pitch black. The electrical conduit cables had been severed by the invading engine. The confined area was thick with bitter smoke. Deep orange flames darted up through the mass of twisted wreckage.

"Bring some lights this way!" Massett shouted to his men. Molony let out a sharp gasping sound as the portable spotlights flared on. No part of his intensive training had prepared him for the sight greeting his eyes. Steel beams, wide as a doorway, had been snapped in two, twisted into grotesque shapes, and tossed like matchsticks over piles of burning rubble. He spotted an arm and part of a leg stabbing out from the shaft that moments before had housed John Monte's car.

Two of the firemen had also spotted the victim. Climbing over the flames, they began pulling at the debris with their asbestos-gloved hands, tossing heavy pieces of steel and smoldering cable to the side as another man played a steady stream of water over their work area. Geysers of dazzling white steam hissed up, shrouding the rescuers in a dreamlike mist.

"Sailor!" Massett shouted, "Over here. Quick."

Molony stumbled over the wreckage to the spot where the fire chief and two of his men were huddled around the shaft of car Number 6. Under the glare of the spotlights Molony saw that the elevator had smashed through the concrete floor, driving itself another three or four feet into the ground. Looking down through the gaping hole in the roof, he saw that the bumper mechansim—a large, round rubber device employed to cushion a car's sudden drop—had been thrust up through the floor. Not even God's Child could have survived a fall like that, Molony thought to himself as he looked questioningly at Massett.

"Do you think you can make it through that hole?" the fire chief asked. He adjusted the spotlight beam, focusing it directly on the jagged passage.

"Sure, I guess so," Molony answered.

"It's too small for any of us, but I think you could squeeze through." Massett was slipping the first aid kit off Molony's shoulder. Almost as an afterthought he added: "We heard her moan. You'll probably have to pull a lot of stuff off to find her."

The Coast Guardsman stared at Massett incredulously for a moment, then quickly scrambled down onto the roof of the car. The hoseman sprayed a stream of cooling water over the opening as Molony eased himself through feet first. He dropped on top of one of the pancaked walls.

"Move the lights," he shouted up, "I can't see where I'm going." He was lost in darkness for an instant, then the interior of the car was brilliantly illuminated. Molony looked up and saw the chief hanging over the edge of the hole, a spotlight in each hand. The stream of water continued to shower over him as he climbed through the wreckage. A glance told him that the operator was not lying on the surface of the rubble. That she had escaped instantaneous death—if the chief weren't mistaken—was miracle enough. But for anyone to survive under the crushing weight of the twisted beams and mountains of brick was a sheer impossibility, Molony thought.

"What's that over there to your right?" Massett called out. Molony turned and saw nothing but a pile of smoking cables and shattered remnants of the car.

"No, no—*there*!" the chief said brusquely. He rotated one of the lights to target the area he meant. Molony turned and followed the beam. There *was* something. A patch of brown cloth and, although difficult to make out until he got closer, perhaps a hand. He ducked under a lean-to of crisscrossed beams and knelt. The chief was right, it was the operator. She was lying face down, all but completely covered by a blanket of bricks and cable. Two steel beams had fallen across her back and legs.

But she was alive! Molony felt a rush of excitement as he saw her try to move her head. She moaned faintly with the effort. He bent close to her ear. "Lie still. Don't try to move," he said softly. "We're going to get you out of here." He straightened and turned toward the chief. "She's alive. Throw down the first aid kit."

Massett tossed the kit down into the car. "What shape is she in?" he called out. Molony had picked up the first aid pack and was moving back toward Betty Lou. "I won't be able to tell until I clear some of the stuff off her. We'll need a stretcher and a body board, something to lay her down flat on. And you'll have to get that hole widened."

He knelt next to the semiconscious operator and opened the first aid kit. Before he could begin extracting her from the wreckage she'd need a shot of morphine. It was clear, even from his hurried glance, that her legs were broken. What concerned him even more was the way her body lay angled under the beams. He prayed that he was wrong, but there was a strong possibility that her spine had been either fractured or crushed. Moving quickly but methodically, Molony had the syringe prepared with a dose of morphine. Clearing some rubble away from her arm, he tore loose what little was left of her uniform sleeve and swabbed her skin with a wad of cotton saturated with alcohol.

She began to moan loudly as Molony injected the painkiller. She moved her head toward him, her mouth struggling to form words. Molony leaned closer.

"What did you say?" he asked.

"Drowning . . . drowning," she muttered, the words barely decipherable.

Puzzled, he was about to dismiss the effort as meaningless. Then he realized what she meant. He turned and shouted to the firemen: "Hey, turn off that hose!" As the drenching shower moved to another part of the wreckage, Molony saw that her face had been submerged in a hollow filled with water. He carefully shifted her head. "Is that better?" he asked. She had passed out. The Coast Guardsman began to lift the wreckage off her body.

*   *   *

Confused and frightened by the crowds rushing through the lobby, Rabbi Avrum Blotner had sought refuge in the doorway of a men's shop next to the cigar stand.

For the better part of the past half hour, he had waited in vain for "Steve" to make his appearance. The black marketeer, a building employee, had promised on the phone to meet Blotner before ten. He had assured the rabbi that their transaction for the heating fuel would take only a few minutes. Once he had the cash in hand, they would set up a date for the oil to be delivered to Blotner's synagogue. The rabbi was to identify him by the name tag on his uniform jacket.

Planting himself directly in front of the small stand, Blotner shifted his eyes like a plainclothesman. Not a single building employee, man or woman, escaped his scrutiny. Being nearsighted didn't help matters any. By mistake, he had taken only his reading glasses, and, so of necessity, he gave uniformed employee a microscopic once-over. Craning forward like a connoisseur examining a Matisse, Blotner had fixed his eyes on their name tags, dismissing each with an abrupt shake of his head. Several times he had duplicated the procedure with the same person, arousing suspicion that the aging, round-shouldered man in the black raincoat might bear watching.

With each passing minute his apprehension that he was *meshugga* to have entered into such an unethical arrangement had grown deeper and more disturbing. The six twenty-dollar bills in his jacket pocket had now taken on the weight of the Wailing Wall. He had found himself hoping that through some guiding act of salvation he had subconsciously chosen to misunderstand the meeting site.

At five minutes to ten, Rabbi Blotner had decided that enough was enough; if this "Steve" person couldn't keep an appointment in the lobby of the very building in which he worked—then how could he be trusted to deliver the heating oil all the way to Brooklyn? With a last self-righteous sweep of the area, Blotner had started for the revolving door leading to Fifth Avenue. He had gone only a few steps when the crash occurred. Through the glass doors he had seen the first surge of panic send pedestrians racing for cover as flaming debris fell in the streets. News of what had taken place reached him seconds later, as people streamed into the building seeking safety.

Characteristically, the rabbi translated the accident into personal terms. God had quite justifiably sought vengeance for Avrum Blotner's transgression. To others, the Almighty seemed to work in mysterious ways, but Blotner long ago had reduced the unfathomable to a simple matter of cause and effect. He had broken the Sabbath. God chose this way to show His displeasure. It was clear to the rabbi that he would have to beg forgiveness, seek atonement in some unique manner. He was reconciled to the thought that it would probably take a lifetime to undo his sins of this summer morning.

Huddled in the doorway of the men's shop, Blotner watched the firemen and police going about their business with military efficiency. Only vaguely above the din of the crisply shouted orders did he hear the policeman's repeated request for any clergymen in the lobby to make themselves known.

"Please!" the officer boomed again. "Are there any clergymen here? You're needed immediately!" This time Blotner distinctly heard the cry for help.

He means priests and ministers, Gentile clergymen, the rabbi was certain. *On the other hand,* came the sudden thought, *what if he truly means* all *clergymen—including rabbis? When people need help, isn't a prayer a prayer?*

"Here!" Blotner shouted, breaking out of the doorway in a run. "I'm a clergyman." As he fought his way through the crowded lobby to the policeman, he saw a priest approaching from another direction.

Responding to the policeman's urgent call, Monsignor Patrick O'Boyle had put aside his attempts to locate a working elevator and reach the crash site.

Minutes before he had abandoned his cab on Sixth Avenue and raced to the burning building on foot. Armed only with veiled sightings of the damaged area, the Monsignor nevertheless had a sinking feeling that disaster had struck the War Relief Services office on the 79th floor. Once inside the building he had discovered that all the elevators in the G bank had been put out of commission. And then had come the policeman's plea for men of the cloth.

With time to exchange only courtesy nods, Rabbi Blotner and Monsignor O'Boyle found themselves being propelled through the lobby and down into the sub-basement.

The devastated area reeked of smoke and acetylene fumes. Hunched over the top of the embedded elevator cage, the clergymen saw a fireman silhouetted against a fountain of sparks as he enlarged the hole with his torch. A few feet away two firemen had placed John Monte on a stretcher and were strapping an oxygen mask over his bleeding face.

Chief Massett spotted the Monsignor. "He was asking for a priest, Father," he said, gesturing toward Monte. "I think he's unconscious now."

Monsignor O'Boyle quickly moved to the elderly operator and bent over him. His eyes were closed. His chest barely rose and fell. In his time O'Boyle had attended enough of the dead and dying to know that this man's earthly hope rested upon the speed with which he could be brought to a hospital. Kneeling beside the stretcher, the Monsignor quickly crossed himself and Monte, and in a murmured whisper gave him absolution. He looked up at the firemen and nodded. They lifted the stretcher and hurriedly climbed the stairs to the lobby.

Betty Lou Oliver had been brought out of the car strapped face down on a wooden board. Hoisting himself nimbly through the roof, Molony assisted the firemen as they placed her on a stretcher. He opened her purse which he had found in the wreckage, and extracting her lipstick, marked a bright red *M* on her forehead—indicating that she had already been given morphine.

"Make sure they keep her face down in the ambulance," Molony told the stretcher bearers. "I'm almost sure her back's broken."

Betty Lou had regained consciousness. Listening to her whimpering cries, Rabbi Blotner tried to ignore the tugging, queasy feeling that always developed in his groin whenever he was faced with someone in extreme pain. Seeing the monsignor kneel beside her, Blotner hesitated, then moved to the opposite side of the stretcher. Perching himself on one knee, he took hold of her hand.

"Miss, you would like us to pray with you?" he asked.

Betty Lou looked from Blotner to O'Boyle. Seeing the monsignor's Roman collar, she shook her head. "I'm not Catholic," she managed to force out, "but I would like to pray." She closed her eyes and gripped the rabbi's hand tightly.

Making the sign of the cross, Monsignor O'Boyle lowered his head, and in a voice that barely carried to Blotner, began. *"Adiutorium nostrum in nomine Domini. Qui fecit caelum et terram . . ."*

Bent slightly forward at the waist, the rabbi had begun a rocking motion. He was chanting in a hushed sing-song. *"Mi sheberakh avoteinu Avraham Yizhak veYaakov Moshe veAharon . . ."*

In that brief moment as the Latin and Hebrew prayers merged into a soothing hum, Betty Lou Oliver was aware of a curious calm replacing her pain. Only vaguely did she hear Donald Molony's footsteps as he ran up the stairs to the lobby.

* * *

In the 102nd-floor viewing station, Lieutenant Allen Aimen, his wife, Betty, and guide Pat Hipwell had been peering out the north windows seconds before the crash.

The young B-24 pilot had been the first to see the silver bomber hurtle out of the cloud bank. Mesmerized, as if disbelieving his senses, he had watched it close on the building. Certain that its nearly vertical climb would carry it directly into their slender tower, Aimen had flung his wife away from the windows. Before he could cry out a warning, the violence of the explosion had knocked the three of them to the floor. Two of the circular windows had instantly blown out. The tower was swaying with a whipsaw motion. Sheets of orange flame and smoke shot up past them. The sudden heat had shattered another window. In a matter of seconds the small chamber had been filled with suffocating smoke.

Grabbing his wife's hand, Aimen shouted at Hipwell, "Where's the exit?"

"We better not try the elevator!" the guard said. "The stairs will be safer." He opened the door leading to the fire tower stairwell. A column of acrid smoke was climbing up from the lower floors. Hipwell pulled a portable emergency spotlight from a wall bracket and led the way as they started down the darkened stairs, their steps echoing a metallic cadence.

* * *

By now, minutes after the bomber's explosive impact, the 86th-floor observation lounge had become a sweltering container. Beyond the locked glass doors leading to the outside deck, a solid wall of flames and pitch black smoke was adding to the fears of the more than forty tourists trapped there.

Although the situation was light years from anything he'd ever experienced, tower manager Frank Powell had quickly and firmly assumed command. Ordering guard Louis Petly to turn up the volume of the waltz music still playing through the loudspeakers, Powell attempted to make phone contact with the building office on the fifth floor. The line was dead. He crossed to the elevator and, without much hope for success, pressed the button. To his surprise, the red light flashed on. He heard the lifting motors thrown into gear, and the car begin to rise.

"Line up in front of the elevator, please," Powell called out in a calm voice. "Families stay together."

With few exceptions, the people began an orderly movement toward the single elevator. Escorting an elderly couple toward the front of the queue, Louis Petly was amazed at the pervading air of composure and generosity. Total strangers for the most part only minutes before, the men and women were acting like a family unit. Men were insisting that the women and children, along with the few aged persons in the group, be placed at the front of the line. Single persons assumed charge of the older children, freeing parents to calm their younger ones' fears.

Forced to break his own hard-and-fast rule by the blistering heat in the sealed lounge, Frank Powell opened his uniform jacket and loosened his collar and tie. Like Petly, he too was impressed with the tourists' level-headed behavior. Only in the first startling seconds after the crash had there been any panic. Several persons had attempted to rush out onto the observation deck, only to discover that the doors were locked. A few had become hysterical when they learned that Powell didn't have the keys. With persistent and calm reasoning, he had pointed out that even if he could open the doors, the raging flames outside were far more dangerous than the heat and lack of air inside the lounge.

Powell allowed himself a sigh of relief as the elevator doors glided open. The operator, a small, chubby-faced man, stood in the center of the doorway.

"Everybody listen to me," he said in a tremulous voice, his eyes darting constantly toward the flames shooting up past the lounge windows. "I can only take twenty-five of you down. The rest are going to have to use the stairs." As if anticipating the group's reaction, he took a defensive step back into the car.

There was a murmur of angry voices. "What are you talking about?" called out a man wearing a snap-brim panama hat. "We can all fit in there!"

The operator held his hands up in a placating gesture. "I know you can—but I got my orders from the Fire Department. They don't want to take a chance on overloading the car. Twenty-five it is!" he said tautly, his eyes rolling fearfully toward the flames.

Standing in the rear of the line, Major Bert Woodstock had purposely chosen to remain in the background. If there was one thing the wounded Infantry officer didn't want, it was to be afforded special treatment because of his war injury.

Now, with the pain in his shattered leg growing steadily worse, he watched the operator count off twenty-five passengers as they filed into the elevator. Just the thought of having to walk down eighty-six floors was again bringing on waves of nausea. It would be so simple, Woodstock knew, to make himself visible. All he had to do was walk toward the elevator with his cane broadcasting his plight. The slender oak rod, the campaign ribbons crowding his chest, his unbending left leg would most assuredly guarantee him a privilege that was now being denied some twenty others in the unbearably hot and airless lounge.

The major watched the elevator doors close. Taking a firmer grip on the handle of his cane, he followed the others toward the stairwell door Frank Powell was holding open. A small smile traced his lips as he remembered the medic's words as they were carrying him on board the hospital ship: "Major, you can at least be thankful for one thing—no more forced marches for you." Gripping the stairway handrail, Woodstock tested his balance with the cane before taking his first step.

*   *   *

Responding to the first alarm sent by Fire Lieutenant William Murphy from Box 681, fire fighting equipment was converging on the building from every part of the city.

Sixteen engine companies, five hook and ladder companies, and the Rescue Squad had delivered more than 300 firemen to the area within the first few minutes after the crash.

Its siren still blaring, Fire Commissioner Patrick Walsh's car slid to a halt in front of the Fifth Avenue entrance to the

building. Walsh, who had made a final inspection tour of the
Empire State on the opening day ceremonies fourteen years
before, now took personal charge of the fire and rescue
operations. Spotting fireman Galvin Gerson with a walkie-
talkie radio pack strapped to his back, Walsh ran to him. "How
many elevators are still running?" he asked.

"Two in the west bank," Gerson responded, "but they
only go up to the fifty-fifth floor."

"What condition are the stairwells in?" the commissioner
asked.

Gerson shook his head grimly. "Last report I got they were
running into heavy smoke from the sixty-first on up."

For the squads of firemen forced to haul their heavy coils
of hose up to the fire area on foot, Gerson's report was a
masterpiece of understatement. Taking the stairs two at a time,
Donald Molony and Fire Lieutenant Edward Ryan, of Engine
Company 14, were in the vanguard of two dozen firemen
racing up the central stairwell. Between the suffocating smoke
and the hundreds of panicked office workers jamming the
stairs, the trek had turned into a nightmare. At the 67th floor,
Ryan ordered his men to cut across the hallway and use the
stairwells on the east side of the building. Molony, a flight
above the firemen and trapped in the downward stream of
fleeing workers, continued his exhausting climb alone to the
crash site.

On the stairs at the south end of the building Joseph
Krajec, of Engine Company 72, had paused a half-dozen times
to use his CO_2 extinguisher on the ribbons of liquid fire that
were racing down the metal stairwell. Thick coils of black
smoke filled the shaftway, forcing the firemen to switch on
their portable lights to read the floor numbers marked on the
corridor doors.

Making the torturous climb with the men of Engine
Company 1, walkie-talkie operator Arthur Myerson was the
first to reach the 79th floor. Throwing his shoulder against a
metal corridor door that had swelled with the heat, Myerson
was hit with a blast of furnace-hot air as he entered the east side
of the hallway. A glance at the holocaust raging at the north

end convinced him that rescue efforts in the War Relief Services office would be unnecessary. Not a betting man, he wouldn't have given a chance in hell for anyone to have survived the bomber's impact, much less the ensuing fire. As the firemen connected their hoses into the standpipe system and began pouring streams of water onto the flames, Myerson contacted the command post outside the building.

"We're on the 79th and pumping water," he reported into his microphone. "The north end and the west corridor are burning heavily. Most of the structural damage seems to be confined to the impact area. So far, there's no sign of any survivors in the west offices."

Working his way down the east side of the corridor, a fireman was using his ax handle to pound on the office doors. Reaching 7901, his shouted "Anybody in there?" brought instantaneous cries of joy from twelve secretaries and bookkeepers trapped in the Ameritrade Corporation office.

Feeding oxygen to several of the women overcome by smoke, members of the Rescue Squad began to lead them down the stairs to an emergency first aid station that had been set up on the 75th floor. Staring at the flames consuming the west portion of the hallway, Myerson thought to halt one of the secretaries.

"Do you know how many were at work in there?" he asked, indicating the War Relief Services quarters.

Numbed by her harrowing experience, the young woman shook her head several times before answering. "I don't know exactly—but a lot." she said, then looked toward the flames pouring out of the devastated area. "Oh, God, a lot of them!" She burst into tears. Myerson put his arm around her shoulder and guided her down the stairs.

*   *   *

Fate seemed to be toying with the seven survivors huddled in the small office at the south end of the 79th floor. Only moments before, Kay O'Connor had heard the firemen's muffled shouts in the hallway filter into their sanctuary.

"We're in here!" she had yelled. The others had joined in, shouting at the top of their lungs, coughing as they breathed in the thick smoke. Ellen Lowe had tried banging her fist on the door leading out to the reception foyer, but the metal was searing hot. She had managed only a few feeble attempts when the firemen's voices, once so close, suddenly faded into silence.

"They didn't hear us!" Theresa Scarpelli shrieked. "They don't even know we're in here!"

Charlotte Deegan ran to the opened east window and thrust her head out. "Help us—won't somebody help us! Don't let us die up here!" she screamed. She pushed herself farther out, taking in great gulps of fresh air. Suddenly, a mass of black smoke shot up from the floor below and enveloped her. She fell back into the office, choking, her face smeared with soot.

Kay O'Connor looked at her and suddenly laughed. "Charlotte, you should see yourself. You look like a minstrel man!" Taken aback for the moment, Charlotte stared at Kay, then she too broke into a giggle. Pointing at Kay, she said, "Well, you finally got your wish—there isn't a trace of white left." Kay pulled down a strand of hair and saw that Charlotte was right. Her once totally white hair was now pitch-black. For the moment, the women's laughter had a calming effect on the others trapped in the sweltering, smoke-filled chamber.

*   *   *

In the 80th-floor office of the Caterpillar Tractor office, Arthur Palmer quite literally had his hands full of Mary Scannell. For the third time since John Norden had hammered a hole through the office wall, the men were attempting to squeeze the chubby elevator operator through the two-foot opening.

Norden had climbed into the empty office. Grabbing hold of the hysterical girl's arms, he yelled to Palmer, "Push, Art!" Straining with all his might, he pulled. Palmer, his hands planted on Mary's buttocks, heaved. With a squeal of pain she exploded through the opening, falling on top of Norden, taking another foot of plaster and tile along with her. Palmer scampered through the hole after her.

As the dense smoke began pouring into the office through their escape route, Norden quickly crossed the room and opened the glass-paneled door. A rush of cool, smoke-free air

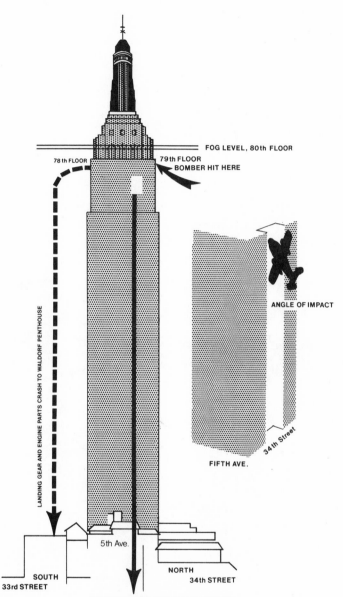

FOG LEVEL, 80th FLOOR

78th FLOOR

79th FLOOR
BOMBER HIT HERE

ANGLE OF IMPACT

LANDING GEAR AND ENGINE PARTS CRASH TO WALDORF PENTHOUSE

FIFTH AVE.

34th Street

5th Ave.

NORTH
34th STREET

SOUTH
33rd STREET

ELEVATOR PLUNGES 79 FLOORS TO SUB-BASEMENT

Diagram shows the plane's impact on the northwest face of the building. The dotted line marks the path the forward landing gear and parts of one engine took as they passed through the 78th floor and dropped onto the roof of the Waldorf Building on 33rd Street.

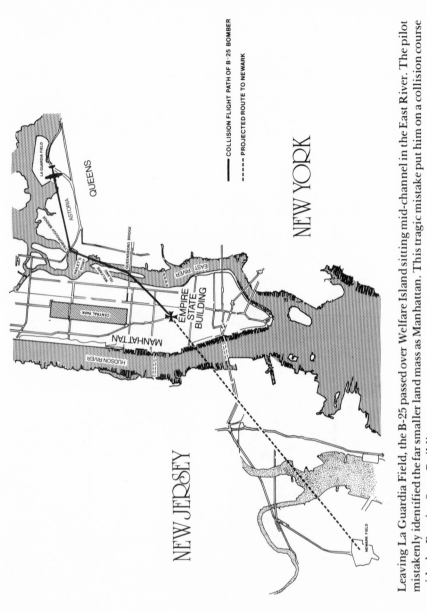

Leaving La Guardia Field, the B-25 passed over Welfare Island sitting mid-channel in the East River. The pilot mistakenly identified the far smaller land mass as Manhattan. This tragic mistake put him on a collision course with the Empire State Building.

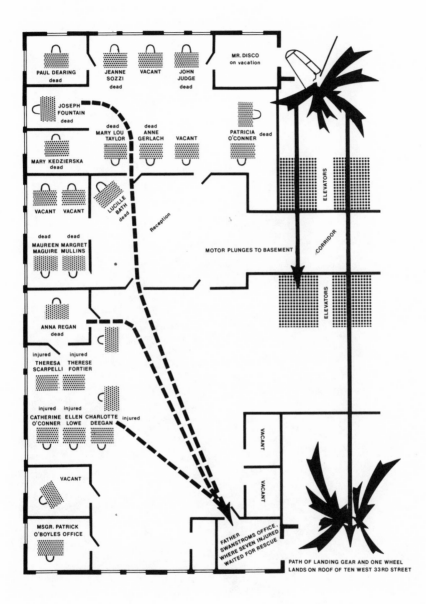

PAUL DEARING
dead

JEANNE
SOZZI
dead

VACANT

JOHN
JUDGE
dead

MR. DISCO
on vacation

JOSEPH
FOUNTAIN
dead

dead
MARY LOU
TAYLOR

dead
ANNE
GERLACH

VACANT

PATRICIA
O'CONNER
dead

MARY KEDZIERSKA
dead

VACANT

VACANT

LUCILLE
BATH
dead

Reception

ELEVATORS

CORRIDOR

dead
MAUREEN
MAGUIRE

dead
MARGRET
MULLINS

MOTOR PLUNGES TO BASEMENT

ELEVATORS

ANNA REGAN
dead

injured
THERESA
SCARPELLI

injured
THERESE
FORTIER

injured
CATHERINE
O'CONNER

injured
ELLEN
LOWE

CHARLOTTE
DEEGAN injured

VACANT

VACANT

VACANT

MSGR. PATRICK
O'BOYLES OFFICE

FATHER
SWANSTROMS OFFICE,
WHERE SEVEN INJURED
WAITED FOR RESCUE

PATH OF LANDING GEAR AND ONE WHEEL
LANDS ON ROOF OF TEN WEST 33RD STREET

Flames rage unchecked from the 79th and 78th floors at the crash site. A passing news photographer hurriedly snapped this shot moments after the impact.

This view of the south face of the building shows flames and smoke
pouring out the Waldorf Building penthouses on 33rd Street. The
B-25's forward landing gear and other parts of the plane were
hurled through the unoccupied 78th floor and plunged onto the
roof of the twelve-story structure.

The use of walkie-talkies by the New York City Fire Department, a recent innovation at the time, played a major role in the quick containment of the fire and greatly aided rescue operations.

A crowd estimated at more than 25,000 persons gathered in the light rain to view the aftermath of the crash. Miraculously, there were no fatalities to pedestrians or motorists.

Skeletal sections of the wings and tail assembly protrude from the 18-by-20-foot gash caused by the bomber's impact. Although parts of the plane fell toward the street, most of the debris landed on lower floor setbacks, as seen in the bottom left of the photo.

Firemen drench the rubble of aircraft parts, masonry, and steelwork on the 78th story to make certain that no embers of the fire that raged through the floor remain.

Another view of the unoccupied 78th floor. Note the steel structural columns bent inward by the bomber's 250-mile-per-hour impact. Sections of the left wing and the tail assembly are lodged in the twenty-foot-wide opening in the building's north face.

The oil buffer mechanism in elevator shaft Number 6, where operator Betty Lou Oliver's car plunged from the 79th floor. The force of the impact drove the safety mechanism through the floor of her car, demolishing it entirely. She was weightless for most of the 1,000-foot fall.

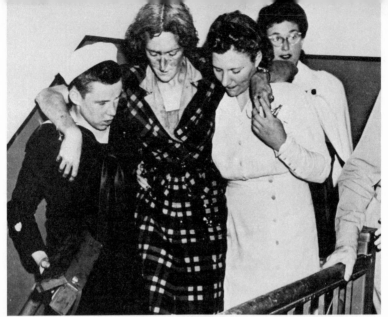

Donald Molony, the seventeen-year-old Coast Guard hospital apprentice who witnessed the crash, quickly became the tragedy's hero. He was credited with rescuing more than a dozen people trapped by the fires that erupted throughout the building's upper floors.

Donald Molony giving first aid to one of the scores of office workers injured by fires that resulted from the plane's exploding gas tanks. Molony was decorated by the Coast Guard and Mayor La Guardia for his cool-headed bravery.

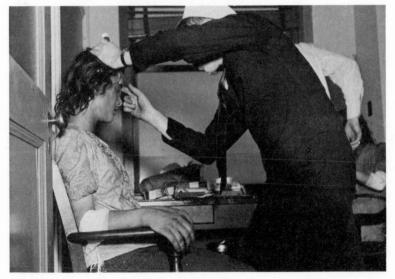

Members of Engine Company I, the first of more than 300 firemen from sixteen companies to respond to the disaster, carry an injured man to waiting ambulances. Twenty-six persons were critically injured. The combination of rain and a half-work day cut down the population working or visiting the building at the time of the crash.

Turning the 34th Street entrance to the Empire State Building into a battlefield scene, municipal and Army ambulances await the dead and injured.

One of the survivors of the flames that swept through the Catholic War Relief Services offices on the 79th floor is led down a stairwell. Eleven workers in the charity's headquarters were killed.

Below: A Catholic priest gives last rites to the charred remains of a victim in the Catholic War Relief Services offices on the 79th floor.

Firemen clear the rubble in sculptor Henry Hering's studio on the roof of the Waldorf Building. Portions of the plane's flaming left engine and its forward landing gear created the gaping hole in the roof. Fire consumed the entire studio but miraculously spared a plaster copy of the sculptor's famous statue, *Pro Patria*.

Below: A Civilian Aviation Administration official examines the B-25's 1,100-pound forward landing gear lying on the roof of the Waldorf Building on 33rd Street. Behind is the shattered skylight of sculptor Henry Hering's penthouse studio which was demolished by fire.

A view of the 80th-floor corridor taken from elevator operator Mary Scannell's car. The explosive force of the blast that flung her against the far wall can be judged by the bent steel pipes and shredded cables.

A policeman performs the gruesome task of placing victims' remains on desk tops in the Catholic War Relief Services office on the 79th floor.

Debris from the B-25 is stacked up in the Empire State Building's lobby awaiting removal for examination by the Army Air Force team of air safety inspectors. Miraculously, this section of one of the bomber's wings landed on 34th Street without causing injury or damage. Sections of the plane were hurled as far as a quarter of a mile from the point of impact.

Policemen carry the last of the crash dead through the Empire State Building's lobby. More than fifty ambulances and morgue wagons along with some 200 medical personnel arrived at the building within minutes after the first alarm.

greeted him as he peered out into an undamaged corridor at the south of the building. Looping Mary's arms around their shoulders, the men hurriedly made for the stairwell.

*   *   *

Ordering his driver, John Peluso, to pull up directly in front of the Empire State, Mayor La Guardia leapt out of the squad car.

"I told them not to fly so goddam low over the city!" he shouted, his face growing more livid as he stared up at the flames and smoke pouring out of the tower. "I warned them something like this would happen!"

La Guardia hadn't been in his City Hall office more than a minute or two when news of the crash reached him over the two-way police radio he kept next to his desk. "Oh, Jesus!" he'd shouted, "that could be bad. I better get over there." On his return trip uptown, Peluso had been ordered to break every speed rule in the book.

Moving into the lobby behind a wedge of policemen, La Guardia saw two priests arguing with an elevator operator. "What's the problem here?" he asked Monsignor O'Boyle and Father Swanstrom.

"We're trying to get up to the Catholic War Relief Services office on the 79th floor," O'Boyle told the mayor.

"It's our office," Swanstrom added. "There may be some survivors up there."

La Guardia snapped a stern glance at the operator. "Why can't they get up there?"

"I got orders from the Fire Department not to take anyone up who isn't a doctor, a cop, or a fireman," the man said with a helpless shrug.

"Does that include the mayor?" La Guardia snapped. He planted his hands on the priests' backs and propelled them into the car, then he pushed past the operator and joined them. "Get this contraption moving!" he ordered. The man hesitated. "This car'll only go to the fifty-fifth. And the fire's still burning on the seventy-ninth, Mr. Mayor. They told me the floor might cave in any minute."

La Guardia's eyes bulged with disbelief. "What's the matter, sonny—afraid to get your face a little dirty? Get going!" The operator blanched and quickly closed the doors.

By now the smoke-filled stairwells had become clogged with a stampeding herd of humanity. More than 500 employees of the Office of Price Administration alone were racing down the central stairs. For the most part the exodus was orderly, controlled in part by the squads of firemen attempting to climb to the crash site. Forced to wait time and again on the floor landings until the evacuees passed, the firemen's presence was responsible for keeping panic to a minimum. Nevertheless, isolated incidents of fear overcoming chivalry were taking place throughout the building. Since abandoning her office on the 39th floor, bookkeeper Shirley Robbie had been bruised several times by men muscling past women slowed by their high-heeled shoes. At the 25th floor, Shirley took off her shoes and continued on, barefooted.

His lungs still bursting from the climb to the 80th floor, Donald Molony was cradling a badly burned woman in his arms as he entered the north stairwell. He had found her wandering in a daze, wearing only a slip, her face and arms charred with third-degree burns. The Coast Guardsman groped his way down the pitch-black stairwell to the 75th floor, then hurried the injured woman into an office which had been set up by the Rescue Squad as a first aid station. She was the fifth victim of the crash Molony had rescued since entering the building a half-hour before.

On the 62nd floor, Dr. Melvin Elting was sidestepping a stream of burning fuel that poured down the south stairwell. For fifteen flights he had been carrying a badly injured and unconscious woman on his back. Like Molony, Elting had seen the crash and had raced into the building. Finding the elevators inoperable, he, too, had climbed on foot up to the crash site. Now the rivers of liquid fire were forcing him to locate another escape route. He threw the corridor door open and found himself exchanging startled looks with a fireman about to enter the stairwell.

"What floor is this?" Elting asked wearily. He shifted the woman's dead weight into a more comfortable position. Without a word, the fireman thrust his axe into the young doctor's hand, then gently removed the injured woman and carried her into the hallway. Propping the axe up against the wall, Elting turned and started back up the stairs to the crash site.

In this, his third attempt to reach the 79th floor, Harold Smith was determined not to be turned back. For the past ten minutes the Army veteran had been desperately trying to tell firemen that he had seen several women hanging out a window in the burning section of the 79th floor. With each attempt he had been turned back, rebuffed by the busy fire fighters.

Climbing up the north stairwell, Smith found himself gasping for air. The blackened shaft was filled with heavy smoke. Trickles of burning oil and aviation fuel ran down the stairs, spilling onto his shoes. Twice he had been forced to stop and stamp out flames that had leapt up and started his pant legs burning. His throat and lungs felt as if he had swallowed acid. At the 70th-floor landing he opened the hallway door and spotted a group of firemen about to enter the south stairwell. Unable to cry out to them, Smith forced his aching legs into a run.

*   *   *

Ellen Lowe was the first to see the trickle of flames shooting under the door leading out to the reception foyer. She stared at them impassively for a moment, then silently turned back to the window and peered out at the column of smoke rising from the floor below.

"Charlotte," she asked, almost casually, "do you think we could jump down to the seventy-second-floor setback?" Looking at her as if she'd suddenly lost her mind, Charlotte Deegan said, "We'd probably break our legs." Ellen nodded, as if in agreement. She was thinking what it would be like in Purgatory. The saddest part of dying would be leaving her family forever. She'd never see her six-month-old nephew Peter again, or her sister Marie, or her four brothers who were still overseas. The heat was making her faint. She leaned over

Charlotte and put her head out the window. How funny and stupid, she thought, to die looking down at the Macy's sign.

Leaning against the wall, Joe Fountain could barely turn his head at the exploding sound that suddenly erupted just outside the door. "What was that!" Anna Regan said with a startled cry.

Since regaining consciousness, she had kept up a nonstop whimper, moaning over and over "Save me . . . save me."

Kay O'Connor listened to the shower of glass splattering against the metal partition. "It's the water jugs," she said matter-of-factly. She remembered that there had been five of the large bottles of spring water sitting next to the cooler.

"I wish we had some of that now," Fountain said with a laugh. "I'd even settle for that drink you offered," Kay said. She, too, had seen the flames licking under the door. She guessed that they had less than three, or at best four, minutes before the room would become an inferno. Resting on her knees with her head out the window, Kay suddenly became aware of a man's face staring at her through a window across the east setback. He waved at her cheerfully, then raised a press camera to his eye.

"Help us!" Kay shouted. "Tell the firemen we're here!"

The women crowded around Kay's window and watched as the photographer, still wearing an unconcerned smile, lowered the camera from his eye. "Lean out more," he called to them. "I can't get all of you in the shot."

Ellen Lowe shrieked, "Save us!" Tell someone we're up here! We can't breathe!"

"Let me get a shot first," the press photographer shouted back, "then I'll get you all the help you can use." He began to focus the camera. As if they were of one mind, the women quickly moved away from the window. When they looked again, the photographer had vanished.

Moving to the south window, Therese Fortier stared down at the burning roof of the Waldorf Building on Thirty-third Street. She could make out dots of firemen scampering about. The thought crossed her mind that they probably didn't have a ladder tall enough to reach them. The heat was unbearable. Her hair felt as if it would explode into flames any second now. It all seemed so useless, the shouts for help, the prayers that somehow they would be rescued before the fire broke through the door. They were going to die, pure and simple—and that was that. Methodically, as if she were preparing for bed, Therese began to take off her wristwatch, rings, and gold earrings. Holding the jewelry in the palm of her right hand, she studied them for a moment, then suddenly tossed them out the window.

"What in the world did you do that for?" Ellen asked.

Therese turned to her with a blank look. After a long silence she shrugged and said, "I won't be able to use them any longer. Maybe somebody will find them. It seemed a shame to just let them burn up."

Pushing open the corridor door at the south end of the 79th floor, Lieutenant Buchanan, of the 54th Engine Company, looked down the smoke-filled hallway.

"You're sure this is where you saw the women?" he asked Harold Smith. Still breathless, Smith could only nod. He pointed toward the glass-paneled door near the corner of the corridor.

"They were leaning out a couple of windows," he finally managed. "I could see smoke pouring out of the office."

Buchanan turned and looked down to the north end of the hall. Squads of firemen were still fighting a raging blaze that seemed unquenched by the tons of water pouring out of their hoses. Smith read the doubtful look on his face.

"I'm telling you they're in there!" he insisted.

"They may be in there," Buchanan said flatly, "but if they're alive, it's one hell of a miracle." He motioned his men toward the door. A solid wall of flame could be seen blazing behind the frosted glass.

"Use your axe," he said to one. "Get ready with the hoses," he ordered the others.

Wielding the axe, the fireman shattered the glass panel with two blows. He jumped back as a volley of flames came bubbling out of the interior of the reception foyer. The high-pressure hoses bucked like wild stallions in the firemen's hands as they directed the streams of water into the center of the blaze.

Inside Father Swanstrom's office, the sudden sound of the door shattering brought mixed reactions. Convinced that the end was at hand, Theresa Scarpelli threw her hands over her face and screamed. Anna Regan continued to sit on the floor, but halted her whimpering pleas to be saved. Instead, in a calm and fearless voice, she began reciting a continuous string of Hail Marys. For Joe Fountain, the sharp sound had a palliative effect. With the thought that within seconds his agony would be ended, he felt his body go limp. He turned toward the door and waited, as if welcoming a long awaited guest.

Hearing the crash of glass and the almost simultaneous sound of water rushing into flames. Kay O'Connor refused at first to believe her ears. Cautiously moving closer to the door, she thought for certain that she had been mistaken; that the combination of heat and panic was making her hallucinate.

"Somebody's out there!" Therese Fortier shouted. "Listen!" She pushed past Kay and grabbed hold of the doorknob. She recoiled in pain as the red-hot metal drew the skin from her palm.

Buchanan's voice boomed through the door. "Stay back— don't come near the door until we cool it down!"

Hard on his words the survivors heard the thudding sound of water being sprayed against the door. An instant later, silhouetted against clouds of gray smoke, the fire lieutenant stood in the doorway. He studied the group with a look of stunned amazement.

"I would've bet anything that nobody was left alive up here!"

"Isn't that funny," Kay O'Connor said between wracking coughs, "just a minute ago I was thinking the same thing."

*   *   *

At 10:25, an hour and a half after Bill had taken off, Martha Smith turned the Buick down the elm-lined street bordering the Brookline Country Club and halted for a red light. With a great shudder the engine suddenly quit. Sliding out of the car, Martha raised the hood and saw that the wires a mechanic at Bedford Field had attached to jump-start the engine were hanging loose. "Damn!" she said out loud.

Glancing around for a phone booth, she caught sight of her sister's car approaching. A chill raced through Martha even before she saw that Mary had been crying.

"There's been an accident, Martha," her sister said finally.

She nodded very quickly. "I know," was all she said. "I know." She opened the door and sat next to Mary, neither looking at the other during the ride home. A half-hour later, when she had finished picking the last flower in the garden, Martha Smith allowed her first tears.

The Aftermath

At precisely 9:55 on Tuesday, July 31, 1945—after lingering in a coma three days—Joseph Fountain died of his injuries. That afternoon, his wife, in her ninth month of pregnancy, collapsed and miscarried while making his funeral arrangements.

For the survivors, the months following the crash were filled with pain and continuing anxiety. Betty Lou Oliver, her back and both legs broken by the thousand-foot plunge in the elevator, made what her doctors described as a miraculous recovery in less than eight months. Returning to Fort Smith, Arkansas, with her husband, Oscar, Betty Lou had three children and is a grandmother of four.

Thirty-two years and sixteen skin- and bone-graft operations later, Mary Scannell has continued her career as an elevator operator, switching several years ago from the Empire State to the United Nations Building. Her coworkers, Sam Watkinson and John Monte, recovered from their injuries and also returned to work at the building.

Since the day of the crash, Kay O'Connor has suffered from a severe respiratory ailment as a result of smoke poisoning. Throughout the years she has been under constant medical care. Therese Fortier married the boy who had given her the ring that looked like a ruby—and that she had tossed out the window when all hope had seemed futile. Amazingly, it was returned to her several days later by the Fire Department, after having been found on the roof of the Waldorf Building. Ellen Lowe, Theresa Scarpelli, Anna Regan, and Charlotte Deegan continued to work for the Catholic Relief Services until recently.

The intervening years saw Monsignor O'Boyle become His Eminence Patrick Cardinal O'Boyle, the retired

247

Archbishop of Washington, D.C. Father Edward Swanstrom, now Bishop Swanstrom, is the retiring executive director of the Catholic Relief Services.

Donald Molony was decorated by the Coast Guard for his outstanding bravery and was given New York City's highest award by Mayor La Guardia. During the Korean conflict he joined the Marine Corps and was wounded eight times in combat.

Martha Smith has never remarried. After her husband's death she returned to school and earned a degree in education. She is currently teaching in the public school system of a Boston suburb. Her son, William Franklin Smith III, served with distinction in Vietnam as a captain in the Marine Corps. He is now an executive with a large insurance company.

More than one hundred claims for loss of life, personal injury, and property damage were filed with the Judge Advocate of the Army Air Forces. The Empire State Building Corporation put in a claim for damages in the amount of $487,352.44. After a brief negotiation, the Army agreed to pay $288,901.90. McCreery's asked for $1,537 for two shattered display windows. The Army whittled the figure down to $1,316. The New York Telephone Company requested and got $1,869.57 without argument. Sculptor Henry Hering, whose studio and works of art were a total loss, put in a claim for $137,000. After two years of legal argument, Hering was offered $25,000 by the Army on a take-it or leave-it basis. He accepted, and it was another year before Congress appropriated his award.

For the families of the dead, memories of that tragic morning were to be recalled many times over the following years. Death claims for the eleven civilian victims were automatically shunted to a Congressional committee, which, after considerable deliberation, offered an average of $7,500 compensation per family. Lawyers were hired, bills were introduced by sympathetic Congressmen and Senators, and personal pleas of extreme hardship were made by wives and parents who had been forced to accept charity with the sudden loss of income. Finally, after eight years of legal maneuvering,

Congress awarded the widows of Joseph Fountain and John Judge $47,000 each. The rest of the awards averaged less than $15,000.

Within three months after the crash, the scar on the face of the Empire State Building had been repaired. Today, not a trace of the incident can be seen by the thousands of passersby who automatically scan the building's upper stories each day. But to the window washers who each week reach the 79th floor, a small blackened crevice in the limestone blocks under the northwest windows is a reminder of that summer morning when a plane hit the building. Not by carelessness but by design, it has been left as a memorial.

Index

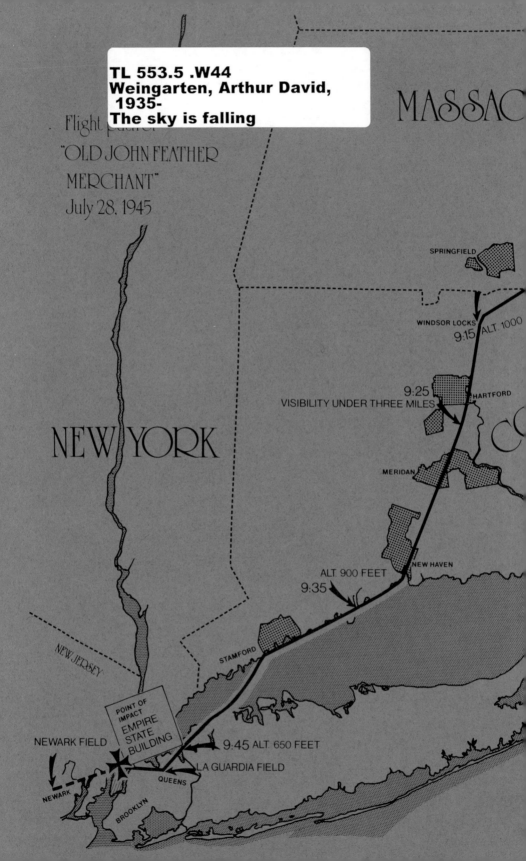

Flight path of
"OLD JOHN FEATHER
MERCHANT"
July 28, 1945

MASSAC

SPRINGFIELD

WINDSOR LOCKS ALT. 1000
9:15

9:25
VISIBILITY UNDER THREE MILES   HARTFORD

NEW YORK

MERIDAN

NEW HAVEN

ALT. 900 FEET
9:35

NEW JERSEY

STAMFORD

POINT OF
IMPACT
EMPIRE
STATE
BUILDING

9:45 ALT 650 FEET

NEWARK FIELD

LA GUARDIA FIELD

QUEENS

NEWARK

BROOKLYN

CO